Challenging the divide
Approaches to Science and Poetry

After graduating from the University of Adelaide with an Honours degree in history, Erica Jolly taught in secondary schools for forty years, mainly in South Australian technical high schools until 1974. In 1978 she completed a Masters degree in English literature at Flinders University. Erica realised early that categorisation and predetermined pathways for students limited their scope. That limitation, reinforced by treating subjects as 'silos', discouraged interdisciplinary approaches. In 1992 she gave up her position as Deputy Principal (Curriculum) at Marion High School. Elected to the Flinders University Council in 1990, she supported interdisciplinary developments. Her publications include social histories *We Came to Marion* (1995) and *A Broader Vision* (2001), and a collection of poetry, *Pomegranates* (2003).

Epigraph

My life's course was set. My father announced, 'You're going to do science'. So that was that. It was the way things were done 50 years ago. I was thirteen and my life's course was set. Gwyn Williams was clear in his reasoning. Science was the means to build the Promised Land, and the British education system made you choose your specialty around puberty. Arts or science: the great divide.

Robyn Williams

Future Perfect: What next? And other impossible questions, p. 33

Challenging the divide

Approaches to Science and Poetry

Erica Jolly

LYTHRVM

Lythrum Press
PO Box 243 Rundle Mall
Adelaide
South Australia 5000
www.lythrumpress.com.au

First published in 2010

Copyright © Erica Jolly 2010; copyright in the individual contributions by scientists, poets and essayists remains with the respective authors. A list of acknowledgements and permissions to reproduce material appears at the end of the book.

All rights reserved. This book is copyright. Apart from any fair dealing for the purposes of private study, research, criticism or review, as permitted under the Copyright Act, no part may be reproduced without written permission. Enquiries should be addressed to the publisher.

National Library of Australia
Cataloguing-in-Publication entry:

Author:	Jolly, Erica
Title:	Challenging the divide: approaches to science and poetry/Erica Jolly
ISBN:	978 1 921013 25 6 (pbk)
Notes:	Includes index
	Bibliography
Subjects:	Science and the arts
Dewey Number:	306.45

Cover design: Stacey Zass
Cover illustration: microphotograph of crystallised sulphur by Hans Fander
Text design and typesetting: Michael Deves, Lythrum Press
Typeset in Adobe Garamond 11/15
Printed and bound by Hyde Park Press, Adelaide

Contents

Introduction

On a Sunday in October 2006 a taxi driver asked me why I was going to the Adelaide Town Hall. I told him I was going to hear the Doctors' Concert.

Doctors as musicians!

He was incredulous. Doctors couldn't be musicians!

Given more red lights on the way, I would have told him that taxi drivers can be artists, mathematicians, musicians, students of engineering, history or computing, clerks or carpenters.

Why, doctors can be poets and poets might be doctors!

The concert was wonderful. Doctors, specialists, pathologists and all those in between brought us proof that no one should make assumptions about human beings – especially in the labelling of students, my greatest fear.

This taxi driver's insistence was timely. His belief that the arts – in this case music – and the sciences – in this case medicine – belonged in separate compartments had prevailed for too long. I became eager to challenge the 'great divide' that had bedevilled school curricula and I was determined to find a way to involve scientists and poets in this challenge.

I have long opposed this narrow approach to learning because it undermines the quality of education. Labelling and division have imposed limits on students' futures. It has forced them into pathways where curiosity has little value. It has undermined the independent spirit of learning. Students have not been learning to make connections that will enhance their understanding of the world we share. They have been learning only to separate subject from subject. For too many it has perpetuated a tunnel vision.

The education consultant Dr Valerie Yule has described how such an approach creates what she has called 'the crisis of human energy'. She made her position clear on *Ockham's Razor* when she said:

> Some teachers threaten classes with, 'If you don't behave I'll set you some hard work'. But I've seen brilliant teachers do the opposite. 'If you are good, I'll give you some hard work.' When teachers ask all the questions, they risk squashing children's curiosity, to turn them into docile or reluctant answering machines, because children are not like Socrates' young adult disciples. Children are still acquiring knowledge to be able to try to answer questions.

> Brilliant teachers have the children avidly asking the questions and seeking the knowledge that will encourage more curiosity.[1]

Evidence of the questioning of this divisive approach to curricula is arriving all the time. It is in a speech by Senator Kim Carr, the Minister for Innovation, Science and Research, to the National Press Club in March 2008. In it he expresses this wish for a richer Australian culture:

> Everybody here knows the rules of professional scientific conduct – think independently, put emotion aside, reject received authority, be faithful to the evidence, communicate openly.
>
> These are good rules – rules I wholeheartedly endorse – but there's one more I'd like to add – remember your humanity ...
>
> The last thing we should be doing is closing off options, rejecting possibilities, making arbitrary decisions about what can or should be known.

Attitudes to learning

Divisions between the arts and sciences did not exist for me in primary school. Natural beauty and calculations were allowed to exist side by side through almond blossom and arithmetic. A nature-loving Headmaster would seek permission from our arithmetic teacher to take us out into the street to paint the soft pink-white petals in July.

Our teacher shared this love of nature and was only too eager for us to have the experience. She could always return later to mental arithmetic. Those early signs of spring might be gone in the next shower or breath of wind.

Even the dropping of atomic bombs in 1945 on Hiroshima and Nagasaki did not mean that non-science and science were separate and incompatible. After all, politicians and scientists had come together to create that tragedy.

Of course, not all scientists agreed with nuclear warfare. George Gamow, the author of *Mr Tompkins in Wonderland* in 1940 and *Mr Tompkins Explores the Atom,* published in 1945, was one who begged the American government not to use these new weapons of war to force Japan to surrender.[2]

Still, the dropping of those bombs had an impact that would resonate for the next half a century. For those of us starting university in the 1950s with the Cold War

---

1 Valerie Yule, interview with Robyn Williams, 'Crisis of Human Energy', *Ockham's Razor*, ABC Radio National, 18 February 2007. Transcript of interview at http://www.abc.net.au/rn/ockhamsrazor/stories/2007/1848554.htm

2 However, it seems that he later had some involvement in investigating the idea of the hydrogen bomb.

replacing the 'hot' one, the stupendous power unleashed by those scientists would have an impact on attitudes.

A friend studying mathematical physics, when irritated by my concern as a student of history about where the USA versus USSR conflict was taking us, would call those of us who were studying the humanities 'clawless tigers'. In the realm of the sciences changes were taking place so rapidly that we, in the humanities, would always be behind.

But we were people first, talking to one another. We were sharing the same culture, only coming to it from different points of reference. I was reassured that we shared the same culture by a young lecturer who came to the University of Adelaide. His name was Hugh Stretton.

Teaching us history in our final year, Hugh Stretton bemoaned the absence of science-oriented students studying history. He would have a more analytical approach in the schools as well as the universities. Students would not be taught to memorise dates and treaties. Theirs would be an evidence-based approach to the interpretation of documents and the motivations of their authors. By his concern for the values of the processes of the sciences, this young lecturer reinforced my sense of the connections between disciplines.

Separation in secondary schooling – Australia and England

Assumptions about students and their future roles in society were made clear to me by the separation of the 'techs' from the 'high' schools. In Australia I first taught in the single-sex girls technical schools. There, general science was of little importance, except in the hands of able teachers who might excite girls and encourage them to move into the 'high' schools.[3] In the 1950s physiology was in the 'techs' for girls in the general course. These girls had been labelled 'non academic'. I would teach students apparently not so labelled, since they had passed the 11+ examination, in an English co-educational grammar school in 1966. The English school system was at that time divided mainly into comprehensive schools in London and grammar schools and secondary modern schools elsewhere.

Trained as a teacher of History, I was asked to teach English in a co-educational grammar school in Bedfordshire. There, I was given two additional jobs that no-one else wanted. The first was to prepare science students at the 'A' level for the comprehension entry test for Cambridge. The next was to organise the inter-house poetry competition. Undertaking the latter task, I discovered Wordsworth's *Prelude*.

3 See *A Broader Vision: Voices of Vocational Education in Twentieth Century South Australia*, compiled by Erica Jolly, for the stories of girls who were interested in the sciences.

Keats's 'magic hand of chance'

I call it that now. Both jobs helped me to learn more about teaching than all the pedagogical classes at the Teachers College. To provide material for the science students, mainly boys, I had to enter their territory. They refused to enter mine. They jeered at Brecht's *Galileo*. Only Ian Fleming's James Bond – sexy, with the right to do anything, to use extraordinary technology, commit any crime in the name of patriotism – was acceptable.

I found Fred Hoyle's novel *The Black Cloud*, the work of Asimov, Ray Bradbury's *Fahrenheit 451*, E.M. Forster's eye-opening novella, *The Machine Stops,* and gave them excerpts from these novels. Most particularly *The Machine Stops*. I also found C.P. Snow's book *The Two Cultures*. The attitudes of these students seemed to reflect the 'chasm' C.P. Snow said existed between the sciences and the humanities, most particularly between poetry and science. They had no interest in or concern for questions of morality. Science, as they saw it, had no place for it.

The separation of 'hands' from 'head'

Back home, in the 1960s, some of the 'hard' sciences had entered the boys technical *high* schools. Biology was being brought into girls technical *high* schools. It was considered 'soft' enough to be appropriate for girls, who might previously have been allowed to study physiology. Or, in the nineteenth century, 'sanitised' botany, reduced by the removal of the sexual elements in Linnaeus's classification that excited Erasmus Darwin (Charles Darwin's grandfather) and made him write poetry delighting in that sexuality, had been considered appropriate for genteel young ladies where flower-pressing and nature study had been optional extras in some schools!

Teaching in a boys tech, I found the impact of labelling even more divisive. The humanities were not valued and some of their technical studies teachers might tell their students not to worry about literature and English because it 'won't get you a job'. These boys had been either labelled as 'non academic' or 'good with their hands'. Given that so much of their work was practically based, they gained emotional satisfaction and pleasure in their sense of achievement. It was not assumed, except by a few outstanding technical studies teachers, that they needed the theory behind their practice.

Boys and girls – separate schools, common humanities

The notion of the separation of 'hand from head' had not been the aim of Dr Charles Fenner – father of Emeritus Professor Frank Fenner – who had once been an apprentice in Victoria. As the Director of Education in South Australia he did not dismiss practically-oriented education as less significant than academic approaches. He established the Thebarton Boys Technical School on the philosophy of the Dalton Plan: it was one of the most innovative student-oriented schools established before the Great Depression. Dr Fenner sent his son, Frank, to that school for the first part of his secondary education to develop a self-reliant approach to learning.

I learnt so much teaching those boys at Brighton Boys Tech. They loved the craft, enjoyed the aesthetics in working with different materials and they could range from woodwork where the grain of the wood gave them direct understanding of what it meant to 'go against the grain', to different metals, electronics, design, photography and art. They could enjoy the 'craft' in a work of literature. My favourite memory, teaching those 'tech' boys is of the day, outside in the shade, I shared with my Year 12 students Shakespeare's sonnet 'Shall I compare thee to a summer's day'. They became aware of the quality of the poet's craft, delighted in his self-confidence and what his poem could give this beauty that Nature could not. Immortality …

In these separate schools, supposedly for the 'non academics' I found concern for the imbalance in their education among teachers. In girls techs, science, humanities and art teachers might cooperate to enable students to discover what their disciplines could offer students in a collaborative way. It might be the sound of water running in a creek after dark, the taste of fresh, cool water from a stream, the wonder of the night sky, or serious discussion of current events such as the reasons why John F. Kennedy had been assassinated. In these informal ways teachers and students would cross the syllabus divide.

In my boys tech, a biology teacher would take students into the Flinders Ranges, where they sang around campfires, wrote stories and poems. One chemistry student's poem, published in the Brighton Boys Technical High School magazine in 1972, made it very clear that his poem did not belong to what C.P. Snow had seen as a separate knowledge system. Robert King had been a student at the school since 1968: his poem was printed under the name of R. King.

Chemistry

Chemistry. What is it?
It's knowing what a protolysis reaction is, or what happens
   when excess phosphorus is added to a halide.
It's a subject that deals with the reactions of chemicals with
   other chemicals to form further chemicals.

It's a study of the structure of atoms and molecules, that the
unassisted human eye has no chance of seeing.
It's the comprehension of amphiprotic substances, acid-bases,
electrolysis, covalency, ionization etc.
It's learning these things off by heart without knowing what
you are learning!
It's cramming facts into heads in three terms of work.
It's passing or failing.
It's wondering what you can make of what you have stored.
It's a hope that those who succeed, who eventually rise to
higher levels of enthusiastic study, will help to create
the future world, not destroy it.

I find Robert King's concern for the future of humanity evidence that we are not two cultures. It is in the hope he expresses in this poem which, according to C.P. Snow, belonged to the emotional side of life not the intellectual side of life.

That artificial separation brought with it a number of unintended consequences, among them the tendency to reduce people and things to smaller and smaller units in the name of specialisation, consequences that are still undermining the quality of our thinking and feeling.

Lateral thinking – working with a student

I think it was 1975. I was asked to tutor a boy from a local high school. He was expected to gain perfect scores in Mathematics I and II, Physics and Chemistry and to fail English. His English teacher had given up. Not that this boy was rebellious. He was a wonderful student, always willing to try, but he did not seem able 'to get it'. As occurs when teaching is at its best, there was shared learning. Antony taught me as much as I taught him. He taught me about electricity. What he needed was access to the language of literature evident in metaphor and imagery. What spark would ignite his imagination? The theatre. We took him to a number of plays.

Once he was able to see the role of metaphor and imagery in exploring the human condition, he entered this literary world with delight in its possibilities and an enhanced depth of understanding in his scientific and mathematical studies. He saw a performance of *King Lear.* In that tragedy, where metaphors for blindness and rage proliferate, he understood what was happening. These daughters, 'tigers not daughters' certainly had claws. The 'blindness' of an old man demanding flattery, refusing to hear the love in Cordelia's straightforward answer in the competition he had set up for his favour between his three daughters. The irony of 'sight' through the agony of being blinded is so intense after the dying Cornwall plucks out Gloucester's other eye.

Antony was learning that there is a place for lateral thinking as well as the linear, straight down the line approach that he appeared to have been used to in the science and maths studies he had undertaken at school. He gained perfect scores in all his subjects that year. He had learnt not only to take time for lateral thinking, but the value of taking time for reflection to explore the possibilities offered by imagery.

Learning in an academic high school

It matters that I experienced four kinds of secondary schools set up for different purposes. This one was designated a 'lighthouse school' among Australian schools in 1984. It was Marion High School and as its Deputy Principal – Curriculum I brought to it all the wonderful experiences from which I had been learning. I was convinced that, with cooperative approaches, students learning across the curriculum, not despising other subjects, could develop deeper levels of understanding. Science, like everything else, is a human activity.

This school was noted for its inclusive approach. There were different pathways for students to reach Year 12. But that did not mean that all areas of study were seen as equally worthy of respect by all members of staff. Schools reflected attitudes in the administration of the Department of Education. The utilitarian approach which found it easier to reduce students to different categories and put them in different schools had only just come to an end in 1970. Comprehensive education was meant to bring with it a broader vision so that young people would leave school with a wider range of experiences across the sciences and the humanities and be able to move from one career to another as their interests expanded.

However, the universities wanted the students to be well prepared for study in their disciplines, particularly in the 'hard' sciences. Many still preferred what they called 'the binary system' of the schools set aside for 'the heads' being separated from other schools set aside for 'the hands'. So practice and public and academic expectations could undermine philosophy. The notion of the 'two cultures' seemed to be entrenched in the high schools.

Luckily that 'magic hand of chance' gave me the opportunity to work with a Principal, Brian Hannaford, who, as the kind of mathematician I had rarely met before, helped those interested to see opportunities in all kinds of opposites, positive and negative. He was often telling us to find ways to make lemonade out of lemons.

Every effort was made to develop an atmosphere that encouraged a collaborative, cross-disciplinary approach where it was appropriate. That was why an inter-disciplinary learning centre, in which students had a say about its formation, was established.[4]

'Don't be shy of integration' – *The Science Show*, 3 May 2008

To hear that dictum on ABC Radio National has encouraged me to describe a major inter-disciplinary event, the student-oriented, whole-of-school engagement called 'Da Vinci is alive and well and living in Adelaide'. Da Vinci's fables were developed by the English senior for all to read. Among them, my favourite remains what happened when the great oak decides to have all the lesser plants beneath his great canopy removed.

The technical teachers and students made brilliant working replicas of machines that da Vinci had invented, the art staff and students produced a gigantic three-dimensional body that little children could crawl through. Science students experimented with falling bodies. The hall became a Florentine market place. Business maths students were buying and selling.

That whole-of-school experience which brought in members of the wider community was followed two years later by one embracing 'Space'. That second project had the advantage of being supported at the grass roots, rather than imposed from above.

Scientists could be poets – experience in a Year 10 English class

One experience was reminiscent of my time in England. These boys and girls were in a Year 10 Advanced English class with a number of very self-assured male science and maths students. English lessons were expected to fit their conservative approach to the subject. I thought otherwise. Marks were not my primary objective. I wanted students to recognise that they were moral beings and that the power of imagery affects the way we interpret ideas. Therefore *The Lord of the Flies* and *To Kill a Mocking Bird* became part of the program.

I also wanted them to recognise that the sciences and poetry could speak to one another, that scientists could be poets. I was lucky. The father of one of the students was a lecturer in biology and a poet. Brian Brock came to school and read his poems to the class: they made the class aware that a scientist could feel emotions and have a conscience.

Marvin Bell, an American poet in Adelaide for Writers' Week challenged this class in a different way. Include ten words, chosen at random around the class, in a ten line poem. The language of the sciences inevitably came to the fore. Their poems were

4 *We Came to Marion 1955–1995*, compiled by Erica Jolly, Flinders Press, 1995

surprising and the boys, in particular, seemed quite delighted by their achievement.

A bio-chemist and computing teacher, and a member of our interdisciplinary learning centre, took this class into the hills. He encouraged close observation of the impact of bush fire on the Governor's summer residence and, at his cherry orchard, provided them with time to reflect on and interpret in poetic form what they had seen and felt.

Over time, I found more and more teachers prepared to support one another in these interdisciplinary ways that engaged the sciences and the arts. In 1989 the Marion High School drama department presented, at the Sturt Theatre, a work-shopped performance of *Stargazers,* based largely on Brecht's *Galileo.*

That production brought an expression of surprise from the CEO of the Information Communication Technology Centre at The Parks about this way of telling the story of one of the greatest scientists. An English teacher was so appreciative of the play, he printed his congratulations and comments on a sheet of A3 paper and blue-tacked it to the door leading out of the staff room so that all staff and students – we did not deny students access to the staff room – could read it.

A 'pas de deux' of a different kind

The program of independent, inter-disciplinary study for senior students developed at Marion High School might have something in common with the 'extended learning initiative' aspect of a student-oriented component soon to be part of the new Certificate of Education in South Australia. This new component is picking up the process of interdisciplinary learning, providing space and time for students' curiosity to pursue avenues of interest. A new senior school Research Project component will enable students to move, if they wish, beyond the narrow boundaries of their senior school subject-oriented program.

Years ago, a student who wanted to explore the physics of dance was discouraged from doing so by her physics teacher. Thanks to a reference by Joy Hakim, I found the essays of Alan Lightman. His essay 'Pas de Deux', a very short essay, connecting physics and the movements of the ballerina, is exquisitely written:

> For an ending, the ballerina does a demi-plié and jumps two feet in the air. The Earth, balancing her momentum, responds with its own sauté and changes orbit by one ten trillionth of an atom's width. No one notices, but it is exactly right.[5]

---

5 Alan Lightman *Time Travel and & Uncle Joe's Pipe,* with ten illustrations by Laszlo Kubinyl, Penguin Books, New York, 1986, p. 80

An astrophysicist and a novelist, acclaimed for his first novel *Einstein's Dream*, Alan Lightman is the first academic to be appointed to a joint Chair of the Sciences and Humanities at the Massachusetts Institute of Technology.

As with Lewis Thomas's essays, there is a place for reason and the imagination, intellect and emotion, in the writing of Alan Lightman. He seems to build on the light touch of Lewis Thomas who does not claim a privileged, unchallengeable, separate position for scientists. Lewis Thomas wants to connect with all of us and he began doing so in the 1970s.

The discovery of his voice made me think that there must be other voices out there, voices of scientists and poets who do not accept the notion of the two cultures as an impassable 'chasm'. Somehow I had to find a way to counter the attitudes that still seemed to dominate the approach to curricula in our schools and which could dominate the national curriculum to be put in place for the twenty-first century. To make these connections I needed the support of scientists. It would not be enough for someone trained in the humanities to make assertions about the need for these connections.

Australian scientists respond

I had written an article for *Five Bells*, the journal of the Poets' Union, suggesting there was a place for scientific writing, other than science fiction, in the study of English.

Among the scientists who agreed to contribute to this book was Laureate Professor Peter C. Doherty. In 2007, he published *A Light History of Hot Air*. Among the essays in that collection is 'Alphabet Soup' in which he says of the writing of Primo Levi – a chemist and poet important in this book – 'We are drawn in and intrigued by the unfamiliar humanity and relevance to daily life that Levi confers on the world of the working scientist.' [6]

I find that phrase 'unfamiliar humanity' revealing. Scientific investigation is a human endeavour. The humanity of scientists, as well as the inhumanity of some, should be there for us to see.

In another essay, Peter Doherty takes us into Charles Dickens' novel *Bleak House* to explore the notion of spontaneous combustion! The connections that can be made between literature and the sciences abound in his book. Professor Doherty does not want us to forget our humanity.

In the most unexpected way, I was encouraged to broaden the avenues of learning

6 Peter C. Doherty, awarded the Nobel Prize for Physiology and Medicine, *A Light History of Hot Air*, Melbourne University Press, 2007, p. 19

when I received an article by Dr David Paganin who had launched a most unusual art exhibition which entered the world of quantum mechanics. In this multi-media world where art takes on new dimensions, the opportunity to include reference to the ways of thinking and feeling of a quantum physicist and a sculptor was irresistible. This is the world that students are in. They are in a world where boundaries are blurred. Too many of us, who were brought up in the world where we were labelled early, have too little understanding of the opportunities these interconnections are creating. The physicist and the sculptor would collaborate, explain the process and help us enter the possibilities they were offering.

Beyond Australian shores: scientific writing with literary merit

So much is going on beyond Australian shores. Besides Alan Lightman's academic position, there is the Lewis Thomas Award established by Rockefeller University for scientists of international renown whose writing crosses that artificial divide and qualifies as work of significant literary merit that is accessible to the general reader. Awarded first in 1993, Lewis Thomas, sometimes called the 'poet of science', was the first to receive it.

Among the recipients have been Max Perutz, Freeman Dyson, Edward O. Wilson, Oliver Sacks and Jared Diamond; some Nobel Prize-winning scientists. Recently the Lewis Thomas Award has been bestowed on Natalie Angier, one of America's most effective writers about the sciences. I found out about her work through Radio National's 'Background Briefing'. She is the science writer for the *New York Times*. She has won the Pulitzer prize for her writing. *The Canon – A Whirligig Tour through the Beautiful Basics of Sciences* is exhilarating. Hers is a voice that has humour, an understanding of adolescents, and she has learnt 'how unintegrated science is into the rest of human affairs'. And she wants it to be integrated. And so do I. In her section on physics, her writing about light is illuminating.

Examples of and reference to these scientists' writings is the core of the third chapter of this book.

In Europe, we will come to Primo Levi and Miroslav Holub, whose works are available in translation. In Primo Levi's collection of short stories, *The Periodic Table,* I found stories about a number of the elements. My favourite is 'Carbon'.

It was Peter Doherty who introduced me to Miroslav Holub; he became even more significant as part of a collection of nineteen dialogues compiled by Robert Crawford of the University of St Andrews, *Contemporary Poetry and Contemporary Science*. The dialogues challenge, question and find connections because, as Kay Redfield Jamison says: 'poetry and science have common roots in observation and they take their cue from the rhythms and patterns of the natural world.'[7]

Science and poetry in the UK

Among other voices in these dialogues, the one that speaks most sensitively to me, talking of poems about astronomy, is the voice of Jocelyn Bell Burnell. In her essay 'Astronomy and Poetry' published in *Contemporary Poetry and Contemporary Science* she is thorough and wide-ranging in her exploration of poets. She speaks to us. We are not lost in abstractions. Directing our attention to poets she admires in both the United Kingdom and the United States, she expands our avenues for investigation.

Among the poets commenting on the scientists in these dialogues, the most provocative is the English poet Simon Armitage. While he reminds us that poets have a role in challenging scientists, his essay is an important counter-weight to those who would blame the scientists for the appalling events of the twentieth century.

In America – the surprising role of Ezra Pound

An American anthology of twentieth century poems has a companion volume of essays discussing them. It is *A Concise Companion to Twentieth Century American Poetry*, edited by Stephen Fredman. There are twelve essays by different contributors. Among the themes chosen is 'Poets and Scientists' by Peter Middleton.

I found, while researching the metaphor for a 'divine creator' in the twentieth-century that, in America, He had ceased to be the 'Divine Watchmaker'. By 1927 'He' was 'the unseen Master of the Laboratory'.[8] It is interesting that Ezra Pound could visualise new descriptions by scientists and poets 'forged under laboratory conditions'. Pound appears to have had the greatest faith that poetry and science would come together in this modern world turned upside down in the way we see everything. The discoveries by Albert Einstein and Max Planck had taken scientific study beyond classical Newtonian science. In his essay Peter Middleton examines a number of American poets and their responses to the sciences.

---

7 R. Crawford, *Contemporary Poetry and Contemporary Science*, p. 192

8 In a critical comment on Eugene O'Neill as a playwright – he also wrote poetry – a critic, Benjamin De Casseres, wrote in 1927 'His characters are chemical and psychological experiments, just as all of us are in the hands of the unseen Master of the Laboratory'.

Via the Internet – a challenge to 'the two cultures'

Among the people I found is David Morley. He has a background in zoology and has been working in creative writing with the scientists at the University of Warwick. He challenges the 'two cultures' division in the following words:

> I began my working life as a scientist, one who also wrote creatively, and I would say that if what you do requires you at best to write clearly, then we are all writers. The Two Cultures, the division of knowledge systems into Arts and Science, was a splintering of the processes by which knowledge and language move and grow. *There are no Two Cultures, and there never were.* [my italics]. The debate between science and arts was based largely on prejudice, fear and a kind of snobbery – a class war between disciplines, their teachers and their students. We might as well say there are a Million Cultures for all the illumination such a debate brings. Creative writing as a discipline may help to shift the debate into a more constructive set of engagements.[9]

Discovering poets engaged with the sciences

Poets who have reacted to or felt the power of the sciences have an important place in this book. First of all Australian poets. Among the contemporary Australian poets is Tony Page, whose poem 'Tutorial with Flowers and Light' fulfils the beauty and enhanced understanding made possible by such connections. These poems are followed by English, European and American poets. An article by Stephen Lawrence, 'The Sounds of Science', introduces young Australian poets (see Appendix).

But the best comes last. Proof that, at school, in an inter-disciplinary atmosphere, the humanities and the sciences can complement, challenge or enhance one another is in the poems of Year 10 and 11 students at the Australian Science and Mathematics School. The Coordinator for the Interdisciplinary Curriculum: English and Humanities was able to engage students and staff in a project that resulted in the production of their anthology, launched in November 2007, *Comets, Conical Flasks & Conundrums.*

The role of respect

In January 2008, the Australian Science and Mathematics School jointly with Flinders University ran the Australian Summer School for Science Teachers. In her keynote address on the last day, Associate Professor Debra Panizzon, the Deputy Director of the Centre for Science Education in the Twenty-first Century established at Flinders

---

9 Morley's essay can be found on the University of Liverpool Centre for Poetry and Science website, at http://www.liv.ac.uk/poetryandscience/essays/creative-recognitions.htm

University, asked an important question. Could outstanding maths and science results be found in schools where all the other results were ordinary?

One of the research team, a mathematician, had thought it was likely. The results of research undertaken in *comprehensive*, not selective high schools, showed that was not the case. What matters is the connection that science and mathematics programs make to link them to the culture of the school.

I would take it further. When we encourage respect for other areas of learning we provide opportunities. We can never predict what the spark will be that excites girls and boys and takes them, one day, into one or other of the sciences. We know that the emotional context in which they study has its role to play. Respect, that human capacity, replaces prejudice and opens minds and hearts to new possibilities.

Erica Jolly
June 2009

Chapter One

My Discoveries Began in the 17th Century

That search took me to Galileo and his conflict with the Church, the discovery by Copernicus – confirmed mathematically by Johannes Kepler – of the heliocentric universe, which ran counter to the belief in the geocentric universe held by the Church, and to the atomist theory of the nature of matter.

It took me to France, in the 17th century, where exiled English intellectuals supporting the Stuarts discussed the ideas of René Descartes who, with his dictum, translated into English as 'I think, therefore I am', found a way to prove that he existed. The intellect, the mind, was the be-all of being.

In England, scientific investigation had been enthusiastically taken up by amateurs and natural philosophers since the time of Elizabeth I, building on the work of William Gilbert. Empiricists, seeking evidence-based investigation of Nature and the universe, the followers of Francis Bacon, and the founders of the Royal Society, were eager to study the planets. Charles II had been given a telescope and became the patron of the Royal Society. When the Royalists returned after Charles II was crowned, with the Restoration of the Monarchy, they brought with them many of the ideas percolating in France.

Attitudes to women

There was one significant difference between the approach in England and the idea developed by René Descartes. Descartes had not insisted on the additional separation of male and female in this intellectual world founded on the Cartesian principle. For him the mind, the intellect, was beyond gender. This was most evident in Voltaire's view of Emilie du Châtelet, a great mathematician, whose intellect he considered superior to his own.

In England, however, the engagement of women in the sciences – as evident in the atomist sonnets of Margaret Cavendish, Duchess of Newcastle, who was fascinated by the theories being discussed in Paris – was discouraged. Women, as a Secretary of the Royal Society wrote, were the 'temptresses' who might intrude upon the pure intellectual pursuits of the male natural philosophers.

So the assumptions that the intellect was male and the body female, the mind pure, the body impure, the power of thought superior and emotions inferior, took root in England. And the approach to the sciences – through the scientific method of William Gilbert, Robert Boyle and the overwhelming discoveries of Isaac Newton – became mechanistic. Once one understood the machinery that made the universe work one could become like a god. Arthur Young thought so. And God Himself became part of the machinery as the Divine Watchmaker. He had set the mechanism in motion. He had regulated time in space. He had done His job. The rest was up to the intellectual power of men.

Impact on attitudes in eighteenth-century 'Enlightenment'

Reason was at the core of the Newtonian Enlightenment in the eighteenth century. The idea was as powerful in France as in England, one difference being that scientific developments in Britain were undermining traditional approaches to agriculture and industry at a time when England was the strongest imperial power in Europe and trade brought wealth. In France – with an absolute monarchy in power – what if Reason, intellect, could develop a society that derived its authority from a meritocracy, not a tax-free aristocracy and clergy? The Encyclopaedists would oppose the *ancien régime* and intellectual challenge would be followed, when circumstances provoked it, by the French Revolution.

So the focus might be different for scientists in both countries. In England, agricultural and industrial changes, as well as navigational changes, were the result of scientific investigations, and it was assumed that the mechanistic approach in the sciences would yield power and profit to England. Every discovery, based on reason and experiment, worked to stimulate English trade, and England's imperial ambitions.

In all the scientific investigation, Isaac Newton and Newtonian laws remained pre-eminent. Natural philosophers and poets, like Pope and Voltaire, maintained that this great genius had solved the riddle of the universe. It would be hard for scientists, building on new knowledge being acquired, to challenge the Newtonian 'laws'.

In England women, like Mary Wollstonecraft (mother of Mary Shelley) saw Reason also as the beginning of female emancipation. Mary Wollstonecraft saw herself joining in the intellectual life of the land on the basis of equality with men and William Blake recognised her right to be there. However, before she could take part she would die in childbirth, as so many women did at that time.

What was happening to the spirit of humanity in 'this age of reason'?

The language of science had a place in the opening stanza of Dryden's 'Song for St Cecelia's Day'. That poet had looked forward to a new age of reason and faith. Pope, an admirer of Dryden, would become sceptical about where science might be leading people in his *Essay on Man.* But, while Pope might have doubts, other English poets did not. Certainly not James Thomson. For him, Newton's refractive law in his study of optics had brought a new, wonderful awareness of the mechanism of the rainbow. But what was this mechanistic approach to everything doing to the quality of English society? Newtonian laws were seen as immutable and it is no coincidence that the eighteenth century 'Classical Economists' put forward what they believed were immutable 'laws' of economics.

Human beings are capable of thinking and feeling, responding to their senses, their emotions and appetites. But an approach to learning driven by 'reason' alone was producing a society that, in his poem urging the return of Milton, Wordsworth called 'a fen' – in his view English society had become a quagmire. Blake had woken up first and challenged the whole notion of the supremacy of Reason as it was manifesting itself in this mechanistic way. Reason was denying the value of the inner, spiritual life. In his poem 'London', Blake attacked the many 'mind-forged manacles' that blighted the lives of people in the city.

Attitudes of English poets – Wordsworth, Coleridge, Shelley

There was not a split between poetry and science but, as it was working in the eighteenth-century, Reason seemed to be permitting such cruelties in the name of that 'Goddess' of Reason. The French Revolution with its catch-cry of *Liberté, Egalité, Fraternité* had fired the minds of young idealists. In England, Joseph Priestley, one of the discoverers of oxygen, would flee to America after his laboratory was burnt down by a mob paid by the conservative English government to attack him for his radical views. Wordsworth would initially be entranced by the possibilities of this 'new dawn'. Coleridge would express less certainty in 'Fears in Solitude'.

But what had an impact on these young English poets, although not on Shelley, was the failure of Reason in that revolution. In France, Antoine Lavoisier, given the palm as the discoverer of oxygen, would be guillotined perhaps because he had humiliated a man who sought his approval. That man was Marat, one of the Jacobins responsible for the 'Reign of Terror'. Terror, cruelty, murder and fanaticism revealed to Wordsworth in particular the twin dangers of both 'mind alone' and 'mindless' human behaviour. For him the refinement of thought by feelings and 'recollection in tranquillity' became central. There had to be a balance between the two. Love, compassion, the spiritual essence of the human being, whatever his or her status, became central. Science, as he perceived it – mechanistic and indifferent to human feelings and the feelings of animals – had to be challenged.

Wordsworth has been seen as the enemy of science. Such a view ignores the fact that he did not deny the intellect. His experience at Cambridge had not been totally a 'vacation' for his mind. He understood that Newton had found pleasure in geometry. He made all of this clear in *The Prelude*. What mattered was the balance of thought and feeling.

In addition, for Wordsworth, Nature was the great healer. For Nature, with her immense power to lift the spirit of Mankind, to be reduced to the categorising science of 'botany' was offensive. The Linnaean sexually-based system of the classification of plants, in which Erasmus Darwin, Dr Solander and Sir Joseph Banks exulted, seemed to undermine the imagination. Not that Erasmus Darwin thought so. He sought to transfer imagination from the realm of poetry to the realm of science.

For Coleridge, interested as he was in every intellectual aspect of life, the same was true. The mindless and thoughtless, those without any feeling for the beauty and innocence of living things, could turn the 'ship of life' into the nightmarish 'Death-in-Life' existence. 'The Rime of the Ancient Mariner' continues to speak to us because, like *King Lear*, it deals with a life without love and compassion, a life in which people are easily manipulated, an existence driven by a kind of blindness.

But Coleridge, also fascinated by science, was a friend of Humphry Davy, and a member of the British Association for the Advancement of Science (BAAS). Humphry Davy, one of the first professional scientists, at one stage offered Coleridge a stipend to free him from his financial worries and let him fulfil the genius so many saw in him. It was Coleridge's challenge at a meeting of the BAAS in Cambridge in 1833 that encouraged Professor Whelwell to coin the collective noun 'scientist' as a substitute for the 'natural philosopher' title that had kept them within the sphere of philosophy. But only men could be scientists. Women would be the admiring supporters of masculine scientific endeavour, although introductions to the sciences were being written by women like Mary Somerville and Jane Marcet.

Shelley and the sciences

Not all of the English Romantic poets feared the influence of a mechanistic or materialistic approach in science. Shelley did not. Science, in his view, could make life better for the poor and wretched. Electricity, for example, could be more than a plaything for amateur natural philosophers playing with Leyden jars. Some of his poems are scientifically accurate and his 'Ode to the West Wind' has a footnote to insist on the scientific accuracy of one of its images.

He understood the difference between imagination and fancy. In his *Defence of Poetry*, however, Shelley makes clear his concerns about life without imagination and what concerned him about the science he saw around him in the early nineteenth century was that people might lack the imagination to realise where it might be taking them. It was poetry that fed that imaginative sensibility.

And, I suggest, it was Shelley's wife, Mary Shelley, who saw where science might take the human race – with the development of artificial Man – in *Frankenstein: The Modern Prometheus.* What would happen to an artificial man created by a scientist when it went seeking friendship? What would happen if it had no way of dealing with emotion? Why was Frankenstein called 'the modern Prometheus'? What had been stolen from the gods this time?

Keats and the rainbow

For the eighteenth century poet, James Thomson, Newton's refractive law in his study of optics had enhanced the image of the rainbow. For Wordsworth, the rainbow was the beauteous natural image capable of lifting the heart of humanity. For Keats, who had some knowledge of medicine, and who believed that the senses had a powerful influence in life, expressed his fear in 'Lamia', that Newtonian law had reduced the rainbow to 'a dull catalogue'.

What would become of Iris, messenger of the gods of ancient Greece and her multi-coloured cloak that flew out from her shoulders as she made her way to the earth from Olympus? What of the iris – the name given to that part of the eye through which the soul was said to depart the earth? What would become of the role of the rainbow in Christian iconography? The richness, the colour, the role in myth, the appeal to our senses, so much was lost, in this poet's view, with the rainbow reduced to part of the Newtonian science of optics.

Generalisations are not always helpful. Generalisations may make subjects seem simpler than they are. And the either/or assumptions that are so convenient for a society that does not want to face the complexity of life make everything worse. Shelley was not opposed to the sciences. However, for Britain, particularly after 1815, the applications of the sciences were often the mechanisms for the expansion of British colonising influence throughout the world.

Imagination and empathy – the anxiety of Victorian poets

Imagination is the human capacity that grows as we develop. Often it comes through engagement with the natural world, which can influence the quality of our feelings. What does a life without imagination mean? It will be a life without empathy, a life governed by machinery and calculation. Is such a life reduced because there is no time for reflection, no time to absorb and respond to the natural world?

That was the fear of English poets in the mid-nineteenth century. Victorian England, industrialised and powerful, had become the hub, 'the workshop of the world'. Materialism was having its effect on what was thought to be appropriate for State schools. Future workers would need to be able to count, read, write and know facts. Imagination had no place in the schooling thought appropriate for the future workers in manufacturing industries.

Charles Dickens would pillory the supposedly scientific, fact-based Gradgrind system of schooling in *Hard Times* in which not a smidgin of sympathetic understanding would be permitted. Feelings of sympathy had no place in the society where reason, as materialistic self-interest, dominated.

For a number of Victorian poets, the industrialised world made them anxious about what was being lost. Tennyson certainly believed Nature was no longer the spiritual healer. In his melancholic and over-dramatised view, in 'In Memoriam', Nature was 'red in tooth and claw' because, through the discoveries of geologists like Charles Lyell, Nature no longer cared about the glories of human achievement, for example, the inspiring Gothic cathedrals.

Nature was indifferent to human needs. That view was reinforced by Charles Darwin's findings about the process of evolution, published in his *Origin of Species.*[1] Tennyson, who would live long and be influential on English poetry, was one of the Pre-Raphaelite Brotherhood, poets and visual artists who believed that beauty was being lost in industrialised England.

The role of Lewis Carroll

Those Victorian poets who were turning away from the sciences because of their feelings about their application could have had a devastating impact. Their refusal to be part

1 Before his *Origin of Species,* Charles Darwin wrote a major treatise on the barnacles he had observed during the voyage of HMS *Beagle*. In *Little Dorrit* Dickens would take Darwin's barnacles and turn them into a metaphor for those holding tenaciously on to power, and clinging so well to the hull of that 'ship of state' which, unlike the real thing, could not be taken into dry dock to have them scraped off its hull.

of what they saw as an ugly world, driven by coal and profit, did revive interest in the mediaeval world. Tennyson's poem 'The Lady of Shalott' is an example of the Pre-Raphaelite influence.

Towards the end of his life, however, Tennyson's melancholy, so evident in 'In Memoriam' was worse. In 1889, when he was eighty, he wrote 'Lockley's Hall Sixty Years Later'. In this poem he expressed his fear that 'Poor poetry', like history, would be relegated to the past.

Not so. Not all Victorian poets shared his pessimistic view of the future. Consider the work of Tennyson's contemporary, Lewis Carroll, the pseudonym for Charles Dodgson, a brilliant mathematician who lived from 1832 to 1893. The imaginative world of Lewis Carroll, in prose and poetry, in *Alice in Wonderland* and *Through the Looking Glass,* with the poems 'Jabberwocky' and 'The Walrus and the Carpenter', as well as 'The Hunting of the Snark' and *Rhyme? and Reason?,* would lighten the lives of children and adults everywhere. Logic, liveliness and delight in the absurd would bring a very different, amusing way of seeing to all who discovered his world.[2]

Lewis Carroll was not the only one. There was Edward Lear. And there would be Edith Nesbit bringing her playful engagement with technological changes to her late nineteenth-century fairy stories. At the same time, in France Jules Verne would be exciting readers with possibilities about the future.

Where were the sciences going? Discovering Michael Faraday

Often, for 'non-scientists', discoveries about the sciences arrive in lateral ways. In 2004, at the birthday party of a physicist who had been a fellow student at the Adelaide Teachers College, I met a man who manufactured bells. Dr John Lowke, a contributor to this book, asked me to read to his scientist friends my poem about Canadian scientists who had chosen the name of a brilliant philosopher, Spinoza, for a robot they were teaching to play soccer.[3] This lover of bells and bell-ringing offered to show me where the poetry lay for him in science and mathematics.

He introduced me to Michael Faraday and demonstrated how Faraday worked out how electricity and magnetism came together as electro-magnetism. He copied Faraday's experiment, using simple objects, and had me engrossed.[4] He made me want to learn more. As I read, I developed a real affection for Faraday who had discovered

2 Lewis Carroll, *The Complete Illustrated Works,* Gramercy Books, New York, 1982.

3 'A Scientist's Spinoza' in *Pomegranates*, Lythrum Press, Adelaide, 2003.

4 Joy Hakim, in *The Story of Science: Newton at the Center* has shown his experiment in Chapter 32, 'Michael Faraday has a Field Day', pp. 344–345.

that the secret of creating the electric current was motion.

Faraday's story reveals the tremendous worth of family support. His parents were poor but did not allow their lack of money to deny their children as much education as they could give them. And for Michael Faraday, there was that 'magic hand of chance'. His employer, a benevolent book-seller, recognised his talent, and fostered it. As a book binder Faraday read about chemistry in the *Encyclopaedia Britannica.* His curiosity was aroused and his passion for learning about it took over his life. The story of his relationship with Humphry Davy reveals more of the role of chance.

Once a Director of the Royal Institution, which was supported by Sir Joseph Banks, Faraday's love of children and his desire to foster their curiosity found an avenue through lectures. He wanted to share with everyone the wonder in Nature. His Friday evening lectures at the Royal Institution always drew a crowd, among them sometimes Charles Darwin.

The Christmas lectures were especially for children. He gave those lectures for thirty years. Renowned scientists were invited to present their work. London was a much smaller place. Albemarle Street was so packed with people eager to hear his lectures that they stopped the traffic and it had to become a one way street.

Michael Faraday and 'the candle' – 'poetic' and 'scientific' truth

In a lecture about the candle Michael Faraday made connection with *truth in a poetic sense as well as in a scientific sense.*

> Now I must take you to a very interesting part of our subject – to the relation between the combustion of a candle and that living kind of combustion which goes on within us. In every one of us there is a living process of combustion going on very similar to that of the candle, and I must try to make that plain to you. *For it is not merely true in a poetical sense – the relation of the life of man to a taper; and if you will follow, I think I can make this clear …* You will be astonished when I tell you what this curious plan of carbon amounts to. A candle will burn some four, five, six or seven hours. What then must be the amount of carbon going up into the air in the way of carbonic acid! What quantity of carbon must go from each of us in respiration! What a wonderful change of carbon must take place under these circumstances of combustion or respiration! A man in twenty-four hours converts as much as seven ounces of carbon into carbonic acid; a milch cow will convert seventy ounces, and a horse seventy-nine ounces; solely by the act of respiration. That is, the horse in twenty-four hours burns seventy-nine ounces of charcoal, or carbon, in his organs of respiration to supply his natural warmth in that time.[5]

---

5 Joy Hakim *The Story of Science: Newton at the Center*, p. 350.

This was long before the invention of the horseless carriage. When Faraday spoke of 'truth in the poetic sense' – in this case the metaphorical sense – of 'the life of man as a taper', he could have been referring to Shakepeare's play and those famous despairing lines of Macbeth:

> Out, out, brief candle!
> Life's but a walking shadow, a poor player
> That struts and frets his hour upon the stage,
> And then is heard no more.

Working in the Royal Institution Faraday had the time and space to explore electricity and magnetism, those separate discoveries of the eighteenth century, that he now brought together as electro-magnetism. His work would further allow British, and American, industrialisation, enabling both nations to go charging along. Faraday made the first generator, the dynamo, and his discoveries formed the basis of the science of metallurgy.

Enter James Clerk Maxwell – scientist and poet

But Faraday's discovery needed mathematical proof. That proof was provided by James Clerk Maxwell, whose work would have a major impact on physics in the twentieth century. I discovered that both Faraday and Maxwell were concerned by the emphasis on trade which Faraday saw as 'vicious and selfish'.

One of Maxwell's hobbies was writing poetry. This poem reveals the role of Nature in helping him to reflect on a subject at the forefront of his mind.

Reflex Musings: Reflections from Various Surfaces (18 April 1853)

> In the dense entangled street,
> Where the web of Trade is weaving,
> Forms unknown in crowds I meet
> Much of each and all believing;
> Each his small designs achieving
> Hurries on with restless feet,
> While through Fancy's power deceiving,
> *Self* in every form I greet.

Oft in yonder rocky dell
Neath the birches' shadow seated
I have watched the darksome well,
Where my stooping form, repeated,
Now advanced and now retreated
With the spring's alternate swell,
Till destroyed before completed
As the big drops grew and fell.
By the hollow mountain-side
Questions strange I shout for ever,
While the echoes far and wide
Seem to mock my vain endeavour;
Still I shout, for though they never
Cast my borrowed voice aside,
Words from empty words they sever –
Words of Truth from words of Pride.

Yes the faces in the crowd,
And the wakened echoes, glancing
From the mountain, rocky browed,
And the lights in water dancing –
Each my wandering sense entrancing,
Tells me back my thoughts aloud,
All the joys of Truth enhancing
Crushing all that makes me proud.[6]

We feel the process that this scientist and mathematician is engaged in. We feel his concerns about what can get in the way. Pride for one thing. James Clerk Maxwell sees evidence of the adverse influence of 'words of Pride' in the crowds passing on 'restless feet', so absorbed by their own 'small designs' that they cannot imagine the broader picture. Reflection in the tranquillity of this quiet spot has let him observe, feel and think about the questions that come back to him as echoes.

Maxwell is not self-engrossed in the ways of those 'entangled in the web of Trade'. And this shouted, echoing dialogue with himself has an important result.

6 Lewis Campbell and William Garnett, *Life of James Clerk Maxwell with selections from his correspondence and occasional writing*, Macmillan, London, 1882, pp. 593–594

Words from empty words they sever –
Words of truth from words of Pride.

Taking it all in,

Yes the faces in the crowd,
And the wakened echoes, glancing
And the lights in water dancing –
'Each my wandering sense entrancing
Tells me back my thoughts aloud,
All the joys of Truth enhancing

This brilliant Scot, a mathematician and physicist, is *not* dismissing his 'wandering senses'. He is finding pleasure in 'lights in water dancing', connecting these meandering natural pleasures that have told '[him] back [his] thoughts aloud.' All this enhances 'the joys of Truth', 'Crushing all that makes me proud'.

James Clerk Maxwell and light

The story of the boy and the man has given me insights into the person behind the scientist. Maxwell was able to confirm Faraday's hypothesis mathematically and to confirm the existence of electromagnetism.

Going further, Maxwell takes up the study of light that Kepler and Newton had explored. Maxwell discovered and proved that light is electromagnetic, that it undulates, travels as waves.[7] Newton had thought that light travelled in a straight line. Not only this, he realised that colours are waves of electromagnetism of differing lengths.

Neither Michael Faraday nor James Clerk Maxwell felt separated from the humanities; they were connected, Maxwell through his poetry, Faraday through his recognition of 'poetic truths' and through his Christmas lectures for children. For Faraday, who had not gone to Cambridge – he was, in the main, self-taught – science was meant to engage all people, not just the wealthy privileged few or those who saw it only as a source of profit, and in this way he was awakening the curiosity of the young.

7 Joy Hakim p. 361 ff. Faraday had expressed his discoveries in language students could understand, whereas James Clerk Maxwell did not have the capacity for simple clarity in the language he used. For a simple explanation of light, see 'The length of light' in *From Atoms to Infinity: 88 Great Ideas in Science,* by Mary and John Gribbin, Icon Books, Cambridge UK, 2006 pp. 84–85.

Fears about the potential uses of scientific applications

Europe was being driven by nationalism during the last decade of the nineteenth century. In the case of Germany, the sciences were at the service of the State. In England scientific applications were racing to increase opportunities for wealth and imperial expansion at a time when Japan was emerging from its isolation at the end of the century.

At the same time pure scientific research was being done with the purpose of expanding the knowledge and understanding about this world and the universe. Some scientists, like J.J. Thomson and Ernest Rutherford, were studying atoms which other scientists, including Ernst Mach, still believed were a fiction. But discoveries were being made that might have an effect on the kinds of weapons that could be used in war. So, the nations of Europe were being, as we would now say, 'pro-active' to limit the weapons that would be acceptable.

The Hague Convention 1899

On 29 July 1899 the International Hague Convention on what were permissible weapons of war was signed by European nations. Chapter II of the Convention made a number of special prohibitions, including no use of poison, no treachery, no killing those who have surrendered, no use of weapons causing unnecessary suffering, no assaults on undefended towns.

The Convention was explicit about a number of other ways of waging war. Maritime war was to be fought according to the Geneva Convention of 1864. No 'projectiles or explosives' were to be launched from balloons. No projectile was to be used that could diffuse 'asphyxiating or deleterious gases'. No bullets could be used that would 'expand or flatten easily in the human body'.

Personal pride, patriotism, peace and adherence to international treaties however, do not always go together. Science was playing a key role in German progress at the turn of the century. John Cornwell, a Cambridge historian, provides the background to the German term for science. *Wissenschaft* 'incorporated traditionally a huge circuit of intellectual disciplines in which the German-speaking peoples, never forgetting Austria, excelled.'[8]

8 John Cornwell, *Hitler's Scientists: Science, War and the Devil's Pact,* Viking, London, 2003, pp. 3–4. Of the sphere of German science, John Cornwell writes, 'Meanwhile, existing for the most part in philosophical and political limbo, while giving impetus to the new technologies with the power to transform the world, the success of the natural and medical sciences in Germany was, before 1933, prodigious: Wilhelm Konrad Röntgen, discoverer of X-rays; Fritz Haber fixed nitrogen in the air; David Hilbert set the world's mathematicians sufficient tasks to keep them busy for a century; Max Planck, a founding father of quantum

Pride, feared by Maxwell, was influencing the way nations celebrated their scientific and technological achievements. Just six months after this important Convention had been signed, there was a question about where the next great international exhibition should be held. Britain had led the way with the Great Exhibition with its centre-piece, the Crystal Palace. Now Germany, 'the Mecca of science' as John Cornwell calls it, wanted the International Exhibition of 1900 to be held in Berlin. However that honour went to France. Paris played host to the exhibition, but the German exhibits 'stretched over fifteen locations from the Tuileries to the Eiffel Tower'.[9]

Light and new ideas in twentieth-century science

So much was happening in the realm of science at the turn of the century. Once more, as a student of the humanities, I learnt about it in a lateral way. I found the writing of Joy Hakim who told me about Albert Einstein's passion to ride, in his imagination, a beam of light that James Clerk Maxwell had already demonstrated comes in waves.

Joy Hakim, a science writer for American students, is doing what I believe needs to be done here. She is making connections that are as valid in the study of English as they are in the study of the sciences and she acknowledges that she is working with 'one of the greatest physicist teachers in America, Edwin E. Taylor'.

Artists had already taken me to the power and delight of light: in England J.W.M. Turner, in France the Impressionists. Now this outstanding science writer was taking me, through *The Story of Science: Einstein Adds a New Dimension,*[10] into the science of light and a world of new ideas. I would find out that 1905 was Albert Einstein's 'Annus Mirabilis'.

Max Planck brought the new knowledge that light comes in waves *and* particles but, he decided, not at the same time. Later Louis-Victor de Broglie would show that all particles of matter have waves and we, too, have 'wavelengths'. Max Planck's formula would describe the nature of light. Einstein would change the way we understand space/time. Rutherford, exploring activity within the atom, would help us to begin to comprehend the power of radio-activity. Rutherford would show us that, within atoms,

---

theory, Albert Einstein and his epoch-making theories of relativity; Werner Heisenberg and quantum mechanics. After more than half a century in which Germany became an unrivalled power-house of chemistry, organic, inorganic and industrial, German nationals in the first two decades of the twentieth century, walked away with more than half the Nobel prizes in every discipline of the natural sciences and medicine.' p. 4.

9 John Cornwell, *Hitler's Scientists,* p. 38

10 Joy Hakim, *The Story of Science: Einstein Adds a New Dimension*, pp. 78, 85

is a nucleus 'orbited by fast-whizzing electrons'. [11] However, it would be Douglas Stewart's poem 'Rutherford' that would reveal another aspect of Rutherford's character, his optimism that people would never be foolish enough to use irresponsibly the power to be released when the atom was split!

Niels Bohr, who had worked with Rutherford, would explain what he called 'the dance of the electrons'. With the invention of spectroscopes, astronomers would begin to read the light coming from the stars. Photons would be found to bring light to the electrons inside the atom. Needing to bring its significance home to American students, Joy Hakim would compare Bohr's discovery with the impact of Columbus's voyage of discovery in 1492.[12] Bohr would be at the centre of what came to be called quantum physics. The understanding of what is inside atoms was made possible by the work in crystallography of the Braggs, father and son.

Among the great developments were the discoveries in chemistry, particularly in Germany.

Chemistry, World War I and Fritz Haber

German success in chemistry began with the establishment of a great laboratory at Giessen by Justus von Liebig. He had discovered the nitrogen cycle, so important in the development of plants.[13] Fritz Haber had made a discovery that would free Germany from dependence on nitrogen imports and double agricultural output for the nation's expanding population.

And it is Fritz Haber, this great chemist, with whom I am concerned.[14] Fritz Haber's biography is informative. He very much saw himself as a patriot, wanted recognition for his achievements by a high position in German academia, gave up his Jewish faith to that end, and converted to the Lutheran form of Christianity because that pathway was more likely to bring the position he craved.

Fritz Haber persuaded the German High Command to break the German government's commitment to the Hague Convention of 1899. He proposed the use of

---

11 Joy Hakim, *The Story of Science: Einstein Adds a New Dimension* Smithsonian Books, Washington, 2007, p. 109

12 Joy Hakim, *The Story of Science: Einstein Adds a New Dimension*, p. 121.

13 *The Ultimate Visual Dictionary of Science,* p. 172. The natural cycles – carbon, nitrogen, oxygen and water – are described.

14 Roald Hoffmann describes Haber's impact on attitudes to science in *The Same and not the Same*. In Part 6, 'A Life in Chemistry', Hoffman makes clear what Haber did in World War 1 (pp. 171–174), and in Part 4, 'The Social Responsibilities of Scientists', he makes their ethical responsibilities clear (pp. 139–140).

chlorine gas, insisting that its use would give Germany victory 'scientifically' in the First World War. He personally supervised the experiments on the Western Front. Another, even more devastating form of poison gas would be used by Germany on the Eastern Front against the Russians. Fritz Haber made his notes about the efficacy of this weapon in what he saw as his objective way. His second wife, also a scientist, appalled by the absence of compassion, committed suicide. The impact of the use of that forbidden weapon is still felt in Wilfred Owen's poem, 'Dulce et decorum est'.

Inevitably, once Germany had broken the Hague Convention it was open slather. World War I has been called 'the chemists' war'. By the end of the war scientists in the name of patriotism had developed a wide range of ways to use chemicals and other forms of technology to kill.

Fritz Haber's assertion about the role of science

After 1918 Fritz Haber enunciated the following idea that became known as the *depersonalisation of science.*[15] The scientist could not be blamed for the way that his (or her) discoveries were used by others. On those 'non scientists', who made decisions regarding the *use* to which the discoveries would be put, would rest the problem of conscience. The scientist was 'the catalyst' and 'the catalyst' was innocent. His discoveries, as a scientist, were outside of his life as a moral human being.

For almost eighty years Haber's assertion has made it possible for many scientists to insist that 'how' is the only relevant question for them, not 'why'. It was quite convenient for him to proclaim that doctrine, that science is 'value-free, neutral and a-political', freeing 'science' and scientists from responsibility for how their discoveries were used. Scientists were not connected, in his view, to the realm of moral philosophy.[16] The view still persists among some scientists to this day.

From chance through certainty to uncertainty

That depersonalisation of science, after 1919, allowed scientists who chose to do so to reduce to nothing any responsibility for how their discoveries were used. We know,

---

15 A side effect of this idea of 'the depersonalisation of science' would occur when, in 1919, T.S. Eliot used the idea of the chemical catalyst – the mind as the 'shred of platinum' – to develop the notion of the depersonalisation of art. See 'Tradition and Individual Talent' in *Selected Essays*, Faber and Faber, London, 1969, p. 18.

16 John Cornwell sees Haber's actions as an exemplar of the 'notion that science is value-free, neutral and apolitical'. 'The scientist discovered the laws of nature and invented applications; the good and evil perpetrated by those applications was on the consciences of others.' (*Hitler's Scientists,* p. 47)

however, that the means affects the ends. The move towards the 'depersonalisation' of science from the scientists coincided with discoveries in science, and particularly in chemistry, that transformed the world, and most importantly warfare.

Once 'depersonalised', science as abstraction was assumed to be objective. The scientist was the intellectual driven by the mind. His or her characteristics as a human being were irrelevant. The scientist was *mind at work.*

The humanities and the arts, by contrast, were supposed to suffer from their connections with the body, feelings, emotions and senses, and had been, and sometimes still are, dismissed as subjective and therefore supposed to be an unreliable basis for making decisions. They were called 'soft', which became an adjective used to undermine their importance. No one considered the role of the connections between body and brain in all of this.

We have always known about the role of chance in life. Call it coincidence, luck or the unexpected, we have known about it. The Greeks had the goddess Tyche: the Romans set up temples to Fortuna. Gamblers have bet on possibilities from the moment people began to imagine them. Blaise Pascal, the seventeenth-century mathematician and philosopher, helped us to consider probabilities. However, the principle of uncertainty gained scientific significance with the work of Werner Heisenberg in 1925.

Heisenberg asserted that, in the world of quantum physics, 'one cannnot measure or know all aspects of the quantum system at the same time.'[17] The Uncertainty Principle appears to suggest that, as we observe anything, our perspective of it can change, depending upon what we bring to that observation. Newton's laws of motion had spoken of a 'body at rest that stays at rest until … '.

The world of quantum physics says that everything is in motion. In his play, *Copenhagen*, performed for the first time in 1998, Michael Frayn[18] puts the 'uncertainty principle' into Niels Bohr's mouth in the following way. 'Then, here in Copenhagen in those three years in the mid-twenties we discover that there is no precisely determinable objective universe. That the universe only exists as a series of approximations (probabilities). Only within our relationship with it. Only through the understanding lodged inside the human head.'[19]

That principle made all the difference in the world. 'Understanding', 'the human head', the collection of aspects of knowledge and learning, and the emotional and

---

17 Joy Hakim, *Einstein Adds a New Dimension*, Smithsonian Books, 2007, p. 153

18 Michael Frayn, novelist, playwright, translator, essayist and writer of non-fiction is also the author of *The Human Touch: Our Part in the Creation of the Universe.*

19 Joy Hakim p. 153

cultural context in which we hold them, had a place in our consideration of everything.

The uncertainty principle and the world of particle physics would make us aware of just how complex our planet and the universe is. The development of remote-controlled rockets and the possibility of war in space, the splitting of the atom and the development of atomic weapons would make some people call World War II 'the physicists' war'. Many important physicists would be brought into the Manhattan Project in the United States which produced the first atomic bombs.

After 1945 the study of particle physics would require massive injections of funds. It is said that after World War II a significant number of physicists felt that there were no new worlds to conquer, until an essay by Erwin Schrödinger, written while he was in Dublin, suggested connections between biology and physics. It was Schrödinger's essay that offered a new pathway, the pathway of biological study through physics. That pathway led to research into DNA; the life of Rosalind Franklin, denied recognition for her work in the Nobel Prize, is an important part of that story in London and Cambridge. Her biography, recorded in *The Dark Lady of DNA* by Brenda Maddox, reveals the significance of the background, the education, the attitudes and experiences of scientists engaged in such life-changing research.

What has all this meant for the post-war world – the role of radio and television

In the whole process the new technologies in spectroscopy, in film, and the power of the visual media to record events, stages in development within ourselves and beyond our galaxy, have been bringing to us an accumulation of knowledge, more and more complex.

Did the governments want us to be kept informed? Did others consider that much of this knowledge would be better kept for an élite? The media can be used just as well to obscure truths as to reveal them.

Luckily in Australia, as with its corresponding public broadcasting organisation in Britain, the BBC, there was recognition that an informed public was preferable to an ignorant one. In 1932 the Australian Broadcasting Commission – now Corporation – would be given the role to inform, educate and entertain. And, unlike the USA, public radio would be government-funded on our behalf. It would not have to rely, as the American Public Broadcasting Service does, on donations from organisations and individuals who value its role.

Among its broadcasting networks, the ABC's Radio National has provided insights through a number of its programs into the complex and interconnected world of which we are a part. For example, my knowledge of the world around me has largely come through 'Poetica', especially during National Science Week, 'Ockham's Razor' and 'The Science Show'. This informal avenue of education, which frequently emphasises the links between the humanities and the sciences, is an important source of ideas and information. On ABC television, and on SBS, we have had documentaries and programs that encourage us to think and feel about the uncertainties we face in our existence on this planet. But in the realm of formal schooling these connections have often not been made for the reasons I have given previously.

Why Roald Hoffmann matters – his rejection of Fritz Haber's position

As Roald Hoffmann, the Nobel prize-winning quantum chemist, puts it, Haber saw himself as a human catalyst. In the chemistry definition, he might bring about change but he, himself – the so-called 'objective' scientist – would remain apart from any matter of morality or conscience. And he held this position in spite of the fact that Germany had been a signatory to the Hague Convention of 1899, which had specifically prohibited the use of 'asphyxiating or deleterious gases'.

Once more, the discovery comes in a lateral way. I have Radio National's 'Poetica' to thank for introducing me to this chemist and poet. In Lecture 33 'Fritz Haber' in *The Same and not the Same*, Roald Hoffmann tackles the consequences of Haber's assertion.

The chemist is *not* separated from the real world 'but it has its own way of touching him, whether at the beginning, the middle or the end of life. In no way has this fact been truer, or played out with more drama, than in the life of one of the greatest of all physical chemists, Fritz Haber.'[20] Fritz Haber's greatest achievement of benefit to the world, according to Roald Hoffmann, was the synthesis of ammonia, so important as a fertiliser in agriculture. But he was also prepared to use his chemical genius to produce poisonous gas, to be used in warfare.

Roald Hoffmann writes: 'Rationalisers of gas warfare, then and now, ask, "Is there a nice, good way to die? What is worse about poison gas than shrapnel?" The answer is to be found in the testimony of the wounded. Something in the psyche, something deep that associates life with breath, is perturbed.'[21] In *Chemistry Imagined: Reflections on Science*, Hoffmann includes this poem:

---

20 Roald Hoffmann, 'Fritz Haber' in *The Same and not the Same*, Columbia University Press, New York, 1995 pp. 167–176.

21 Roald Hoffmann, *The Same and not the Same*, p. 172

Fritz Haber

invented a catalyst to mine cubic miles
of nitrogen from air. He fixed the gas
with iron chips; German factories coming
on stream, pouring out tons of ammonia,

fertilizers, months before the sea-lines
to Chilean saltpeter and guano were cut,
just in time to stock powder, explosives
for the Great War. Haber knew how catalysts

work, that a catalyst is not innocent, but
joins in, to carve off the top or undermine
some critical hill, or, reaching molecular
arms for the partners in the most difficult

stage of reaction, brings them near, eases
the desired making and breaking of bonds.
The catalyst, reborn, rises to its match-
making again; a cheap pound of Haber's

primped iron could make a million pounds
of ammonia. Geheimrat Haber of the Kaiser
Wilhelm Institute thought himself a catalyst
for ending the War; his chemical weapons

would bring victory in the trenches; burns
and lung cankers were better than a dum-dum
bullet, shrapnel. When his men unscrewed
the chlorine tank caps, and green gas spilled

over the dawn field at Ypres, he carefully
took notes, forgot his wife's sad letters.
After the War, Fritz Haber dreamed in Berlin
of mercury and sulfur, the alchemists' work

hastening the world, changing themselves.
He wondered how he could extract the millions
of atoms of gold in every liter of water,
transmuting the sea to the stacked bullion

of the German war debt. And the world, well,
it *was* changing; in Munich one could hear
the boots of brown-shirted troopers, one paid
a billiard marks for lunch. A catalyst again,

that's what he would find, and found – himself,
in Basel, the foreign town on the banks of his
Rhine, there he found himself, the Protestant
Geheimrat Haber, now the Jew Haber, in the city
of wily Paracelsus, a changed and dying man.[22]

Roald Hoffmann made clear, in prose and poetry, that Haber's position involved special pleading. My conviction that such division has handicapped students and undermined the quality of education had found confirmation. Roald Hoffmann was helping to bring the two cultures together. He would make clear how important it was to remain connected with 'our friends in the humanities'. In addition, there were other essays by scientists, whose beauty, wit and the capacity to enlarge our horizons should be available to students of English.

The humanity of Lewis Thomas

Among the scientists writing for the general reader, one of the most influential has been Lewis Thomas. He is outraged by the separation of knowledge into supposedly incompatible systems. I was attracted first to the beauty of his essays. In the early 1980s he confirmed my view that the sciences and the humanities and, in particular poetry, can have connections.

I wanted to share his ideas and his approach with senior students in English. Lewis Thomas refused to see decisions in life as a series of inevitable alternatives. The first essay I found that challenged the assumption that all life, for example, must be competitive

22 Roald Hoffmann, *Chemistry Imagined*, pp. 93–94. See also Chapter 3 – 'Fritz Haber' in John Cornwell's book *Hitler's Scientists: Science, War and the Devil's Pact*, pp. 47–60 and Chapter 4 – 'The Poison Gas Scientists', pp. 61–70.

is 'The Medusa and the Snail' where unusual and unexpected collaboration keeps both creatures alive. His delicate poem 'We Live Inside Each Other' takes the idea of that essay much further.

It seemed to me that in his sharp, witty, amusing essays I had found a voice that everyone, open to the sciences and arts, could enjoy. He brings together beauty and knowledge, curiosity and analysis, imagination and reason, discovery and creativity, and sometimes music and sometimes laughter to whatever he offers us. And Lewis Thomas insists that such shared knowledge is an essential part of a liberal education for all young people.

Chapter Two

Responses from Australian Scientists

There is a haunting sense of climax in all of this. At the very moment man gains his greatest power he runs his greatest risk. It is almost as though humanity were being put through a kind of 'fitness trial'. If we are worthy trustees of life on Earth then we will come to understand that terms like 'the brotherhood of man' are not empty phrases but patents for survival. If we are unfit to take the reins of evolution into our hands, then the selfish sectarianism that now divides parties and nations will destroy us. In that case I doubt that our demise will trouble whatever gods may be.

Darryl Reanney[1]

The point is that disciplines intermingle.

Robyn Williams[2]

Research for this project began some years ago, nominally in 2001. Some time later, in 2006, invitations to scientists to become involved in the project were posted out. Not all responses would come as a result of that invitation. Some information revealing the connections scientists found with the poetry, the humanities and the arts might come through Radio National. For example that is how I discovered Miriam Rothschild and her delicate connection of the scientific precision of observation in nature with the writing of poets and the work of artists in *Butterfly Cooing Like a Dove*. Chance meetings, conversations, or following up names given to me led to scientists willing to make contributions.

Once the process was in place, further evidence of the desire of scientists to engage with those of us designated non-scientists could be found in different books. Such was

1 Darryl Reanney, 'Dangerous Harmony', *Age Monthly Review*, April 1982

2 Robyn Williams, *Future Perfect: What Next and Other Impossible Questions*. Allen & Unwin, Crows Nest, NSW, 2007, p. 46.

the case with Professor Peter C. Doherty who had responded swiftly to the invitation. I found his essays in *A Light History of Hot Air*. Even the title was amusing. We need hot air for balloons and, in idiomatic terms, we speak of people spouting so much 'hot air', heated in debate or slanging matches across an ideological divide. The juxtaposition of the science and the human capacity for the light-hearted touch is in that title. In the essays that delicate touch is maintained – for example in 'Alphabet Soup: On egg sandwiches and chemistry'.[3]

Peter Doherty's desire to communicate his twin focus on science and humanity is clearly evident in the concluding paragraph in 'Beacons'.

> Beacons for human progress like the United Nations, global treaties that preserve the air and the oceans, accords that respond to the rights and needs of persecuted women and children, and the international courts of justice that bring criminals at every level to account do not always burn as brightly as they should. We need to work out how to enhance such positive flames, to clean the lenses that focus the twin beams of the intellect and moral consciousness that protect the human family.[4]

His concern that people are swayed by the 'hot air' of soaring rhetoric appears in his ironically titled essay 'Soaring with Eagles: On turkeys and Aryan demagogues'. Here, dealing with rhetoric that encouraged the killing of children, mothers, babies, grandmothers, grandfathers, uncles, aunts, cousins, carpenters, pianists, book-keepers, invalids, and so many more, he tackles the 'power of soaring rhetoric' in a paragraph that should be read by everyone.

> Those who doubt the power of soaring rhetoric, the social conflagration that can result from the corrupting mix of fear, ignorance, racism, intellectual laziness, targeted paranoia and political hot air, should pause and reflect. Think about it next time sensibilities are jolted by one of those 'shock jock' sociopaths who infiltrate the world of talk-back radio. Whether the particular zealot is driven intellectually from the 'right' or 'left' of the political spectrum, the essence of totalitarianism is that nuanced, balanced, evidence-based discourse is considered 'weak' and has no sway. Like most predators, eagles are not subtle, and they are basically about death.'[5]

The writings of scientists in this book are of a more balanced kind and act as a counterweight to the rhetoric that so often appeals to people. I found this collection of

---

3 Peter C. Doherty, *A Light History of Hot Air*, Melbourne University Press, Melbourne, 2007

4 Peter C. Doherty, p. 175

5 Peter C. Doherty, p. 44

Peter Doherty's essays after I had asked him to contribute to this book. I included both of these examples of his outlook because they reinforce his commitment to humanity.

Metaphors can awaken the imagination, stimulating the senses as well as the mind. They can encourage reflection. Images invite connections in different ways, enhancing our understanding or provoking a way of thinking and feeling that can feed the human spirit. The scientists who talk on ABC Radio National, knowing they are speaking to a wider audience, many of whom have no knowledge of their discipline, make an effort to be understood. In that process they use metaphors that connect their world with ours. Often they quote from poems that provide them with a metaphor which might bring cultural experiences together.

That happens more and more frequently. For example, on 'Ockham's Razor', for 1 April 2007, Professor John Bradshaw of Monash University, whose area of study is neuroscience, made a comparison between James Elroy Flecker's poem 'The Golden Road to Samarkand', that Central Asian city with its history of mathematics and science in its architecture, with the golden road to scientific discovery.[6] As a child he had played the part of Hassan in a performance of the poem at school. Now, he quoted the rich, exotic language of the poem, commented on the connection between the two cultures that C.P. Snow had seen as separate, and took us willingly to the idea of the golden journey of curiosity in science. And he was not afraid of making connections with those personal experiences as a young man, in the 1960s, that had taken him to 'rose red Petra' in Jordan and the glories of Baghdad, with its history of connections between the arts and the sciences.

The voices of these Australian scientists speak to the problem created by that separation fostered in schools and by the concept of the 'two cultures' challenged by this book. They are presented in alphabetical order.

JANINE BAKER

Janine Baker is a scientist and poet who lives and works in South Australia. Much of her writing is influenced by an itinerant upbringing in various parts of Australia and New Guinea, including isolated islands. Although academically she excelled in undergraduate and postgraduate degrees in biology and environmental research, and is completing a PhD part-time during her working life, her choice to study science at university was against the advice of mentors who considered that a background in arts and humanities

6 'Ockham's Razor', named for the medieval English philosopher, William of Ockham, is on ABC Radio National at 8.45 am on Sunday.

would be a disadvantage. Janine has authored or co-authored more than 60 scientific publications, including papers, reports and more recently, electronic books. She has been writing poetry intermittently since childhood, when she won medals and other prizes for her poems and prose. Since 1996, about 80 of Janine's poems have appeared in Australian and American print journals, magazines and in on-line collections. In 2006, one of Janine's poems was selected for an anthology of 30 Australian and New Zealand poets, used for teaching in secondary schools in England. Her first collection, *Circus Earth*, was published in 2008 (Friendly Street Poets Inc. and Wakefield Press).

Writing poems is my other way of understanding, respecting, and chronicling the non-human world

Biological sciences and poetry are subjective human constructs. Both an experiment and a poem are a person's considered opinion of the way in which they think the world works, and another human may approach a scientific question or a poem in an entirely different way. 'Repeatability' as the basis of objectivity in science is a myth – the fact that an experiment is repeatable does not mean that it is correct – it will always be a human opinion of the world's workings. As scientists, we are taught that there is a 'truth' to be proved or falsified, but the 'truths' are discounted, or superseded, as human knowledge (opinion) of the way in which the world works improves (changes) over decades and centuries. One look at the contents of a *Science* volume from 1910 shows this: many of the postulates of the early 20th century biologists are now pooh-poohed, but at that time, were highly regarded revelations about the workings of Nature. Another case is systematics and taxonomy, study of the evolutionary relationships, categorisation, and naming of organisms on Earth. What is described as a 'species' does not usually conform to the notion of what can and cannot interbreed. Both meristic and molecular methods separate myriad natural variations in form into distinct boxes, depending on how much variation in a character or a gene that the scientist considers worthy of distinction. If we undertook the cataloguing of people in the exact way in which we approach the taxonomy of many non-human organisms, how many species of humans would there be? As part of this process, the Latin binomials given to every living thing on Earth are subjective human constructs, and many of these names change over time as particular groups in turn attract the interest of human 'lumpers' or 'splitters', who are driven to categorise life forms. Humans group or separate what they consider to be species (and higher order taxa) on complicated sets of characters. As one of millions of examples, a species of a particular genus of red algae is distinguished from closely related species mainly by minor differences in reproductive structures, including size: '(i) conspicuously elevated cystocarpic (100–150 µm high) and tetrasporangial (80–110 µm high) nemathecia; (ii) tetrasporangia with or without a unicellular pedicel; and (iii) large (25–45 µm in diameter by 70–115 µm in length) tetrasporangia and (iv) the production of double chains of spermatangia (*Peyssonnelia harveyana*-type spermatangial development).[7]

For almost any subject or object, there is a scientific aspect of 'the way it works', but also an emotional perception of it, a personal understanding of the way it influences our lives. In my poem 'Lunar-cy', the physical and technical, spiritual and emotional aspects of the Moon are contrasted (with all due respect to Shakespeare, the master wordsmith who seems to have had an unprecedented and paranormal understanding of the influence of the non-human world on human thought and action):

> 380 thousand Ks from the Third Rock
> spins *the natural satellite*,
> reflected in sunlight,
> the puller of tides, of whales, of shoals:
> it's the white glass ball on a 30-day roll.
> A jutting mass of maria and highlands;
> it's *the one small step*,
> the *one giant leap*,
> the source of fertility rites and seasons;
> the Artemis; the Yin; the Sun's good wife;
> the smugglers' enemy and the sulkers' reason.
> Maugham's muse, and the fuel for '50s crooners.
> The bleeder of women
> and the blinder of men.
> The excuse for idiots, flashers and killers,
> aimless wanderers, and howling dogs.
> It's Will's *sovereign mistress of true melancholy*
> By the light of the …
> The dark side of the …
> The cow jumped over the …
> I see the Moon and the Moon sees me.[8]

---

7 A. Kato and M. Masuda (2003) A new crustose red alga *Peyssonnelia rumoiana* (Rhodophyta, Gigartinales) from Japan. *Phycological Research* 51(10): 21

8 Janine Baker, *New Poets 13: Circus Earth,* Friendly St Poets Inc. and Wakefield Press, South Australia, 2008

In my writing, I often try to convey the significance of non-human living things that surround us every day, that we often overlook. In 'Monera', the overwhelming influence of bacteria on human existence is highlighted:

Bacteria rule the Earth:
gliding, whipping, twisting their way
on/in/under mankind.
While some bugs grow feed crops
and their kin sweeten wine,
their comrades rot our lungs,
spot our skins, send us blind.
Blue-greens turn clean water to soup,
E. coli kill through binary fission,
spirochaetes make sex a misery,
cocci bring us cheese and infection.
They even eat fuels our bodies oppose:
sulphur, petrol, methane, salt,
forming armies of bugs in protein coats.
Bacteria are smaller, and smarter, and more:
not bombs nor guns
will spell human doom
but killer bacilli
bred in the back room.[9]

In a number of my poems that anthropomorphise animals in a humorous way, I present the world from the perspective of the animal (another arrogant human practice). For example, 'Oh to be a Chiton' pays homage to the beautiful, carnival-coloured inter-tidal organisms that kids love to try to pull off rocks:

Yes, you don't ask for much, still the snoops come along
and prod at your periostracum. So you cling all the harder, and fasten your lip,
resisting the urge to attack 'em.
Your description's so solemn! All those names for your parts,
right down to your spiculose fringe.
A nomenclature nightmare, bestowed with such terms:
(At least they haven't named every valve hinge!)

---

9 Janine Baker, *New Poets 13: Circus Earth*.

Animal behaviour is a wonderful subject for a poem, perhaps as useful and satisfying a way of cataloguing the moment, as any brief note in a naturalist journal. 'Feeding the Babes' is an observation of two juvenile terns on a rock at West Island, out of Encounter Bay. One sat quietly and patiently, waiting for the parent to bring food, but received none. The other made a loud fuss, cheeping and running around wildly, and was promptly fed:

Little lost tern, perched on the ledge
with your speckled wings folded
searching the sky, peering over the edge
till your cheeping is scolded
by the graceful fishers
with their Art Deco shape –
you aspire to be so adept at the catch
but you're confined to the shore
to wait, mouth agape
relying on handouts from the moment you hatched.
With black orbs alert and your down blowing 'round
you circle yourself, and face the squawks in the sky:
give an up-tempo peep as the adults plunge down –
missed out again! If only you could fly!
Another swoops closer – could this be your chance?
A beak full of promise might fill up your maw.
Another false hope, as it zooms up to dance
with the other folk, flying now they've finished their chore.
You peep a bit louder, search over your shoulder,
see your brother approach and put on a turn,
with arms flailing wildly, running out from the boulder: attracting attention's
his only concern.
One plummeting swoop and a mouthful of fish
satisfies him – he knows how to protest
while you've peeped here for hours for a piscean dish.
Lost tern, you must scream to be noticed.[10]

10 Janine Baker, *New Poets 13: Circus Earth*.

An interest in spatial and temporal scales of human impact on the rest of the world is ever-present in my writing, as both a scientist and a poet. As indicated in 'Coastal Impact', various creations of weeks, months and centuries can be destroyed in an instant, by a single human footstep:

> We're here to turn back time
> without meaning
> crushing in our wake:
> sea-spurge
> that took months to stake its claim
> in a swathe of dunal sand
> fossilised twigs
> that took a century to cement
> the grains that form their cast
> winkle-blue jewels
> that took sea-weeks to settle
> on the smooth granite face of the shore.
> The impressions we leave
> where earth and sea meet
> mark human advance
> to the Coastal Retreat.[11]

The relationship and parallels between the human and non-human world pervade my poetry. 'Some Sentimental Stuff about the Gallery of Ants in the Window Sill', documents the killing of an unwanted colony of ants inside a room, but also tries to show the vulnerability of human existence in the 21st century, in the face of nuclear (or chemical) annihilation.

> Wingless workers filed out each spring
> to survey the surface
> found nothing (fly specks and crumbs)
> and filed back
> to build a few more rooms.
> In summer, mating pairs took to the wing
> in a frenzied attempt

11 Janine Baker, *New Poets 13: Circus Earth*.

to make more ants
to guard their fort
to extend their suburbs.
In autumn was found a chemical weapon
to lure them all
in lively procession
till they circled a pool
of deadly sugar.
Their graveyard of shiny black specks:
confused survivors
wrapping antennae
'round the dead and dying.
Line broken.
Nowhere to go.
Two slow crawlers left to start a new teem. These tiny twitching machines
run only on crumbs and formic acid:
work like nerves, for their days are numbered –
nuclear winter in a can of Mortein.

In my scientific work, I document marine plants and animals in southern Australia; describe and map exactly where they live, and (out of deep respect for the non-human world), try to publicly promote some of the impacts we may be having on them, in the hope that more and more people over time will appreciate the diversity and abundance of what is here, and what is being lost. Writing poems is my other way of understanding, respecting, and chronicling the non-human world. Both endeavours will likely end as a soon-forgotten account of what was there at a single brief point in human history, but is no longer.

MARCELLO COSTA

Professor Costa of Flinders University told me that he is not a poet. At first, he did not feel qualified to write about poetry and science. However, he is a neurophysiologist. When I spoke of the tendency in curricula to discourage interdisciplinary connections across the 'great divide', a separation that relegates the intellect and reason to one area and imagination and emotion to another, he decided to contribute.

Born in Torino, Italy, Professor Marcello Costa migrated to Australia in 1970, where he was one of the founders of the new discipline of neuroscience and the Australian Neuroscience Society (ANS), of which he later became President. Marcello holds a personal Chair in Neurophysiology at Flinders University – the first ever awarded in Australia – and has published over 200 scientific papers, written two books and numerous reviews.

A co-founder of the South Australian Neuroscience Institute (SANI), Marcello contributes widely to the public understanding of neuroscience by, among other things, writing articles in the national magazine, *Fast Thinking*, and through his involvement in public events such as 'Science Outside the Square'. He was elected as Fellow of the Australian Academy of Science in 1988, and received the Centenary Medal, Australia 2003.

In 2007 he contributed to the multi-disciplinary program, 'With the Body in Mind'. It was held in the Flinders School of Medicine as part of the contribution of Flinders University, Flinders Medical Centre and Arts in Health to the extended Science Outside the Square program bringing the sciences, in an inter-disciplinary way, to the public. Marcello Costa paints and plays guitar as a hobby.

Above all both require imagination

When the words poetry and science are sided together, we usually think of the profound differences between these two very human activities. Science is supposed to be precise, cold, constrained by rationality, objective and in modern times also useful. Poetry is associated with creativity, freedom of concepts and beauty, rather than usefulness. Those of us who have been involved in a lifetime of science know better. Although not a poet I find myself, more often than not, noticing similarities between these two apparent opposite worlds. Both are the result of creative human activities. Both use language and symbols. Both require intelligence and insight and above all both require imagination.

Imagination appeared in evolution as the very ability to make up situations that do not exist in the present. This ability is unique to *Homo Sapiens,* that is to say, to us, the latest addition to the family of hominids and apes which appeared around 5–7 million years ago. The ability to rehearse situations before they actually happen is well embedded in brain circuits that are not immediately involved in the response to what happens in the present, in the here and now. The brain of humans is larger than that of apes or that of the preceding hominids precisely because it has grown in the extensive outer shell (cortex = bark) areas that 'associate' different senses into 'imagination' before providing guidance for behaviour. When we sit quietly just thinking, other people may assume that our brain is idle. But usually the brain is active even when there is no external sign of activity. We can even say that mental activity is what goes on in our brain when we are doing nothing, just thinking.

Up until recently no one could tell if anything was going on inside the brain. It appeared to psychologists of the 19th and 20th centuries as a 'black box', with no way to find out what is going on inside. In the past 20 years brain imaging has been made possible with the development of tools to visualise what part of the brain is active and when. Although this approach is quite recent and still at its infancy, it has given neuroscientists a view of what happens inside our brains when we think, when we imagine. The results are most telling. When we imagine something, the same parts of the brain become active as those we use when we actually see things in the real world. This is true whether what we imagine does or does not exist: it requires as much imagination of a scientist to visualise an electron swirling around an atom's nucleus one million times per second as for a poet to visualise a girl following a white rabbit down into a netherworld of talking cats and smoking caterpillars.

What does this tell us? It is likely that the power of imagination is associated with the human ability to extend the perception of the real world into imaginary worlds, and that this ability has had a tremendous influence on our ability to adapt and evolve into a world-wide species. Humans have migrated from Africa, over several tens of thousands of years, into new lands into Asia, then arriving in Australia (over 50,000 years ago) before arriving in Europe (around 40,000 years ago) with the Americas being populated last (about 11,000 years ago). This remarkable ability, prominent amongst mammals, is probably linked to the ability to imagine what is beyond the local scene, for example behind a hill, or on the other side of a river, a lake or even an ocean. Human migration advanced at about one kilometre a year over the past 100,000 years. While that may seem slow nowadays, it implied not just some daring members of tribes exploring, but the moving of entire communities. Those explorers almost certainly had 'imagination' of what could be beyond their horizon, and they had another important motivator: curiosity. Curiosity can be interpreted as the drive for novelty. Humans from early childhood show a remarkable degree of curiosity, which if fostered leads to poets, artists and scientists.

Since prehistoric times, curiosity and imagination are the hallmark of all explorations, not only geographic but also in the use of ideas and concepts in both science and poetry. Imagining something new and being driven by the curiosity to find out about it is the main characteristic of science and exploration. The power of such imagination in science has been responsible for the most incredible ideas developed by human cultures. One of the greatest examples of human imagination is the realisation that we live on a ball hanging in space swirling around a burning star driven by a force we call gravity according to very precise rules (those first set out by Isaac Newton). Another great example is the thought that there may be particles that come into existence and disappear at a very sub-microscopic level of the quantum world (explored by many physicists in the early 20th century). The very idea that time and space are not absolutes and that they can be bent by matter is an example of remarkable imagination, that of Albert Einstein. Even the idea that we have evolved, just like other animals on Earth, was a big leap of imagination by Darwin. Now all these ideas have been proven to be quite right in that they explain a lot of apparent mysteries. Imagination and curiosity were the main motivators of these advances of humanity's view of the world, which was not simply given by some more ancient beliefs, myths or religions. So science flourishes when imagination and curiosity merge. And so does poetry. The endless exploration of imagery using words is the hallmark of poetry.

Both poetry and science also share rigour. That is to say the need of being in full control of the means of exploration. A scientist must know the proper use of language, of concepts and must master instruments in order to explore the unknown. They must also subject their imagination to the rigour of providing evidence to other peers. A poet must know the multiple meanings and inferences of words and be aware of the long history of concepts to be able to express a combination of words in a novel way. It is not a random choice of words. When one reads Dante Alighieri's *Divine Comedy*, the words in Shakespeare's theatre, or the rap of Eminem, one feels that every word is there for a precise reason and cannot be changed. The poet's writing is unique and specifically chosen.

Poetry is about beauty. But so is science. The search for harmony in nature and the sense of awe a scientist feels when confronted with a new discovery are intrinsic to this exploration. Even allegedly dry mathematics becomes a part of this sense of beauty in the universe. Mathematical proofs often are described as 'elegant' and 'beautiful' by mathematicians. Indeed mathematics requires a greater degree of imagination than most other human activities.

The best minds perhaps are capable of merging these qualities – poetry, mathematics and experimental science – into one activity, thereby creating the best condition for broadening the horizon of human existence. Both poets and scientists are engaged in a journey, searching for what lies beyond the present. Both are humble as they face an endless choice of ideas supplied by their imaginations. It is often said that the world is more imaginative than the human mind. The human mind is all that we have to explore this mysterious, rich and open world. Poets and scientists are our explorers of this endless world. Both have the power and the responsibility to change our world and ourselves.

PETER C. DOHERTY

Peter Doherty trained as a veterinarian, then went on via various twists and turns to a career as a research immunologist. Being awarded the 1996 Nobel Prize for Medicine led to his being named the 1997 Australian of the Year, an event that brought him onto the public stage. When that happened, the fact that he had always read widely in literature, history and even poetry stood him in good stead and helped him greatly in communicating with a broader audience.

He believes passionately that we must continue to embrace those values of reason, debate and rigorous intellectual analysis that characterised the European reformation and the enlightenment. Putting evidence ahead of superstition and ignorance has driven enormous advance in human well-being. However, while science enables real progress, anyone who has read history knows that there is no guarantee it will always be used for good purposes. Great literature, poetry, music, art keep us human and, if what's happened so far is anything to go by, we're going to need every drop of that humanity through this coming century.

Thinking about poetry, science and the two cultures

Though the activities are very different, the poet and the scientist are in the same business of illuminating underlying realities. Each looks at 'the thing itself' and tries to distil meaning. The starting material for the poet can be any aspect of experience, a breeze moving pampas grass, the cry of a timber wolf, the light in a 'fine old eye'. The scientist, on the other hand, is driven by intellectual constructs, experiments and a view of reality that is limited by the available data. Where the two come together is that each, in a different way, tries to tell some basic truth.

Both poetry and the major findings of science are for all of us, though public understanding of some of more complex scientific issues can require the involvement of professional communicators, like Robyn Williams or Karl Kruszelnicki. Much of science is, of course, concerned with obscure detail that adds to the body of knowledge in the field but does not merit community attention. We can read a minor poet, but even scientists will ignore the minor contributions in areas that are not of very direct importance to what they do.

Can scientists be poets? One of my former bosses was a private poet and a great clinical investigator. In my field, immunology, the Czech Miroslav Holub (1923–1998) was both a very substantial scientist and a widely read poet. Here's Holub's poem on animal experimentation and the animal liberation movement, published in translation in *Vanishing Lung Syndrome.*[12] The tone is, of course, ironic.

Animal Rights

Pity for dogs
        that cry
(boundless pity).
Pity for mice
        that squirm.

Pity for earthworms
        that wither helplessly
(limited pity).
(Pity for protozoons
        that sway their cilia
        so desperately.
Pity for cells
        that crawl away
        for life).
Pity for the central nervous system,
        microglia excepted.

Patients
with progressive amyotrophic lateral sclerosis
can just fuck off. They shouldn't have been born.
Hieronymus Bosch be with them
for ever and ever amen.

---

12 Miroslav Holub, trans. David Young and Dana Hábová, *Vanishing Lung Syndrome,* Oberlin College Press, 1990, p. 64.

Some areas of science deal with material that is extraordinarily beautiful. A case in point is the stained, complex structures that can be seen with various types of optical and electron microscopes. We marvel at the extraordinary movement of cells and their processes that we can access through modern video and imaging techniques. Companies that sell microscopes, for instance, have promoted public exhibitions and competitions that show such material. People who have no scientific leanings can be surprised and delighted when they see these images. In my experience, the individuals who dedicate themselves to such activities are often as much intuitive artists as scientists.

What of C.P. Snow's two cultures? Quite frankly, I think that any educational system that promotes this division is a disaster. Given the complexity of the modern world, and the fact that many people will be involved in a diversity of activities throughout their careers, the more that we can do to give our young people a solid acquaintance with both the sciences and the humanities the better our society will be. We make a great mistake when we force children to narrow their area of interest too early. What is the problem here? If it is the way we gauge university entrance, then it should be a simple matter to make the appropriate changes.

So far as the sciences are concerned, every high school student needs to be equipped with some basic understanding of how science works, how their bodies and minds function and the nature of the chemical and physical principles that have direct consequences in their every day lives. This doesn't need to be at a high level, but it does need to stick. Given the reality of global warming, for instance, no kid should now be leaving school without a basic understanding of the carbon cycle. We can't afford yet another generation of opinion makers, political and clerical leaders who are scientific illiterates.

Any professional scientist who cannot write good, clear, concise English is at a great disadvantage. The mark of most highly successful scientists is that they write well. When we look at our young colleagues, we see enormous scientific talent and creativity that, too often, is not matched by a commensurate ability to write. Where has our education system been failing such bright young people? Acquiring the grammar and discipline to write good, readable English is helped enormously by familiarity with another language. Because of the derivation of English, the most useful foreign languages are probably Latin and French. We think in both words and pictures. Learning to write well also promotes clarity of mind.

We must all know some history and have at least a little sense of the long march of humanity. The generals who commanded at Mons and Gallipoli in 1914 and 1915 seemed to be totally ignorant of the mass slaughter of the American Civil War, the first to use modern weaponry. How could anyone who had some acquaintance with the 20th century history of the Middle East and even the most minimal understanding of the Sunni/Shia divide have supported the disastrous military adventure in Iraq?

The health of any democracy depends on the active engagement of a well-educated citizenry, and on good information systems. If you want to experience a frisson of cold horror, look at the Australian statistics for viewing various television programs. We can only try to provide everyone with a broad, satisfying and comprehensive education. This means developing mechanisms to deal with a spectrum of interests and intellectual potential. As we do that, we may need to abandon some of our assumptions about the best ways to reach people. In my limited experience, good memorable stories that are seen as relevant to people's lives always work. Maybe there's also a role for the poetry, or even the limericks, of the carbon cycle that is central to all life.

SUSANNAH ELIOTT

Susannah Eliott has a PhD in cell biology from Macquarie University, a Graduate Diploma in Journalism from the University of Technology, Sydney, and 15 years of experience in science communication with the media as her primary focus. She has published a number of scientific and popular articles and worked on numerous communication projects in Australia and overseas including the successful 'Horizons of Science' forums for the media, 'Science in the Pub', 'Science in the Bush' and the Earth System Science Ambassadors program. In 2000 Susannah moved to Stockholm, Sweden as Communications Director for the International Geosphere-Biosphere Program (IGBP), an international network of scientists working on global environmental change. In September 2005 she became CEO of the Australian Science Media Centre, a unique national initiative that aims to inform public debate with science by providing news journalists with better access to experts and information.

Of slime moulds and poetry

If I could speak to my great, great grandchild, what would I say? Would I talk about how life is now – the cars, the clothes, the people? Or would I apologise for all the damage we have done?

No, I would probably talk about slime moulds.

'Slime what?' I hear him or her say with disgust. Images of brownish, greenish layers of muck hardly sounds like the stuff of poetry. Yet if only you could see it through my microscope eyes it wouldn't look ugly at all.

Among the petri dishes, test tubes, chemicals and microscopes is the fact of life itself. And what a remarkable life it is. Living most of its life as a single cell in the dark underworld of the soil, it sometimes undertakes a breathtaking transformation. Driven by hunger, the single cells find each other, forming small chains and then massive spiralling streams. Once the dance is complete hundreds of cells have coalesced to form a single being, a tiny slug, an animal without a brain. No nervous system to co-ordinate its movements or muscles to power it. How do they do it?

And having found each other in the darkness, they move as a unit, working their way up to the surface of the soil where the final stage of their metamorphosis takes place. Moulding and squeezing themselves into a new shape, they finally form a tiny plant-like structure, a perfectly shaped bud of spores atop a long slender stalk. Here they wait for the rain, wind and passing insects to carry the spores off to new realms and hopefully more food.

As one of the most ancient creatures on Earth, slime moulds have been doing this for millions of years. Long before humans, the dinosaurs or even the first primitive fish.

The secret of its transformation has kept teams of people around the world discussing, researching, arguing and lying awake at night with the sheer wonder of it. I sometimes imagine the small slime mould slugs laughing in unison at the international network of scientists, working frenetically to solve their riddles.

To unlock such secrets one must become completely immersed in the nature of the being. Whether it is a slime mould, a new strand of physics or the dance of a honey bee, immersion in the subject allows you to break beyond the barriers of limited imagination and cliché. You need creativity and wonder and a lot of patience.

Like a lover, you may simultaneously love and hate your subject but you cannot stop thinking about it, dreaming about it. And flowering from such obsession comes humility and deep respect for life. Though science is not magic, there is magic in science.

And so what do I hope for my great great grandchildren? That they will know that science, as with poetry, is about life and about passion. And with this knowledge they will have more humility and respect than we have shown the life around us.

TIM FLANNERY

Science writers, wanting to wake general readers to the ideas they are presenting, make felt connections with the world we know. That is what Professor Tim Flannery does. He gave support for this project when I spoke to him at the South Australian Museum where he was Director. Busy with his writing and his campaign to wake us up to climate change, he gave permission to include material from *The Weather Makers*. He wants us to have a feeling for and the desire to learn about the complex interactions that are bringing about climate change.

Consequently, I have included the following material from that important book. He wants us to take action to decrease our use of energy. In fact at the end of the book he has a list of actions we can take to begin the process of making a difference to ease the burden that is being placed on our children.

Imagining the Earth as an onion – Excerpts from The Weather Makers

Consider this paragraph from Chapter 2 'The Great Aerial Ocean'. In itself, that is an unusual way to describe what we call the sky. He writes:

> We are so small and the great aerial ocean so vast, that it seems hardly credible that we could do anything to affect its equilibrium. Indeed, for most of the past century humans have held to the belief that climate is largely stable, and the flea on the elephant's buttock that is humanity can have no effect. Yet, if we were to imagine Earth as an onion, our atmosphere would be no thicker than its outermost parchment skin. Its breathable portion does not even completely cover the surface of the planet – which is why climbers on Mt Everest must wear oxygen masks. And the gases that comprise it are so insubstantial that more gas lies dissolved in the oceans than floats in the atmosphere, and more heat energy is stored near the ocean's surface than in the entire great aerial ocean itself.'[13]

He wants us, the voters, the citizens whose decisions can influence the future, the people who should be having a say in our future for the sake of our children and grandchildren, to understand both the vulnerability and the dynamism of the atmosphere.

Tim Flannery presents us with chapter headings that invite our attention. He knows we do not have the level of technical language that might revel in an academic treatise. He is not afraid of using headings that engage our hearts as well as our minds. For

13 Tim Flannery, *The Weather Makers: The history and future impact of climate change*, Text Publishing, Melbourne, Australia, 2005, p. 22

example, in Chapter 8, 'Digging up the Dead' refers to mining, but first of all Professor Flannery awakens us to what the land means, eager for us to feel and be aware of the whole picture rather than just focus on a narrow part of it.[14] To do so he takes us to an epic poem by Big Bill Neidjie, an Elder of the Kakadu country and quotes these lines from its section on Land.

> We walk on earth
> We look after,
> Like rainbow sitting on top.
> But something underneath,
> Under the ground.
> We don't know.
> You don't know.
> What you want to do?
> If you touch,
> You might get cyclone, heavy rain or flood.
> Not just here,
> You might kill someone in another place.
> Might kill him in another country.
> You cannot touch him.[15]

The Weather Makers is easy to read. All that is needed is the desire to become more aware of the globe on which we live. Tim Flannery takes us to the depths of the oceans, to discoveries by scientists at Wood Hole in America and by Australia's CSIRO, and makes us aware of the increasing discomfort and major problems that climate change will bring for the people of Earth.

---

14 That narrow focus is known as reductionism, an approach to the sciences which believes that by studying a very narrow aspect of one of the sciences, one can know everything. It involves increased specialisation and fragmentation. On Radio National, the repeat of the Science Show, at 7 pm on 22 January 2007, scientists discussed Gaia and warned of the danger of reductionism which denies the significance of the holistic view. The program also dealt with the 'problem of inertia', 'the pandemic of apathy' which makes too many of us unwilling to look beyond the present moment.

15 Bill Neidjie, *Gagudju Man: The environmental and spiritual philosophy of a senior traditional owner*, Kakadu National Park, JB Books, Marleston, South Australia, 2002, pp. 34–35. In *The Weather Makers*, Tim Flannery wants us to consider the challenge that Bill Neidjie had thrown down; see pp. 69–79. Here he examines the long-term consequences of the Industrial Revolution.

Chapter 22 poses another challenge: 'Civilisation: Out with a whimper?'. To put this question about our future, Professor Flannery has chosen the conclusion to a poem that T.S. Eliot wrote after World War I. The massive expansion in the kinds of weapons of war that governments were prepared to use made us afraid of the damage we could do. That is why the League of Nations, inadequate as it proved, was founded to try to establish a peaceful way to resolve national differences through international arbitration.

T.S. Eliot's poem, of 1922, 'The Wasteland' concludes with despair as he lists the 'fragments [he has] shored against [his] ruin'. Three years later, in 1925 Eliot wrote 'The Hollow Men'. It is 'the dead land' and he ends with

> This is the way the world ends
> Not with a bang but a whimper.[16]

Those of us who are old enough remember the original impact of this poem and its images, and ponder the question Flannery is asking us to think about now.

Readers might be aroused by the title he has chosen for Chapter 26. 'People in Greenhouses shouldn't tell lies'. The author has been clever. The 'greenhouse' is the hot house for exotic plants. With temperature increasing, Earth is becoming closer to a 'greenhouse' in some ways. The 'glass house' is the reminder. The original proverb advises that 'People who live in glass houses shouldn't throw stones'. Who is lying about the problems facing the planet?

To reinforce the title of the chapter, Flannery quotes from *The Merchant of Venice*.

> The Devil can cite scripture for his purpose.
> An evil soul, producing holy witness,
> Is like a villain with a smiling cheek,
> A goodly apple rotten at the heart.
> O, what a goodly outside falsehood hath!

He points out that 'in the 1970s the US was a world leader and innovator in energy conservation'. What happened? Who has the money to fight the propaganda war? The evidence is in that chapter. He takes us towards the solutions he sees and, in 'Over to You', the final chapter, he gives the warning in lines from 'Truth' a poem by William Cowper, an eighteenth century poet.

At every stage, throughout his book, Tim Flannery has shown us how the disciplines can intermingle in the writing of someone who has a broader-based education. Through that intermingling, the general reader is brought into 'the heart of the matter.'

---

16 T.S. Eliot, *Collected Poems 1909–1962*, Faber and Faber Ltd, London 1974, p. 92

IAN GIBBINS

Professor Ian Gibbins, a colleague of Professor Costa's, is a scientist and a poet. He now presents his poetry at Adelaide's centre for open poetry readings, Friendly Street.

Professor Gibbins was originally trained in zoology at the University of Melbourne. After a couple of years in the USA, he arrived at Flinders University, where he has been Professor and Head of the Department of Anatomy and Histology since 1993. He teaches extensively in functional anatomy, neuroscience and embryology. He also has coordinated major components of the medical program, and more recently a Graduate Certificate in Neuroscience (Learning). In addition Ian's research uses combinations of microscopy and electrical recordings to investigate the nerves that control the internal organs. Outside work, Ian windsurfs, writes poetry, experiments with electronic music and cooks. Over the past couple of years he has become interested in the cultural history of anatomy and its place in the emerging science of early modern Europe.

With Marcello Costa, Professor Gibbins has made valuable contributions to the 'Science Outside the Square' program at 'The Gov' and, in 2007 in the 'With the Body in Mind' program at Flinders School of Medicine. His contribution was the interdisciplinary 'Know thyself: art and the cultural history of anatomy'. Ian has worked on a number of projects with groups of students at the Australian Science and Mathematics School. Currently he is mentoring a group researching the emotional content of music. He gave a public lecture in association with *The Australian Book Review* on the Body/Mind connection in 2007 and was interviewed by Natasha Mitchell for 'All in the Mind' on ABC Radio National.

Imagined Worlds: Neuroscience and Poetry

1. In the laboratory

I am a neuroscientist. I am interested in how nerve cells communicate with each other. Today, I will be doing an experiment. I am sitting alone in my room, a small dark space without windows. Once, in the years before the digital imaging revolution, we used this room to develop photographic films. It is easy to forget how much time we spent carefully controlling the temperature and light, the volume and concentration of chemicals that made your eyes sting and your finger tips turn sepia brown: all to get that perfect picture of a tiny nerve cell, the ideal illustration of the microscopic relations that underpin the almost inconceivable complexity of the nervous system.

Now, my corner of the room is packed with sophisticated electronic equipment. There are oscilloscopes, amplifiers, timers with banks of flashing lights, as if they are part of a Hollywood sci-fi set, and the ubiquitous computers to control the circuits, to record the data. The air hums with the whirr of a dozen cooling fans, punctuated every so often by the clicking of solenoids or the flicking switches of stimulators and microscope optics. Why do we need all this gear? What will I actually be doing today?

Imagine this: each individual nerve cell is minute, only a few hundredths of a millimetre in diameter. It communicates with other nerve cells via a long fine process, perhaps only a few thousandths of a millimetre in diameter. The surface of the nerve cell works like a chemical battery that discharges an electrical impulse in just a fraction of a second. Imagine if we could measure this impulse, using an electrode so fine that you'd need a microscope to see its tip, as it is placed right inside a living nerve cell. This is exactly what physiologists did imagine, and in the 1950s and 1960s, they figured out how to record the electrical activity of single nerve cells. It was such an outstanding achievement, that some of them, including the Australian, Sir John Eccles, won Nobel Prizes for their discoveries.

These days, with the benefit of improved electronic and computer technology, you can buy ready-made, albeit expensive, equipment to do these recordings. But the procedures remain difficult. You need patience and practice, not to mention the rock-steady hand and dexterity required to manipulate the nerve cells and electrodes under a microscope. And you need to concentrate on the job. No distracting conversations about football or the budget or someone's latest romantic involvement. Odd, isn't it, how we cannot talk while focusing on skilled motor tasks, but that is another story ...

As it is, there are many things that can go wrong during an experiment like this. Everything has to be just right, and even the best technology can fail on occasion. More importantly, we do not know exactly how the nerve cell will behave this time round. After all that is why we are doing the experiments! In planning the experiment, we try to predict alternative outcomes, based on what we know from previous trials or from data produced by scientists in other laboratories. If we are sufficiently fortunate or clever (or, more often, a bit of both), and we do find something new, we have to replicate the experience, so that we can confirm that the world of the nerve cell really operates the way we think it does. If so, we have made a small step in predicting how the nerves might react in different, novel circumstances.

This last point is important, because predicting the future, imagining models of the world, is what our brains do really well. We go about our lives constantly faced with a barely perceived tension between predictability and novelty. On one hand, most of us like new things, new sights and sensations. On the other hand, we usually do not feel comfortable if all this novelty is too distant from our prior expectations or experience. There is a famous book by Robert Hughes on the history of modern art called *The Shock of the New*: the title sums up the dilemma perfectly. In science as in art, new ideas, new conceptualisations, new approaches and techniques, can challenge and threaten as much as they ultimately can enlighten and inform.

Back in my laboratory, my experiment has gone well enough. The nerve cells responded to my electrodes and biochemical manipulations pretty much as I had expected. No big breakthrough, but satisfying, with data that other neuroscientists should find useful and interesting. As I clean up and turn off all the machines at the end of a long and tiring day, I find my mind wandering. Imagine what it would be like if someone recorded the electrical activity of my very own nerve cells …

Stereotactic

you know the way it is
the words the words
the words rushing out from somewhere
somewhere, you know, between my ears
and all the hidden questions
all the flashing liquid crystals
while I rattle my joystick buttons
simply trying to keep to time

I don't care what the plan may be
double blinded and under control
my head encased in magnetite
false alarms, yes, rising and falling
or the plates in my skull
just kind of, you know, separated
to let the needles buzz and probe
and my cathode rays light up their room

2. In the classroom

Tomorrow, I will be teaching. Neuroanatomy. Which bits of the brain are which, and which bits do what. It can all get very complicated. But then, it is often said that the human brain is the most complicated thing in the known universe. A big call, typical, I suppose, of our self-centred view of the world. Still it's all we have, and that well-worn catch phrase does help to get the point across: the brain really is complex and if you want to learn how it might function, you had better pay attention to some of the key facts, you'd better get some of these general principles of organisation straight. Or you may never get it right. And if you are planning to be a doctor, for example, that may come back to haunt you. But let's move on …

The students will need some guidance. I've written some notes, a sort of beginner's guide to the brain. Although they were updated last year, I suspect there may still be a mistake somewhere. Nothing much: a misplaced word or two, but annoying nevertheless. By now it's too late to fix. Anyway, we'll do the class a different way next year and we'll sort it out then.

Yes, it is annoying. The words matter. Just like any field of human endeavour, there are the special words that define what we mean, that create the fine grained concepts, the links, the meshworks of ideas and metaphors that let us both encapsulate and expand what we know about the interlocking components of our world.

Tomorrow, the students will come to their class in the Anatomy Museum and they will begin this process. Little by little, they will come to learn that this area is the occipital cortex, where visual information begins to reach consciousness; that one is the supplementary motor area, where we plan our skilled movements. They might remember that the anterior cingulate gyrus has something to do with emotion, or that the curiously-named insula holds a map of our internal organs.

For most members of the class, this will be their first opportunity to see, to hold, to handle a real human brain. What a privilege! What a responsibility! They will be surprised. Not by its complexity, but by its dullness, its flatness of texture, despite the folds and wrinkles, and its near uniform colouration, all but obscuring the subtle nuances of grey and white matter. Unlike the images from biology texts or confronting murder-mysteries, these brains will not be soft and mushy. They will not bleed if they are cut.

These brains are different. These brains are special, even more special than that usual run-of-the-mill Most-Complicated-Things-in-the-Universe. Think about it. How did they come to be in our anatomy class room? Why are we allowed to use them for teaching at all?

The answer is at once both simple and wondrous. They are here because at some stage, when each was the living, thinking, dreaming core of a human, a person, a life, they decided that this would be their fate. They decided that, once they were dead, their physical selves, their mortal remains (to use the terms of the Anatomy Act), could be used for teaching and research, for the future benefit of students and the society within which they will live and work. They decided that, once they were dead, their blood could be replaced with preservative and their brains put on display so future generations can observe and learn.

By the end of these classes, some of the students, the lucky ones, will have glimpsed a little of what it is that makes us what we are. If they had paid attention to what they were really looking at, if they looked deep into their own minds, they might begin to grasp what once seemed almost unknowable: the real but elusive connections between the physical existence of a complex biological system that forms a brain, and the all pervasive feeling of being one's self.

Perhaps some of my class, when I challenge them, will dare to imagine that mysterious transition from a decision made in fine spirit and good health through an unknown death into that anonymous specimen, the precious relic, lifeless but giving of life, on the bench before them.

museum

No-one is likely to argue
that, any time soon,
we will be moving far from here.

Not because our bones
have become soft and yellow,
carefully exposed

below these white cotton sheets.
Nor because our nerves,
now slack, without tension or tone,

no longer sing like piano strings.
Nor even because our
rich red blood and

dark shining muscles
have ceased to pump, to pulse.
As you can see, we are done with action:

all we have left is intent and desire;
all we wish is for
you to feel our warmth.

3. In the street

In some ways, it's a bit like walking. Like walking through a town or landscape where we haven't been before. We have some directions. We may even have a map. Although we know more or less where we are heading, the details of how we will get there are not so clear. We'll see as we go along. We'll seek advice, if required, from a friendly local.

People used to talk about 'rambling'. Not a bad thing, like a rambling speech, or worse, a rambling mind, but a pleasurable activity, heading out across the open fields with a certain sense of adventure or the hint of a promise of coming across something that little bit unexpected. Perhaps this was in the marketeers' minds when they called a popular American car of the 1960s the 'Rambler'. Too bad it was ugly, even by the sensitivities of that era, and its manufacturer ended up going broke.

These days rambling doesn't seem such a valued concept. It implies vagueness of intent and a tendency to wander off the track. But that was certainly not the case when the pioneering neuroanatomists first started constructing detailed maps of the physical body, collected into beautifully illustrated atlases. They called one of the longest, most widely distributed nerves in the body the 'vagus': the vagrant, the wanderer, the rambler. Arising from near the base of the brain, near where the skull meets the bones of the neck, the vagus rambles out to your lungs, your heart, your stomach and other parts of your internal organs you rarely need to think about. It has a great diversity of functions sending information and instructions to and from the brain. For example, the vagus can slow down your heartbeat or sense how much food is in your stomach. All this is done with a precision that is truly remarkable. How it does so is something that neuroscientists are actively investigating in laboratories around the world.

We may not understand the vagus fully, but we certainly understand a lot more than those early anatomists. They saw that the vagus extended from the brain to organs that they thought to be responsible for the control of our emotions, an idea inherited from Galen and the ancient Greeks. Thus, there was the heart, a source of heat; the liver, the source of bile and bad temper; and the lungs, taking in the vital air. Perhaps, they wondered, the vagus connected between the brain and the organs via a system of pneumatic pumps. Perhaps, they hypothesised, the vagus was a conduit for an unknown ether-like fluid.

Now we know that the vagus, like any set of nerves, transmits information by a complex series of electrochemical processes, just like those I measured in my experiment. However, the language associated with those early ideas persists to this day in those slightly archaic descriptors of personality: someone may be melancholic (full of black bile, according to Galenic principles) or phlegmatic (an excess of water or phlegm) or excitable and hot headed. This is a really amazing element of our culture: our history, including the history of our science, is embedded in the words we use. Our language is like a vast evolving organism, built up from a series of neural circuits along the sides of our brains, an organism made from the minds of individuals living and working and talking together over many generations. Language allows us to build on these reservoirs of past experience, of by-gone meaning, and integrate contemporary interpretations of our webs of knowledge to construct new futures, to imagine new worlds. This is a key to the art of science. This is a key to the science of art.

electrocardiogram

light hearted
heavy hearted
soft hearted
broken hearted
heartache
open hearted
cold hearted
empty hearted
kind hearted
heart of gold

goodness of your heart
bottom of my heart
heartfelt
heartless
change of heart

lion hearted
stout hearted
heart like an ox
your heart's desire
learnt by heart

hale and hearty
his hearty laugh
her hearty broth
heartburn
your heart on your sleeve

down hearted
faint hearted
bleeding heart
heartened to hear
the heart of the matter

sweet heart
this heartland
this heart of the country
this heartbeat
this heart to heart

JOHN J. LOWKE [17]

Dr John Lowke is an Honorary Fellow at CSIRO Industrial Physics, Sydney. Earlier in his career he was a teacher of science and mathematics at high schools in South Australia, a Lecturer at Adelaide Teachers College, Senior Physicist at Westinghouse Research Laboratories, Pittsburgh, USA, Senior Lecturer then Reader, University of Sydney, Chief, CSIRO Applied Physics, and Chief Research Scientist, CSIRO Telecommunications and Industrial Physics. His many research papers are frequently quoted in text books on the physics of plasmas, lightning, welding, lasers, circuit interruption and discharge lamps. He is a Fellow of the Australian Academy of Technological Sciences and Engineering.

17 I am indebted to my wife Karil and also A.B. Murphy and P Watterson of the CSIRO for comments on the manuscript.

Feelings of awe, imagination and inspiration in physics

Among the people on earth who are concerned with the search for truth, beauty and meaning, I believe there is a commonality of mental processes, usually going through the three stages of firstly, feelings of awe, secondly the mental activities of imagination and thirdly and finally the inspiration of the final solution. I include both scientists and poets in this group of people! The final outcome is, respectively, science and poetry!

I am writing as a scientist, and from the particular point of view of a physicist. I would like to mention three aspects of science and physics that are markedly different from poetry. These differences need to be stated and understood, as they help us to understand the chasm that often separates the two cultures. Having understood and observed these differences, it is then possible to arrive at a wider understanding and appreciation of the commonality of both cultures and their mental processes and to appreciate the beauty of these most advanced achievements of the human mind.

Firstly, I mention the rather obvious and immediate differences between poetry and science, which is the use of words. Great care is taken in science, and in physics in particular, to convey exact meaning. When physicists use the word 'power' they mean 'joules per second'! But poets use poetic license and the word 'power' can have many different meanings. The application of a strict scientific or linguistic analysis can demolish poetry. Wordsworth 'wandered lonely as a cloud'; but clouds are not lonely and do not wander. R.L. Stevenson observed 'faster than houses, faster than ditches' from his railway carriage; but houses and ditches do not move. Such differences are not the shortcomings of poetry, but are the core contributions of poetry in providing meaning in terms of rhyme, rhythm and correlations of differing pictorial imagery.

But the second big difference between science and poetry is that while the language of poetry is words, the language of physics is not words at all, but mathematics. I will never forget the feelings of awe and inspiration that I experienced in my last year of high school when we finally studied the differential and integral calculus, developed initially by Newton in the late 1660s. We had spent years in our earlier high school studies doing many exercises in removing and inserting brackets in algebraic expressions, 'rationalising' the denominator of fractions, developing laws of the indices etc. Then finally we climbed to the top of the mountain to see the promised land of calculus in all its beauty. We could calculate areas under a curve exactly. We could calculate speeds and accelerations from distances as a function of time. All encapsulated in those few symbols of dy/dx! Calculus is truly one of the greatest achievements and most beautiful creations of the human mind.

Mathematics is not poetry. My shop-keeper father kept asking me 'What are maths?' and treated mathematics as inconsequential gibberish. But mathematics does have poetic undertones. It ever so succinctly encapsulates meaning. Maxwell's equations describing electromagnetic properties have a beauty yet elegance of symmetry which is astounding. Furthermore the meaning is many faceted. If you look at the equations in a slightly different way, completely different meaning is revealed, yet all of the meaning is contained in the original expression. Poetry can have very similar features, with multiple meanings involving different symbolism.

The third aspect I wish to discuss is the role of 'awe' in these human creations. The heavens and motion of the stars have been a source of wonder and awe throughout history for poets, lovers, and scientists and physicists. Newton was concerned with the puzzle of why the planets in their motion across the sky obeyed peculiar laws as observed from the telescopic observations of Tycho Brahe and the generalisations of these observations made by Kepler. It was the triumph of Newton that all of these observations were explained through an application of the calculus to the postulate that the gravitational force of the sun obeys a law that if the distance between the sun and the planet is doubled, the force is divided by four. Newton showed that the solution of the differential equation following from this simple law of gravitation leads to the conclusion that planets must travel around the sun in an ellipse. This proof is by no means simple. When Halley, of Halley's comet fame, asked Newton as to the basis of the proof, Newton had to go home and send the proof to Halley days later. The conclusion of elliptical motion of the planets was the triumph of Newton's career and has been one of the major achievements of science in all history.[18]

But in science one problem leads to another. Seven of the eight planets go round the sun in orbits that are very close to being circular, but a circle is a very special case of an ellipse, having equal major and minor axes. Furthermore the orbits are all almost in the same plane. And six out of eight of the planets themselves rotate in the same direction. Why does the solar system have all of these additional regularities? It is likely that there is a mechanism that can explain such regularities in terms of some physical mechanism resulting from the basic laws of motion.

It could be argued that the result of such scientific explanations is that having found the explanation, the initial reason for the poetic awe is lost. The planetary motion at first sight is mysteriously regular and inspires feelings that there must be some intelligent design or even a designer behind it all. But after the physicist has formulated explanations, the reason for the awe is gone. The planetary motions are just

18 R.S. Westfall, *Memoirs of the life, writings and discoveries of Sir Isaac Newton*, Vol. 1, p. 297.

a consequence of a few simple laws of behaviour in the presence of gravity.

Similarly the light and power of thunder and lightning have inspired poets and novelists throughout history. Early mankind would plead with thunder-gods. But the physicist's explanation is just that different electrostatic charges on hail of different sizes within a thundercloud, combined with the separating effect of high wind, causes voltage differences that result in a spark, which is lightning, and electrical heating of the air, which causes thunder. On a finer scale of observational detail, it has been shown that each lightning strike is preceded by a series of fifty metre steps from the cloud to the ground, each lightning up for a millionth of a second, but then going dark for fifty millionths of a second. Such a series of steps can become branched, but when one of the branches touches a high point on the ground, there is a 'return stroke' of very high current from the ground to the cloud, which is the lightning we see. But again this complex behaviour can be explained simply in terms of the motion of electrons, positive ions and negative ions. All of the details of the steps and pauses between the steps follow from a solution of the equations for the motion of these particles.[19] The mystery is gone. There is no need for any 'awe', the world just follows from relatively simple physical laws of physical behaviour. Scientists might follow the dictum of R.H. March[20] in his book *Physics for Poets*, who says 'The worst possible attitude with which to approach the study of physics is one of awe. Physics has prospered largely by sticking to business!'

No! I believe that there is indeed a strong component of awe driving all of the significant advances of physics. The mental processes behind the principal advances of physics are feelings of awe, imagination and inspiration – similar to those at the basis of poetry. I believe that the total picture of the explanations in terms of physics and mathematics makes the regularities of the solar system, or the light and power of lightning, *more* awe inspiring, not less. The activities of the major physicists, starting with Newton and Einstein, were more than mere mathematical mechanics. Newton spent twenty years of his life studying alchemy and theology. He said 'I keep the subject of my inquiry constantly before me, and wait till the first dawning opens gradually, by little and little, into a full and clear light', and 'If I have seen further it is by standing on the shoulders of giants'.

In conclusion, it is evident from the many published quotations of Einstein[21], arguably the greatest physicist, he, and I believe most physicists, have the mentality of

---

19 J.J. Lowke,On the Physics of Lightning, *Proc. IEEE Trans. Plasma Science*, 32, 4–17 (2004).

20 R.H. March, *Physics for Poets*, Mc Graw-Hill, New York, 1970.

21 A. Calaprice, *The Expanded Quotable Einstein*, Princeton University Press, Princeton 2000.

poets. Einstein said 'Every day I remind myself that my inner and outer life are based on the labours of other men, living and dead, and that I must exert myself in order to give in the same measure as I have received and am still receiving'. Also 'The most beautiful thing we experience is the mysterious. It is the source of all true art and science.' I believe that poets, in their interaction and involvement with language could endorse these words as their own.

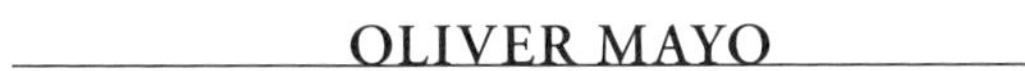

OLIVER MAYO

Oliver Mayo is a statistical geneticist who has worked in human, animal and plant genetics and livestock production science. He is a post-retirement research fellow with CSIRO Livestock Industries and an Adjunct Professor of Biometry in the University of Adelaide. He is a Fellow of the Australian Academy of Science and of the Australian Academy of Technological Sciences and Engineering and a Foreign Member of the Russian Academy of Agricultural Science. He has written over 100 scientific papers and books on various topics, from evolution, to Australian wine, to a biography of a Victorian detective story writer.

Poetry and genetics? 'Nature to advantage drest'

> Up to the age of thirty or beyond it, poetry of many kinds, such as the works of Milton, Gray, Byron, Wordsworth, Coleridge and Shelley, gave me great pleasure; and even as a schoolboy I took intense delight in Shakespeare, especially in the historical plays. I have also said that pictures formerly gave me considerable joy and music every great delight. But now for many years I cannot endure to read a line of poetry: I have tried lately to read Shakespeare, and found it so intolerably dull that it nauseated me. I have also almost lost my taste for pictures or music …
>
> My mind seems to have become a kind of machine for grinding general laws out of large collections of facts; but why this should have caused the atrophy of that part of the brain alone, on which the higher tastes depend, I cannot conceive.
>
> [I]f I had to live my life again, I would have made a rule to read some poetry and listen to some music at least once every week; for perhaps the part of my brain now atrophied would thus have been kept alive through use. The loss of these tastes is a loss of happiness.

Darwin, *Autobiography* in F. Darwin (editor) *The Life and Letters of Charles Darwin*. London, John Murray, 1887, pp. 100–102.

Darwin's loss is well known among literate biologists. What is less well known, perhaps, is that Darwin used poetry in his work. In his charming as well as startlingly original work on *The Expression of the Emotions in Man and Animals*, he quoted Shakespeare when he needed a description of disgust or envy or jealousy or modesty or patience or rage or the integration of thought and movement, Homer for laughter and grief and Plautus for perplexity (but in translation, for Darwin was very bad at languages), Spenser for suspicion and Somerville for grinning in dogs. This book was published when he was over 50, so his loss occurred relatively late in life.

Many of us, whose contribution to science is not a ten millionth of Darwin's, have not lost the love of poetry. It is somehow comforting to read Philip Larkin's bleak view of death as the end, expressed in so few words, for example,

> Life is first boredom, then fear.
> Whether or not we use it, it goes,
> And leaves what something hidden in us chose,
> And age, and then the only end of age.
>
> from 'Dockery and Son'

It is (sometimes) warming to read Les Murray. It is funny and horrible by turns to read Browning's excoriation of false prophets in 'Mr Sludge the Medium'. One can be awed by Dante or Milton and always astounded by Shakespeare.

Lines of verse, not always poetry, run through my head when I'm working, but if one threatens to turn into an ear-worm, to use the German expression, I can be rid of it by thinking of a few others. Verse forms have their own attraction to anyone who likes structure, symmetry, economy, wit, above all structure: what can be fitted into a particular form, such as a sonnet? Rilke's 'Panther' comes to mind: the famous last line that stops short, constrained like the panther inside its cage.

I wrote a little book called *Natural Selection and Its Constraints* twenty-five years ago, and one of my inspirations for doing so was the thought that natural selection works within tightly defined rules (the strength of gravity, the spectrum of electromagnetic radiation, the nature and magnitude of chemical bonds and so on), just like a poet. And of course 'natural selection' is a metaphor as fraught with emotional baggage as anything a poet might use, indeed has used, if one recalls Tennyson's 'nature red in tooth and claw'.

It is rare for poetry to have a direct influence on my work of the kind I've just described. Usually verse, whether one's reading it or writing it, is a recreation, a pleasure, a parallel activity, a constant comfort in the back of the mind. It's even more rare for poetry to come out of the work. The beauty of a result (for a statistical geneticist usually the form of a relationship, or a new relationship, or a clarified mode of causation) is a prime motivation for many of us, but it's only part of the thrill of discovery, and discovery, by its nature, is vanishingly rare for the individual scientist.

A final word on language, taking Darwin as a cautionary tale: I've been learning a little French, German and Italian so I can begin to read Dante or Goethe or Rilke or Rimbaud without the interpolation of a translator. I think this aids my enjoyment of English verse as well, not to mention the suppleness of mind needed to read statistics.

Executive forum: 'a mere bundle of sensations'

When I remove my spectacles
The world softens, edges fray,
Leaves disappear. So do high tackles
From the sidelines – on the day
At least. But a clear vision
Of our paymasters
Is no misprision.
Anticipate disasters:
'In science and sport we lead the way,
Always ready to see fair play.'

Tall cedars fractal as snowflakes
Loom over the synagogue.
Anthony Edens, fedoras, bowlers
Stroll, scuttle or stride across the slate below the willows.

Culture is 'values in action'
Our culture values inaction.

Scientist I am, I have a starting point,
A purpose, a set of unstated presuppositions.
Do I know what they are? Let me enumerate.
Whatever I apprehend results from internal treatments,

By means I do not yet understand, of sense impressions.
Whatever is in the world, whatever happens, has
A material basis.
There is no god, no immaterial soul, no afterlife.
There is free will and, as a result, altruism is possible.
(Not certain, mind you, or even highly likely.)
Every phenomenon has a causal explanation, except perhaps at
The quantum level.
(Not too certain about that, either.)
Properties at one level of hierarchy may be described at a
Lower level but not necessarily predicted for that level.
Correlation is not causation but causation should be
Manifest in some pattern of correlation.
Chance events may be no more than chance events,
Rain on the slate.[22]

DAVID PAGANIN

An invitation was sent to Dr Rosemary Mardling, a physicist at Monash University who, though she was unable to contribute directly, praised this project when we spoke at the University of Melbourne. She had heard the following address given by Dr Paganin when in Melbourne he opened a collaborative work, by a collective group of artists, that explored quantum physics through sculpture.

With her recommendation that Dr Paganin was a lecturer at Monash University who engaged his students and recognised the importance of collaboration between the arts and the sciences, I asked to see the address he had given. While it is not a direct address to young students, it is a variation on the theme that provoked this project and it is a theme that will be taken up in a different way by Dr Elizabeth Truswell.

I felt convinced that some senior students and teachers would be engrossed by the information he has given about the difference between quantum and classical physics, appreciate his love of beauty, delight in the verbs he uses, enjoy the connections he makes and, as a result, broaden their horizons in both the sciences and the arts. This contribution is the joint work of Dr Paganin and the sculptor Marc Rogerson.

---

22 *All We Like Sheep*, Oliver Mayo, Fastbooks, Sydney, 2002, pp. 5–6.

Biographical notes

David Paganin is a theoretical physicist from Monash University, who has worked in a variety of areas spanning the spectrum from the fundamental to the applied. Areas in which he has published include quantum vortices, superconductivity, superfluidity, non-linear quantum fields, topological defects, Bose-Einstein condensation, X-ray imaging, electron diffraction, tomography, medical imaging, polymer scaffolds for tissue regeneration, next-generation lithography for the manufacture of integrated circuits, microscopy, holography, atom optics, condensed matter physics, neutron optics and visible-light optics.

Marc Rogerson is a Melbourne-based sculptor and painter whose practice involves illuminated sculpture, architectural–sculptural installations, abstract painting, figurative painting and portraiture. Not formally trained, he started executing mural commissions in 1988.

DAVID M. PAGANIN & MARC ROGERSON

Αστρων παντων καλλιστος (Sappho)[23]

When words and worldviews decay: thoughts on the art–science nexus, on how a poem can be as beautiful as a scientific theory

1. Introduction

The Plump trio – comprised of sculptor Marc Rogerson, together with sound artists Philip Samartzis and Dave Brown – is a Melbourne-based group whose latest project operates at the isthmus between the arts and the sciences. In April 2008 this Australian trio, augmented by video artist Marcia Jane, presented a fine-art installation titled 'Cluster' at the Victoria College of the Arts Margaret Lawrence Gallery.[24] In this exhibit, translucent illuminated fibreglass pods were juxtaposed with fields of both

23 D.A. Campbell (ed.), *Greek Lyric: Sappho and Alcaeus*, Harvard University Press, Cambridge Massachusetts, 1982.

24 Website for installation at www.clusterbyplump.blogspot.com.

sound art and video projection (see Figure 1, together with Section 2). Feedback sensors allowed the sculptures, sound and light to react to the presence of any observers in the space. Jointly supported by both the City of Melbourne and the Australian Institute of Physics, this exciting conceptual exhibit served both as an artistic metaphor for the quantum mechanical realm,[25] and a means of strengthening a nascent bridge between the fine-art and physics communities.

The remainder of this report is broken into three sections. Section 2 briefly documents some key features of Plump's 'Cluster' installation. Two related readings of this installation are then given, one from the perspective of a physicist (DMP, see Section 3), and one from the perspective of a sculptor–painter (MR, see Section 4). It is hoped that this report will serve to contribute to a core theme of the present volume, that of challenging the traditional divide between the arts and the sciences, by exploring some of the points of nexus between them.

2. Description of Plump's 'Cluster' installation

The visitor to the gallery enters a darkened space – four walls, floor and ceiling. Within this space are clusters behind clusters of Marc Rogerson's large floating fibreglass sculptures (see Figures 1 and 2). Pod-like, illuminated, amorphous, catching fan-generated air currents. The pods are animated and illuminated by a hidden interactive logic, brought about by electronic motion detectors, relays, electric fans and motion sensitive lights. This rich visual field is drenched in an exquisite auditory field, with eight speakers surrounding the exhibition (one of which can be seen to the left of the presenter in Figure 1), from which Philip Samartzis's composition pulses and emanates. Two further speakers lie inside the pods, from which radiate the sounds of Dave Brown's composition, as triggered by the observer via the motion detectors. The combined effect is that the visitor is partly a co-creator in the experience of visiting the exhibition, their presence serving to substantially change the composition of light, movement and form. To be close to the suspended pods invites a tactile, visceral urge to push in amongst them, which many did, thereby creating a most direct way of interacting. Even to stand totally still in itself is rewarding as according to the exigencies of human traffic flow, the room may empty, leaving the visitor in total darkness and silence, but with a sense that the installation is alert and upon the slightest motion will react accordingly or in kind, with all of its sonic and visual sensibility.

25 To keep this contribution self contained, Section 3 seeks to give an accessible outline of the salient concepts of quantum physics, needed for a reading of this essay.

3. Edited transcript of introductory talk, by David Paganin

What follows is an edited transcript of David Paganin's talk at the opening night of Cluster by Plump, which was intended both to introduce the gathered artists and physicists to the installation, and to explore possible points of resonance between these communities.

3.1 Introduction

Marc Rogerson, sculptor for this installation, gave me the brief to 'Express the shared nature of art and science in the most beautiful part of both their manifestations'. This I now do, as a preface to the exquisite installation of illuminated sculpture and sound art in which you are immersed.

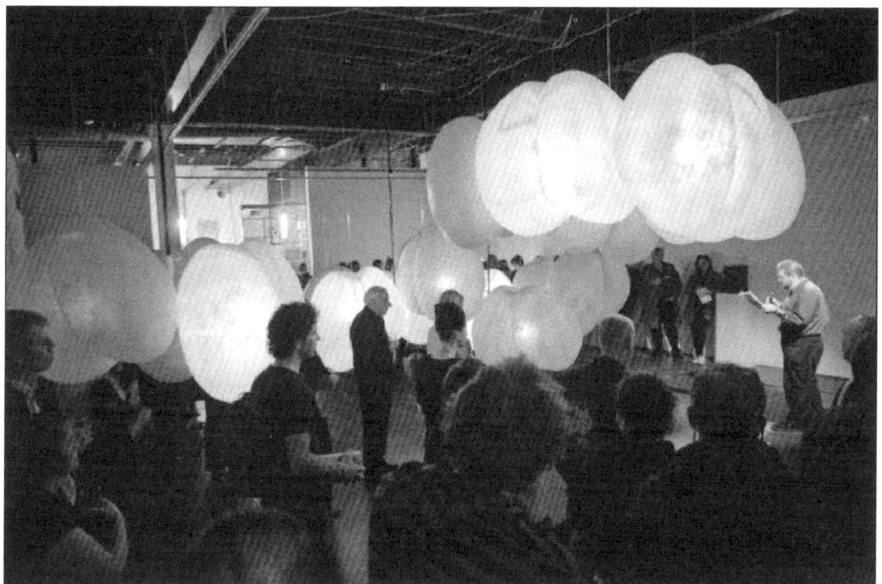

Figure 1. Opening night of Cluster by Plump, showing clusters of illuminated suspended pods. Image courtesy of Michael Blamey.

3.2 Three plus one: the creators of 'Cluster'

This installation was created by four members of an artistic trio known as 'Plump'. Marc Rogerson, the sculptor, sculpts the quanta of matter, the atoms. And let me point out that the word 'quanta', which is the plural for 'quantum' (as in 'quantum physics') refers to something very simple. It simply refers to pieces, to discrete lumps, to packets, to bits. So, when we speak of 'quanta of matter', we mean the individual pieces or building blocks of matter, namely the atoms. So, Marc Rogerson, the sculptor, is responsible for the quanta of matter. Philip Samartzis and Dave Brown, the sound artists, sculpt the quanta of sound ... this is quantum mechanics after all, and in quantum physics the quanta, the lumps of sound, are known as phonons. Marcia Jane, who augments the trio, is a video artist, and she sculpts the quanta of the light field, known as photons.

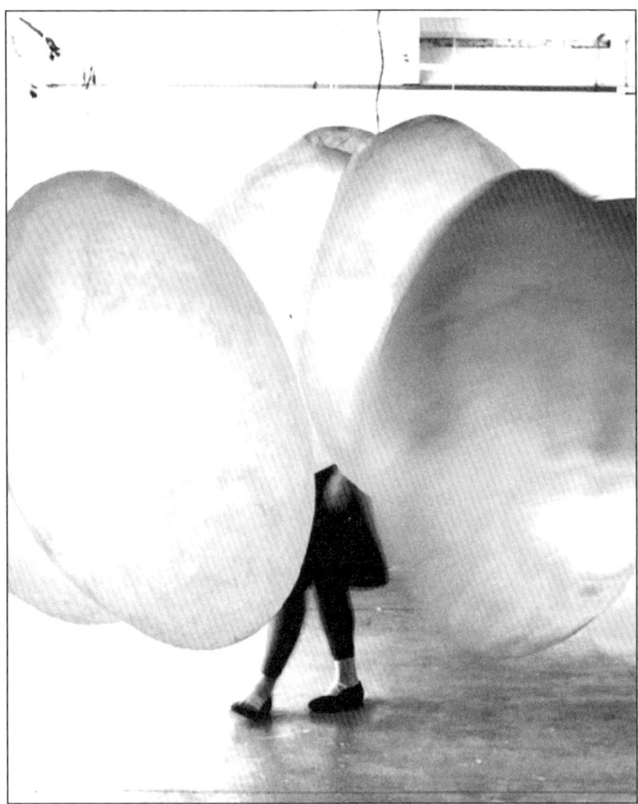

Figure 2

3.3 On beauty as a nexus point between art and science

The account I give tonight is personal. My opinion. I am not telling you that 'this is the way it should be', I am not telling you that 'this is the way it is', rather I am telling you that 'this is the way I feel' about certain interfaces, certain parallels, certain kinships between the arts and sciences, about the 'shared nature of art and science'. Let's give this 'shared nature' a name, let's call it the 'art–science nexus'.

And with regard to this art–science nexus: beauty, the creation and appreciation of beauty, for me, is very much a point of nexus between the arts and the sciences. This I want to explore now. I want to explore this nexus point via a question: 'In what sense can a poem be as beautiful as a physical theory?'

Let's begin with a poem. Choose Sappho, the great ancient Greek poet. She wrote a gorgeous line, which I'll translate into English as: 'Of all the stars, you are the most beautiful'. Even in English translation, this is a stunningly beautiful verse, an evocative, brilliant line of genius poetry. Now, you appreciate this beautiful line of poetry, you appreciate this beautiful verse when you hear it in English, but trust me when I say that you would appreciate it all the more deeply if you were to spend several years studying ancient Greek. You want to more deeply appreciate Sappho? Then knuckle down and learn the language of Sappho.

In what sense can a poem be as beautiful as a physical theory? We've just mentioned a poem, so let's now mention a physical theory. For now, I want to concentrate not on quantum physics, but on classical physics, namely the brand of physics that is in at least reasonable accord with our everyday common sense. The classical physics of the light that fills this room – let's call it the 'electromagnetic disturbance' that fills the room – classically speaking, this electromagnetic disturbance is considered to be governed by a certain set of physical laws, differential equations known as the Maxwell equations. These are the equations of classical ('common sense') physics, which govern the evolution in space and time, the ebb and the flow, of the light field, the electromagnetic field in this room. And these equations, these Maxwell equations, are stunningly beautiful. I am not going to justify this last statement. I am just saying, that as far as I am concerned, these equations are stunningly beautiful. Many physicists would agree with me. But again, in order to deeply appreciate the statement I have just made, regarding the sublime beauty of the Maxwell equations, one would need to spend several years studying mathematical physics, the language of nature.

Now, I'm a fan of both Sappho and Maxwell. Both are stunningly beautiful. And I don't mean that they are beautiful in a cold, distant, merely intellectual way – nothing wrong with being intellectual, nothing culpable in having a few brain cells stretched, as it were, with either the finer points of ancient Greek grammar or with a particularly challenging piece of mathematical physics – rather, I am talking about how both Sappho's poems and Maxwell's equations are beautiful in a visceral way,[26] that hits you in the stomach, that sends a trill/frisson/shock through the blood, that excites a quiet spasm of emotional thrill – this is what I speak of, this is what I want to focus on, this is what I want to feel, this is what I want you to feel, when I speak of the beauty of both Maxwell's equations and Sappho's poems.

As another point of nexus between the arts and the sciences, I would argue, again for

26 This statement was intended to resonate with Marc Rogerson's intention for the audience to have a 'visceral response' to his sculpture, and to the Plump trio as a whole.

me personally, that the urge to create and appreciate something beautiful, either alone or in collaboration with others, is what I aspire to as a scientist, as a physicist. The urge to create something beautiful, this is 'research', in the strong sense of the term, when one is researching physical ideas, physical ideas that no-one has seen or appreciated before, to create something new, to create something beautiful. This is the urge to *create* something beautiful. The urge to *appreciate* something beautiful in the physics realm – such appreciation is about learning, learning about the researches of others – learning from books, learning from papers, learning in person from dialogue with other physicists. Again, the urge to create and appreciate something beautiful, either alone or in collaboration with others, is what I aspire to as a physicist.

The urge to create or appreciate beauty is also what I aspire to as an artist. Now, I'm an amateur artist, very much an amateur ... I enjoy composing and performing music, I enjoy creative writing, I enjoy painting. The urge to create and appreciate the beautiful is what I aspire to as a scientist ... the urge to create and appreciate the beautiful is also what I aspire to as an amateur artist.

Again, again, again: beauty as a point of nexus between the arts and the sciences. Be it a poem by Sappho or Gwen Harwood, a mathematical theorem of Euclid or Emmy Noether, a painting by Russell Drysdale or Jackson Pollock, a physical theory of Albert Einstein or Stephen Hawking, a musical piece by Peter Sculthorpe or Olivier Messiaen, a scientific discovery by Marie Curie or Edwin Hubble – all are most beautiful, almost unspeakably so.

3.4 On research as a nexus point between art and science

What of other points of nexus between art and science? More generally, and as always for me personally, both the arts and the sciences are expressions/outlets/cathartic vents for the urge to create, to perceive, to represent, to depict, to overturn, to transcend, to understand, to see or create or construct or synthesise the hitherto unseen.

To focus on the latter point: to see or create the hitherto unseen, this is what we do as professional physicists, knocking/beating/pushing against the boundaries and limitations of our understanding, the boundaries of our appreciation, the boundaries of our knowledge, the boundaries of our perception, the boundaries that form an interface between what we think we know and what we do not know.

By the way, some non-physicists are surprised to hear that the process of physics research can be very 'organic', in a sense that I now outline. As physicists we throw up ideas, we argue for hours, we argue and search for days, we argue and search for weeks, we argue and search for months, tossing up physics ideas and hunches and leads and 'running them through the mill'. I'll throw something up and my colleague will shoot it down; my colleague will throw something else up and I'll shoot it down, or at least modify/evolve it; and we evolve and evolve and evolve until we reach some sort of distilled essence, out of this communal research effort. And this process, as I experience it almost every day as a working physicist, the essence of this creative process is not too dissimilar to the process of artistic creation which I observed between several members of the artistic group creating the cluster of illuminated and aurally immersed pods that now surround us ... thrashing ideas around, following hunches, evolving, evolving, evolving, collaborating, pushing the boundaries, creating that which has not been created before, a new beauty. It's all research – be it physics research or artistic research.

With a view to illustrating the parallels that we are here tonight to explore, to celebrate, I went to various background materials and texts which several of the artists in the group had provided for me. Let me focus on one such text, from the online biography of Marcia Jane, the projectionist. A line from this online bio spoke of her work as involving a process in which 'intensive editing and the application of structure abstracts images away from real-world origins and combines them in new, graphic and rhythmic relationships'.[27] Let us take this same text, written in the context of a creative art, in this case video art, and see how much alignment it might have, as a statement pertaining to the physical sciences. (i) 'Intensive editing and the application of structure abstracts images away from real-world origins' ... this makes me think of physical laws. What are physical laws? One has an otherwise bewildering array of sense impressions, measurements in a suitably wide sense of the term – measurements of light, measurements of electricity, measurements of magnetic fields, measurements of billiard balls and springs, measurements of water waves and winds, planets and suns – and from this otherwise bewildering array of sense impressions, one tries to abstract the essence, 'away from (the) real-world origins', to abstract a physical essence (rather than images) in a few beautiful laws of physics, to abstract the simple compressed beautiful mathematico-physical essence, to summarise that data in a beautifully concise/dense/essence-ial way ... this is the formulation of physical laws in the quantitative sciences.[28] (ii) The latter part of Marcia Jane's statement, regarding combining these abstracted

27 See Marcia Jane website at http://www.permutations.net/, accessed 24 April 2008.

28 In the words of Wheeler, 'The yield of decades of research, hundreds of investigators, and thousands of experiments, turn out to be derivable from principles of almost trivial simplicity.' See J.A. Wheeler, *International Journal of Theoretical Physics*, Volume 21, 1982, pp. 555–572.

images into 'new ... relationships' – does not this have a direct parallel with the idea of a physicist exploring a new and hitherto unknown/unseen prediction or consequence of existing physical laws?

Artists and scientists ... we work with different materials ... we might work with images, with sounds, with clay, with fiberglass, with measurements, with mathematical structures ... for the artist, the sum total of human experience is the raw material to be mined and mutated and evolved and morphed and metamorphosed and filtered and reworked and sculpted into art ... for the physical scientist, the raw material is a subset of the sum total of possible human experience, this raw material being provided by the physical world, the universe as a text, quantifiable measurements of the universe considered as raw material to be mined and mutated and evolved and morphed and metamorphosed and filtered and reworked and sculpted into science.

3.5 On extrapolation

Let us change tack, and talk about gardening, about roses. I really like gardening. I love growing/nurturing/tending roses, and particularly climbing roses. Suppose that the climbing roses in my garden were to grow one metre in one year. So, here's the observation: my roses grew one metre in one year. Suppose I was to conclude, as a brilliant deduction based upon this observation: 'My roses grew one metre in one year, therefore they will grow one million metres in one million years'. Now, if I were to say this, what would you say to me? You'd say, 'You're mad/crazy/wrong'.

What this simple scenario is intended to show, to exhibit in a slightly silly simple stark form, is the idea of the dangers of extrapolation, of taking an observation, a harmless observation, and making an unwarranted extrapolation.

The history of physics is littered with unwarranted extrapolations, the challenging of which has stimulated and continues to stimulate the ferment of ideas, a realignment of worldviews, a suspension of common sense, with the old common sense being discarded as a previous prejudice. Some examples: (i) The earth is flat. I don't know what you reckon, but the earth is flat, you go outside and the earth is flat. Play cricket, play lawn bowls, play football, and you behave/act/play according to the common sense that the earth is flat. The earth *is* flat. To conclude that the whole earth is flat because it looks flat in our immediate vicinity, is one example of an unwarranted extrapolation. The flat-earth hypothesis, the flat earth theory is fine if you are playing lawn bowls or cricket or football, but it's not fine if you're wanting to circumnavigate the earth. (ii) As another example, of a physical theory that represents an unwarranted extrapolation, one has the idea that matter is a continuum. Let me illustrate. Suppose that I am holding in my hand a glass of wine – I don't know about you, but when I look at a glass of wine it looks like a continuous liquid, a continuum, it looks infinitely divisible, there do not seem to be any gaps. This is another observation, another everyday observation (cf. the flat earth) – and for me to make the extrapolation, that because the liquid in my glass appears to be continuous, *therefore* it must be continuous down to the very smallest length scales, down to infinitely small scales – this extrapolation, like the roses and the flat earth – this statement that matter is a continuum down to arbitrarily small length scales, this is also an unwarranted extrapolation ... as the idea of atoms asserts.

And what each of these examples of unwarranted extrapolations is meant to show – the rose, the flat earth, the wine – is the idea that common sense (and common-sense physical theories) have domains of validity. Theories have domains of validity. The earth is close enough to flat, in sufficiently small patches, for most everyday purposes. The theory that the earth is flat, this is a good theory, provided that you do not try to push it too far, beyond its domain of validity. The idea that matter is continuous, this too is a good theory, provided that you do not try to push it too far. The idea that my roses grow about a metre per year, this is a good theory, provided that you do not try to push it too far.

(iii) Now as a last example, of the history of physics being littered with unwarranted extrapolations, let me get towards the point I am really trying to make, regarding 'everyday notions of common sense'. To this end, let me state a few tenets of common sense, a few statements of 'obviously true' everyday common sense in the physical world. Consider the idea of a 'trajectory'. As I wave my hand slowly through the air in front of me, one has the common-sense notion that at each instant of time my hand occupies a particular position in space, a particular well-defined position in space at each instant of time, a 'trajectory'. As another example, of an 'obvious' statement of common sense, if I am playing billiards, as my billiard balls bang/clack/collide into one another one never has the situation that a given billiard ball spontaneously starts travelling backwards in time.[29] As another example of everyday common sense, if I throw a tennis ball at a wall, I never get two tennis balls coming back.[30] As yet another example of everyday common sense, if I laterally stretch out my arms, such that my left thumb points up

29 Here, I have in mind physicist Richard Feynman's interpretation of anti-particles as particles travelling backwards in time. Adopting this viewpoint, one may consider the virtual electromagnetic process of an electron-positron pair annihilating to give a single photon, as an electron emitting a photon and then scattering backwards in time.

30 In making this statement, I have in mind the famous 'Klein paradox' of relativistic quantum physics.

and my right thumb points down, then it is meaningful for us to speak of 'the state' of my left hand and 'the state' of my right hand. This demarcation is rather anti-holistic, by assuming/asserting that one can indeed meaningfully speak in isolation of the state of each sub-piece of a given system.[31] As a last example of everyday common sense, one has the notion that there is a clear separation between that which observes and that which is observed.

3.6 Quantum physics for artists

Now, all of the above examples of everyday common sense are like the flat-earth hypothesis, like the million-metre-mega-rose hypothesis – insofar as these are theories, and they therefore have domains of validity. All of these common-sense statements break down in the quantum world, the world of the very small.

Why is this so? Think about it. What is the smallest mass that we can directly apprehend with our unaided senses? Let's say that it's a thousandth of a gram. What is the smallest time interval that we can directly apprehend? Let's say that it is roughly one hundredth of a second. What is the smallest length that we can directly apprehend with our senses? Let's say that it is roughly a tenth of a millimetre.

Well, the mass of one of the building blocks of atoms in our body, known as an electron … this has a mass that is a million million million million times smaller than the smallest mass we can directly apprehend with our senses. Certain ultra-transient phenomena in physics (the decay of certain elementary particles known as 'hadron resonances') can occur over timescales that are a thousand million million million times shorter than the smallest time interval that we can directly apprehend with our senses. And an atom is 'only' a million times smaller than the smallest distance we can directly apprehend.

It was bad enough when I tried to make an unwarranted million-fold extrapolation of my observation that my roses grew a metre in a year. So if one has a sub-atomic particle with a mass that is a million million million million times smaller than the smallest mass we can directly apprehend, or a particle that only lives for a time that is a thousand million million million times smaller than the smallest time we can

31 'Entangled' quantum states transcend this classical notion. In this context, I often introduce entangled 'Schrödinger cat' states to my Honours Quantum Mechanics class in the following way: (i) I laterally extend both arms, with my left thumb pointing up and my right thumb pointing down; (ii) I then ask the class to consider the *superposition* of this state, with a state in which the direction of each thumb is reversed; (iii) The question 'What is the state of my left hand' is thereby dissolved, in this rather strong analogy for an 'entangled' quantum-mechanical state.

apprehend, or an atom that is a million times smaller than the smallest length we can directly apprehend – why should our everyday notions of common sense hold true at such tiny levels, for distances/masses/times millions of times smaller than the ken of our everyday experience, upon which our common sense notions of space/time/causality are based? Our everyday notions of common sense have a domain of validity, and there is no *a priori* reason why these everyday notions of common sense should extrapolate down to describe masses that are a million million million million fold smaller than the smallest mass we can directly perceive. Again, there is no reason why all of our everyday notions of common sense should necessarily be operative or meaningful at the level of atoms and subatomic particles, where a billionth of a second may be an eternity – there is no *a priori* reason why, at the level of atoms, a million times smaller than the smallest thing we can see, there is no reason why our everyday notions of common sense should hold true.

So let us zoom into this quantum world, let us zoom in to the size of atoms or smaller, at least a million times smaller than anything we can directly apprehend, let us zoom into this quantum world. Again, there is no *a priori* reason why our everyday notions of common sense – those tenets of common sense that I mentioned before – there is no *a priori* reason why they should not break down, because physical theories have domains of validity and cannot be extrapolated too far. Indeed these everyday notions do break down – in many cases spectacularly so – and this, my friends, is the quantum world.

Welcome to the quantum world. This is where world views decay, where we transcend everyday common sense. Things are counterintuitive, as they should be. Remember the roses – it would be arrogant, implicitly arrogant, to assume that common sense should extrapolate down to this quantum level. Quantum physics *should* be weird.

Having zoomed down to this quantum world, we have a different world, different rules, a different game. As Marc Rogerson aptly put it, 'Normal thinking is suspended, we have transcended the paradigms that we know'.

3.7 Welcome

And so here we are, we scientists, we artists – we artists, we scientists – anticipating an installation, immersed in an installation which is a metaphor for this counterintuitive quantum realm, transcending the paradigms that we know. The matter and the light and the sound, in this space, is evocative of the quantum world. As one example, this is an interactive installation, your presence changing the space in a non-intuitive way, as a metaphor for the idea that in quantum physics there is no clear distinction between observer and observed. But enough – I do not want to speak in detail about the installation, let it speak for itself, to each of you as individuals.

As you enter this space – I know that you are physically here already, but as you enter this space in a more total way, I want you to feel/remember/re-experience a childlike sense of wonder, that childlike sense of wonder that you might feel when you gaze at a beautiful pattern formed by a twirling tendril of smoke, or a particularly singular cloud formation, or a delicately veined leaf, or an ant (pondering the size disparity as you watch the industrious ant striding around). The sort of childlike sense of wonder that you might feel when you stare at a particularly pretty bolt of lightning, or when you stand gob-smacked by a particularly poignant painting or measure of music, a sublime sculpture, a gorgeous mathematical theorem, an exquisite equation, or a beautiful physical law.

May you feel this childlike sense of wonder, this childlike open mindedness, as you approach this installation. May this installation overwhelm your senses. May it overturn intuition. May it strengthen the bridge between science and art, such that each inspires the other. May it transcend language and concrete representation. May its beauty both challenge and inspire.

4. The Unobservable in Art and Science, by Marc Rogerson

4.1 Creation

The moment of creation is a tricky subject. It has pre-occupied far better minds than mine and, I dare say, as an area of enquiry, it hasn't finished its run yet.

Any artist or scientist can't help but to look back with envy and longing at moments in history when the epiphanic moment has struck some lucky ideological forebear.

Luck? Luck or design? Design or serendipity? Artistic or scientific creation as a manifestation of inner genius or the catching of the plump apple of chance?

The contemplation of this moment has to be accompanied by a quiet thrill that such moments of creation are tucked away, hidden around us too. Serendipity midst deliberate process, synchronicity popping of a hard, muddled, day, a eureka moment rumbling just below the surface. It is probably, in part, a drive to practise in the arts and sciences and compels the toiler to keep going.

The attempt to penetrate a scientific problem can give an unexpected serendipitous yield into an artwork. Was it luck or design that delivered the fruit of da Vinci's toil in the study and sketching of a sphere (for the sake of scientifically understanding its properties) into the skills he needed to paint the Mona Lisa's head perfectly in the round? Well, I find it too beautifully happenstance to weigh the creative moment down by the idea of pre-meditated design. This example, of course, draws on a moment in the working life of one of the most famous minds and one of the most famous paintings. It is, however, in the daily business of the nature of art and science that I'm interested in finding the parallels and differences.

The purpose of this text is to attempt to define, via science, a different, hitherto unexplored definition of the moment of creation. I shall attempt to go beyond the ideas of study, work, serendipity, design and luck into the provocative and intoxicating area of unobservability in quantum physics and its effects on creativity. I shall consider this both generally and in the context of a particular sculptural project that attempted to consider ideas in art and science.

4.2 Quantum mechanics to the wide-eyed innocent

The sheer mystery of both celestial and quantum mechanics has held a grip on the popular imagination far different from the other sciences. The practical updates in chemistry, biology, engineering and so on comfort the non-scientific world with the assurance that we're all moving forward in a fabulous, utilitarian congo line – adding new members to a steady procession of goodness and practicality. But the seeming arcana of bent space-time versus the uncertainty principle shocks us. The more we know, the more bizarre it appears to be. This can be a deeply emotional concept for the artist who's been without religious mystery to inform his work since the systematic unveilings of the enlightenment in the 18th century. Gradually, with the sheer exoticism of the science of the sub-atomic, a world appears that can feed a mind primarily interested in aesthetics.

I was having a cup of coffee with a physicist friend when he nailed me by his penetrating (and probably exasperated) gaze. The evolution of our language dealt, he said, with ideas of understanding the world. Trajectories of flung objects, seasons, the elements and so on all contributed to the structure of our language and its attendant cerebral substrates. But the world at a sub-atomic level defies language. A table cannot have a superannuation fund; a tree has no anxiety over a publishing deadline. But this level of apparent mental and conceptual fluidity is needed to consider the workings of the world at a sub-atomic scale.

Considering the moment of creation in a materialistic world with all the accumulation of practical facts heaped upon it makes a grave picture. How ordered and dull. But suddenly mystery is allowed to occur again. It has been expunged and tidied from our imaginations by a good couple of hundred years of technological advance. Farewell ye gods. The mystery of a sub-atomic world where language breaks down needs a new species of imagination to consider entities bi-locating, time reversing, entities being unobservable and so on. Suddenly along with mystery there appears a possible reason to create art: the creation of the inexpressible into the expressed.

Which leads me to the creation of the Cluster exhibition.

4.3 Cluster

The creation of Cluster had a number of small, technical, aesthetic, historic and personal rumblings before the satisfying 'pop' of the work as an idea came into being.

(a) Unobservability as a vast relief. It is a relief to be utterly unable to observe a quantum entity without robbing it of its mysterious ability to be in many contradictory states at once. It is a relief to be impotent in the face of nature. It is a relief to see our apparent omniscience take a knock or two as we tramp around the planet. An electron assumes dimensions of time and space to humour us, happy to be many contradictory things at once, it's even happier to be something that we can understand after beaming our inquisitorial photon at it. Lovely. What a relief. 'Glad you could come to the party,' it tells us. Anyway, enough of this anthropic irreverence … the idea of unobservability is the point of creation that informed Cluster's birth.

(b) But it doesn't work! I wanted there to be a slightly maddeningly counter-intuitive quality to Cluster. It should be frustrating. Frankly, it was. I could never get it to follow my commands. It anticipated my observation and changed itself accordingly. Fabulous, existential impotence at last!

4.3.1 General Description

Cluster was an interactive, kinetic, illuminated sculpture exhibition with soundscape. I invited two sound-art composers, Philip Samartzis and Dave Brown, to form a trio called Plump. Thereby we had spatial and time-based arts covered.

I wanted to have an immersive environment which responded to the visitor and reacted in a non-intuitive way. There would be no text but large, illuminated pods suspended in space with a soundscape generated from surrounding speakers and speakers internal to the cluster of the pods. Motion detectors triggered the switching of electric fans and audio speakers, the fans caused the pods to knock against each other and thereby switched lights inside the pods.

The visitor, upon entering the space, could find the installation in a state of stillness, darkness and silence, or in total, animated, illuminated, noisiness. Perhaps somewhere in between, however, the approach of the visitor changed the combination of the above kinetic, illuminated and sonic aspects of the piece.

If you walked towards a cluster of pods a fan on the other side of the room may be activated whilst someone else in the room may activate a speaker in a pod near you. The sound artists had their compositions on CD loops with Dave Brown's emanating from within clusters and Philip Samartzis's surrounding the installation.

By having the lux levels on the motion detectors finely adjusted, they may have or may not have been activated by motion because the pods adjacent to the visitor may or may not have been activated, thereby creating the light necessary to activate the motion detector

All in all, there was life there but not as we knew it.

Aesthetically, Cluster was gently and slightly disturbing; the soft, floating pods were tactile and invited people to touch them, push them or mingle through them. But it didn't make sense. While not a sentient entity, it knew you were there.

4.3.2 The unobservable system

I wanted there to be a sense in the observer that there was definitely a greater idea informing the environment which no amount of observing could determine. Indeed, the harder the attempt to observe, the more the installation would react and change. The randomness of human agency brought the standard observer–observed nature of art exhibitions to its knees. The analogy of the subatomic world, whilst oblique, held true.

4.3.3 The forming of the pods

Ah my pretty pretty things. I formed the maquettes in clay over a couple of months while at the beach in Southern Victoria, Australia. The shape that I finally settled on had a quality of life bursting from its seams. Two lobes of a pod bulbously protruding out from themselves like the moment of cell division that one sees on TV documentaries as a child.

They were carved in polystyrene to the correct scale, coated and finished in plaster and then moulded in fibreglass. From this mould were pulled fibreglass-skin replicas of the original shape.

The next task was to illuminate them with a technique that pulsed light as a result of their motions. Simply suspending a globe on a wire which struck the electrode, both hooked up to 12 volts DC, did the trick.

4.3.4 The performance
Cluster was performed as one large sound and light instrument. Drawing on the enormous experience of Dave and Philip as improvising musicians, the piece came alive as a sometimes jostling sometimes supremely calm manifestation of time-based and spatial arts.

4.4 Mystery regained
As an artist I have found the contemplation of the ideas supporting quantum mechanics to have been as nourishing as Christianity once was to a pre-enlightenment world. The use of art to communicate something at which traditional language fails is an enormous increase in the validity of art and its departure from mere aesthetics into something else. The observing of the unobservable.

****

The Author Meets Professor Plimer

Curiosity has significance throughout this book. Professor Marcello Costa has already reminded us of the importance of curiosity as a motivator. Speaking of how 'government and big business may want to dowse mental energy, preferring passive non-thinking voters and consumers', Valerie Yule, interviewed by Robyn Williams on ABC Radio National, and quoted in the Introduction, emphasised the role of curiosity. 'Mental energy' she said, 'drives our curiosity. Curiosity is like handling gunpowder, so many cultures and parents have tried to squash it. Curiosity adds spice and thrills to life, and nothing is humdrum when it is fizzing.'[32]

That present participle, 'fizzing' describes the state of my mind when I visited the South Australian Museum during National Science Week in 2006. Walking between the white marquees set up by scientifically-oriented organisations, with the work of primary students on display on one side, I saw an invitation. 'Munch on science during luncheon'. I looked at the menu on offer. The next day, if I decided to miss Tai-chi, I could 'eat recycled stardust' with Professor Ian Plimer. That set my brain fizzing. He was offering this special dish to the general public. There was no contest. I had to be there.

32 Valerie Yule, interview with Robyn Williams, 'Crisis of Human Energy', 'Ockham's Razor', ABC Radio National, 18 February 2007. Transcript of interview at http://www.abc.net.au/rn/ockhamsrazor/stories/2007/1848554.htm.

At the University of the Third Age (U3A) at Port Adelaide, I had begun a program 'From Seeds to the Stars' connecting the work and writing of scientists and poets. Professor Plimer appeared to be offering a new way of seeing and understanding. I could not resist the invitation. He is a geologist (Professor of Mining Geology), a renowned expert on the behaviour of volcanoes. Bringing my ignorance and interest with me I was there early to ensure I had a seat at this 'luncheon' with its imaginative main course.

He began by telling us that geology is the history of our planet, where it came from and why it is as it is. He had my attention from the moment he drew from his pocket bits of gold which he passed around to students, most of them students who had come as refugees from African nations.

Professor Plimer began by telling us that our universe might be 10 billion years old and that the recycling process began possibly 12,000 million years ago. He mentioned our teeth that consist of calcium, phosphorus, oxygen and hydrogen.

So when did we come into the universe? It had to be when oxygen was present. Gold came into the universe before we did: it came in about 2,500 million years ago. Gold does not need oxygen. We measure the age of rocks using uranium and strontium. Iron was the heaviest element that could be made through nuclear fusion in a star. It is essential for all living beings. In human beings, it carries the oxygen to the lungs; the haemoglobin in our body contains iron.

Professor Plimer showed us a shaving of iron ore that had been very finely sliced to reveal the bacteria it carried within it. What had happened 2,500 million years ago? Micro-palaeontologists noted the change in the bacteria to a cell with a nucleus and a second cell wall. Ninety per cent of the bacterial organisms in our body attack and dissolve the food we take in. Some protect us from oxygen. Others are 'refugees' and hide in the stomach.

Our bodies recycle everything. We breathe out carbon dioxide and breathe in the 'waste' materials of plants. Over 40,000 tonnes of meteorites and comets have come from space bringing bacteria to earth.

There was so much in what he fed us during that hour-long muncheon. Was the planet hit by something the size of Mars? We were bombarded by asteroids. There were no oceans. When did this planet first have water? Was water first on earth in Greenland 3,800 million years ago? Mars once had water. Where did it go? What of the centre of the earth with its magnetic core? Old glacial rocks of 800 million years ago in the Flinders Ranges' magnetic field must have been formed at the equator.

How have we been finding out all of this? Scientists in different disciplines cooperate. Mathematicians provide the statistics, chemists the understanding of the elements, astronomers the understanding of space, astro-physicists, biologists and geologists, all work together to explain the history of our planet. I came away with my mind fizzing. But, before I came away I asked Professor Plimer whether he would consider writing about his approach for this collection of essays by scientists. He responded as follows.

> I am really interested in the unity of science and religion, with science dealing with the world without and religion dealing with the world within. Science is married to evidence which derives from observation, calculation, measurement and experiment. Scientists argue about the validity of the data, the weakness in data collection and the veracity of data. This data must be coherent with other bodies of data, even from other disciplines. This data can be tested and it matters not whether one is in Poland or Patagonia, if the test cannot duplicate the data then the data and the resultant theory must be rejected. By this way science is international, transparent and validated. If data can survive a validation process, then the next stage of science is to explain the phenomenon, and this is a 'theory'. A scientific theory is a very powerful explanation and can change with more data or more thinking. This is the falsification of Karl Popper. We hear today in the press about consensus, a tool of politics but not science. Science does not work by consensus, and if one piece of data conflicts with the theory, then the theory must be abandoned. As solar astronomy and geology are in conflict with ideas of human-induced global warming, then the scientific idea of human-induced global warming must be rejected. This is not to say that humans do not change climate, it is that the evidence presented to show that humans change climate cannot be validated. Furthermore, a religious experience or trauma that could induce a road to Damascus conversion might occur with one person but an adjacent person who experiences the same events might not be affected.
>
> For me, the unity between science, religion and the arts (which includes poetry, painting, etc.) is the concept of awe. I can view matters of Nature with great awe – awe at the complexity, the beauty and the fragility. I too can view Nature through the eyes of a Spinozan theologian, be in awe of Nature and think that if there is a G(g)od then he/she resides in Nature. I can even understand the view of some Christian fundamentalists who see Nature in all its complexity and interpret this to mean that it must be the creation of an intelligent designer. However, if there was an omnipotent omnipresent all knowing deity then why did He/She/It design the shinbone at the same level as a towbar. With a painting we can scan it and reconstitute it using billions of pixels This is a mathematical process. However, when we look at a painting, we do not see pixels, we see a painting and feel all the emotions that this painting evokes. Other people looking at the same painting have a different emotional feeling from the painting despite the fact that the pixels are all the same. To me, this separates the arts from science. Science is unashamedly unemotional although when we get into areas of pseudo-science such as creationism and the myth of

global warming, emotions become intertwined with data and interpretations. Unemotional science is one of the main problem-solving methodologies that we humans can use. We may get emotional about millions of deaths every year from a curable affliction like malaria but there are solutions which also create emotional responses. The use of DDT, although it may weaken shells of birds, can greatly reduce malaria by attacking it at its source. It is then for those who talk politics, religion, ethics, etc. to decide what solution will be used (bearing in mind that politics, religion etc. change over time).

The use of language is extremely important. Science has a formal format for the presentation of data and interpretations based therefrom. This is an attempt to reduce ambiguities. By contrast, the language of literature, poetry etc. can be beautifully ambiguous thereby allowing each reader to share a different emotional experience. Music is probably an even better example. We have reams written on philosophy (e.g. the philosophy of science, the philosophy of literature) but there is no philosophy of music. Why not? Music is an emotional experience. While I write, I am listening to the adagio movement of Mahler's 10th Symphony. This is to me hauntingly beautiful and achingly challenging but years ago I could not listen to this piece which I would then have regarded as achromatic and atonal.

For me, the unity of science with religion, art, literature, poetry and music is awe. We can stand in front of a painting in awe. We can read a poem and wonder in awe how a poet can be so economical with words that say so much. We can be in awe of Nature. We can be in awe of the almighty.

SCORESBY SHEPHERD

Dr Scoresby Shepherd AO is a marine ecologist. After graduating in classics and law, and practising as a lawyer or teaching legal studies for a decade, he joined the Department of Fisheries in 1968, and has spent his life studying marine life, mostly underwater. He is currently a Senior Research Fellow of the South Autralian Research and Development Institute at West Beach. He has worked in the waters of Alaska, Mexico, Oman and France, as well as in South Australia. He has co-edited eight books, and written over 120 papers on many aspects of marine life. For his contributions to marine science, he was awarded the Jubilee Medal of the Australian Marine Sciences Association in 1997, made an Officer of the Order of Australia in 2006, and awarded the Sir Joseph Verco Medal of the Royal Society of South Australia in 2008.

Janine Baker is a marine ecologist in Adelaide, and Dr Lisa-Ann Gershwin is a marine scientist of Queensland studying jellyfish biology, and a world authority on the Irukanji stinging jellyfish. Brian Brock is a poet and biologist, with interests in marine taxonomy (bryozoans), freshwater and terrestrial fauna.

Poetry and science to a water-borne biologist

My first degree was in classics in the days (1950s) when they were studied in their original splendour. The magic of Homer, Virgil, Horace and Pindar were glimpses of another world, but were soon overwhelmed by the mundane need to work, and then forgotten. Yet not quite, as they were rekindled in a different way on a summer day just a few years later (1956) when I first tremulously strapped on an aqualung and slid into a cool, calm sea. What I saw was more exciting than I had ever imagined. I was in a gully, with kelp-covered rocks on my left and tall seagrasses on my right. The kelp and seagrasses swayed rhythmically in the swell, and I in unison, while fishes peered from crevices at this strange invader. I decided at once that this was the real world, and that in all my previous gravity-bound life I had been trapped in Plato's cave, merely watching shadows on the wall. It was like a return to pre-natal amniotic tranquillity.

Spirituality is the sense of submergence of the self and the union of the spirit with another world beyond. Were my feelings of wonderment on that day of my first dive a spiritual experience, or merely a transient euphoria? Over the next 48 years I have done many thousands of dives in almost all oceans of the world, and this spiritual sense of absorption in a greater world has never left me, and has become a powerful driver to know more of that world, and make it known. These two elements – the intellectual challenge to learn, and the spiritual feeling of absorption into something greater – were to fill my life. The former was fulfilled by marine science studies, and the latter by poetry. But in reality the two were tightly interwoven. I saw science as a wonderful reason to be underwater.

What I had unwittingly experienced in those earliest years was the Ionian enchantment[33] – the belief in the unity of the sciences and humanities – reflecting the naturalist's conviction that unravelling the secrets of nature is stimulated by the imagination as much as by writing or reading poetry. The Ionian enchantment had its source in Homer, who never separated reason, myth, theory, philosophy and poetry, and the unity was unquestioned by later Greek philosophers. Science itself was the poetic expression of the spiritual perception of an unknowable world. The pre-Socratic philosopher, Xenophanes[34], said in words much loved by modern philosophers:

---

33 G. Holton, *Einstein, History and other Passions,* American Institute of Physics Press, New York, 1995.

34 *Elegy and Iambus,* Vols. 1 & 2. J.M. Edmonds (ed.), Loeb Classical Library, Heinemann, London, 1931.

As for certain truth, no man has known it
Nor shall he know ...
And even if by chance he were to utter
The final truth, he would himself not know it
For all is but a woven web of guesses.

The Roman poet, Lucretius, followed the same Homeric tradition, and beautifully expounded science and his philosophy in the poem *De Rerum Naturae* (On the Nature of Things).

On the other hand, in the classic period poetry had a more prosaic duty. By the classical theory of mimesis poetry and the arts were supposed to mimic reality. So Plato[35] encouraged poetry lovers 'to plead the cause of poetry, and show that she is not only delightful, but beneficial to orderly government and human life'. To the Greeks, science was poetry and poetry science.

Yet, inexorably over the succeeding millennia, science has fragmented into many independent sub-disciplines, which have drifted far apart from poetry, and risked becoming mere desiccated and unimaginative expositions. Scientists are forced to find their poetic outlets in other milieus. Yet there is the occasional *cri de coeur* of a protesting scientist. One such was Bacon who had a deep sense of the unity of knowledge. He believed that science must stimulate the imagination, as did fables and poetry, and that the humanities were well employed in expressing science. Steinbeck affirmed the same:

> Most of the mystical outcrying ... of our species is the attempt to say that man is related to the whole thing, related inextricably to all reality, known as unknowable ... A St Francis, a Charles Darwin and an Einstein ... each discovered and reaffirmed with astonishment the knowledge that all things are one thing and one thing is all things.[36]

And most recently, Edward O. Wilson[37], saw in the Ionian enchantment and the later Enlightenment the origins of Consilience, the belief in the unity of knowledge, which, with a new ethic, was the only hope for the future of mankind. From the other side of the chasm, literary scholars have begun to apply evolutionary science to theories of literature in the hope of progressing their discipline in the same way as science[38].

---

35 Plato. *Republic,* Book. 10.

36 John Steinbeck, *The Log from the Sea of Cortez,* Penguin Books, New York, 1986, p. 257.

37 E.O. Wilson, *Consilience: the Unity of Knowledge*, A.A. Knopf, New York, 1998.

38 J. Gottschall & D.S. Wilson, *The Literary Animal: Evolution and the Nature of Narrative* Northwestern, 2005.

I return to my own pursuit of marine science over the last four decades. A spiritual dimension is still present. Each discovery of some aspect of nature, exciting and surprising in itself, suffuses an inner charm, and creates yet more mysteries. There is no end in sight to this infinite submarine diorama of nature, and its deepest realities. My ideas and interpretations may be the merest glimpses of fleeting events, coloured with preconceptions of coherence and elegance. Yet, this is precisely the entry point of poetry, which alone captures something of the spiritual dimension – the other worldliness, the magic, the infinity, and beauty, to say nothing of the humour, the absurdities and the tragedies – of the sea and its life. The magic is hinted at by Ibsen in *The Lady from the Sea*:

> We talked about the whales and the dolphins and the seals who lie out there on the rocks in the midday sun. And then we talked about the gulls, and the eagles and all the other sea birds. I think – isn't it wonderful? – when we talked about those things it seemed to me as if both the sea beasts and the sea birds were one with him.[39]

The challenge is offered by Longfellow:

> 'Wouldst thou' so the helmsman answered
> 'learn the secret of the sea?
> Only those who brave its dangers
> Comprehend its mysteries.'

and the sense of eternity by John Betjeman:

> And all the time the waves, the waves, the waves
> Chase, intersect and flatten on the sand
> As they have done for centuries,
> As they will for centuries to come …
> When mankind has blown himself to pieces. Still the sea
> Consolingly disastrous will return
> While the strange starfish, hugely magnified,
> Waits in the jewelled basin of a pool.[40]

---

39 Henrik Ibsen, *The Lady from the Sea,* Act II, Everyman 1958. J.M. Dent & Sons, London, p. 193.

40 John Betjeman, 'Beside the Seaside', *Collected Poems,* 4th edn, J. Murray, London, 1979.

The poignancy of sea creatures captured by trawl net, is pictured by Janine Baker[41]:

> They're hauled and slaughtered; death feels slow,
> Expiring on the decks.
> They're scaled, and chopped, and neatly boxed,
> Awaiting final checks.
> While lesser kinds don't make the cache,
> Tossed back, to stay afloat –
> Aquatic resource, whatever you be,
> Your chance to live's remote.

and the capture of the giant crab in a lobster pot, by Sarah Day:

> Hanging on to the pot's mesh
> with his oversize right claw,
> elevating through seventy dark green fathoms,
> the Giant Crab has recourse to consider
> that there is much security within a rock
> and that he has always felt at home on the sea bed.[42]

I, too, have often felt more at home on the seabed than on land, and been equally disturbed by human contamination, as Brian Brock wrote:

> The diver watched us closely
> With his salt clean eyes,
> Caressed the hollow head
> he cradled on his arm
> At length he shook his seaweed hair
> Then asked us: Did you have a question?
> Yes – we answered shyly –
> What sunken treasures did you find
> Spread about the ocean floor?
> Plastic bags, he said.[43]

---

41 Janine Baker. 'Ode to Aquatic Resources'. Fisheries Newsletter 25 October 1990.

42 Sarah Day, 'Seventy fathoms up'.

43 Brian Brock, unpublished.

Poetry far surpasses science in describing nature, as, for example, the beauty of a paper nautilus, described by Oliver Wendell Holmes:

> Year after year beheld the silent toil
> That spread his lustrous coil;
> Still, as the spiral grew,
> He left the past year's dwelling for new,
> Stole with soft steps its shining archway through,
> Built up its idle door,
> Stretched in his last-found home, and knew the old no more.[44]

and Judith Wright:

> Out of its birth it came with this.
> The smallest spiral holds the history
> of something tiny in the battering sea,
> that carried on its obstinate gathering,
> till the years swelled in it to one last perfect
> ballooning curve of colour laid by colour.
> All was implicit in its hold on time.[45]

Or (less seriously) the lobster by Edward Kravitz:

> Hail to thee most noble of crustaceans !
> No predator dare match thy might;
> Who choose with thee to fight?
> No spindly jaws or furry paws
> Dare tamper with thy mega-claws.
> Inventor of contraception! Thou scoff? Thou doubt?
> What other creature neatly packs
> All its sperm cells up in sacs?
> Thou matest but once a year, tis true,
> But that one time is quite a time! [46]

---

44 Oliver Wendell Holmes, 'The Chambered Nautilus', *Complete Works of Oliver Wendell Holmes*, Houghton Mifflin, Boston, 1895.

45 Judith Wright,'The Nautilus', *Colllected Poems: 1942–1985*, Angus & Robertson, 1994, p. 189.

46 E.A. Kravitz,'The rime of the ancient scientist', *Biological Bulletin* (1991) 180: 329–331.

Or jetty fauna by Brian Brock:

> A çuttlefish
> backs deeper into its algal lair.
> A spotted stingray
> mimics a stone in humped stillness.
> Sponge crabs
> lift their hats
> as they promenade on the pylons ...[47]

Or the stinging cells (nematocysts) of a jellyfish, by Lisa-Ann Gershwin:

> Wondrous little organelle of death;
> O to know your mysteries.
> A coiled harpoon of lightning speed,
> Revealing species' histories.[48]

Or the coat-of-mail shell, the chiton, by Janine Baker.

> What a curious sort in its colourful coat
> Is the well-armoured beast named the chiton;
> With your magnetite teeth buried deep in the folds,
> Timid sea squirts are bound to be frightened.
>
> With your granules and pustules and bumps of all kinds
> You could pass for the feat of an artist.
> Flash your blotches and stripes in fantastic array –
> Of the molluscs you're surely the smartest.
>
> You've a girdle of iron, suckered close to the rock,
> Lest some evil seasider dislodge you;
> Whilst you nibble at weed, or feast on a sponge
> (Naïve amphipods do well to dodge you).[49]

---

47 Brian Brock, 'Night dive, Edithburgh', *Autumn Peonies,* B.J. Brock, Adelaide.

48 Lisa-Ann Gershwin, 'Ode to the nematocyst', *Zootaxa* (2006) 1232: 1–57.

49 Janine Baker,'Oh, to be a chiton', unpublished poem.

I once added to a scientific paper I had written about the diet of the wrasse, a major fish predator of abalone, these lines:

> The wrasse likes crabs and shells –
> Bigger ones for bigger mouths. O well,
> Choosy? Sure, and seastars are no go
> And limpets just so-so.
> A keystone she? Now why be drab?
> And sushi is top class. So if you're a youthful ab
> Take my advice. Just mind your wrasse!

but the editorial board of the journal thought it too irreverent for a serious scientific publication!

Now in retirement I am still enchanted by the sea. I feel liberated and comforted by the philosophy of nature and its deeper reality, sketchily outlined above. For me still:

> The sea chants its perennial laments,
> Beating its murmuring shores,
> While I reminisce of old affections,
> Of creatures gone and past events.

Of course, it is possible that I am suffering the malaise of Prometheus, as told by the Chorus:

> Your wits do wander in your sore despite,
> Even as a fumbling doctor
> Finds himself diseased,
> Not knowing his own remedy.[50]

---

50 Aeschylus, *Prometheus Bound,* ll. 467–475. A.O. Prickard (ed.) 1931 Impression. Oxford University Press, Oxford.

ELIZABETH TRUSWELL

Dr Elizabeth Truswell was born and spent her early childhood in Kalgoorlie, Western Australia. She holds an Honours degree in Geology from the University of Western Ausralia, and a PhD from Cambridge University. A long career in the earth sciences followed, as a palaeontologist – mostly with the Australian Geological Survey Organisation in Canberra, where she was Chief Research Scientist from 1992–97. Her scientific work was acknowledged with election as a Fellow of the Australian Academy of Science in 1985. Her research deals with the vegetation history of Australia and Antarctica, and she continues to pursue those interests as a Visiting Fellow in the Research School of Earth Science at the Australian National University.

In 2000, in response to a long-held interest in drawing and painting, she graduated with Honours in Visual Arts from the ANU, winning an award for environmental art in that year. In 2005 she held her first solo exhibition 'Drawing on the Past' in Canberra; a second exhibition followed in 2007, entitled 'Flowers of Stone', based on the fossil forms that are the earliest evidence of the flowering plants. In 2008 a major exhibition, 'Unearthing the Past – a Celebration' was held at the Goldfields Regional Gallery in Kalgoorlie, consisting mainly of large drawings reflecting the local landscape recollected from childhood. A number of the works have been acquired by Curtin University in WA. She has a wide interest in the art/science interface, and has spoken on this issue at a number of conferences. She was a contributor to the 2006 conference 'From Stars to Brains', in Canberra, presenting there an overview of the development of art as part of the evolution of human consciousness.

Poetry and a journey in science

I am writing as one who has always had a strong feeling that the arts and sciences are two sides of the one coin. Their close relationship is at the motivational level, and stems from the fact that each has its origins in a felt need to understand, and respond to, the natural world. The aesthetic sense plays an equally strong role in each; in fact scientists are often more comfortable with the word 'beauty' than are artists.

My own story reflects this interaction. As an undergraduate, at the University of Western Australia, I was not sure what direction my working life would eventually take. I had enrolled in a geology degree – and more of that later – but had always had a love of painting and drawing. I resolved, as I approached my honours year, that the decision would be made somewhat arbitrarily. I would make just one application for a scholarship to take me to England and do a PhD in geology. If that failed then it would be art school and painting full time. The scholarship arrived, so I was set on the track to become a geologist – a palaeontologist – and the art would have to wait.

Well, wait it did, through long years of a very rewarding career in palaeontology. I specialised in pollen analysis, in using the tiny, often extremely beautiful cells as tools to understand the past. Much of it was day to day and applied, such as dating rocks and correlating rock sequences between sedimentary basins, all activities that were of value to the practical world of mapping and petroleum exploration. But most of the work was infused with a sense of wonder at the enormity of time that I was routinely dealing with, and the variety of life that I was privileged to view through the microscope. I followed a career path that is perhaps all too common in scientists; first to work in the discipline you love, then gradually to accept more and more administrative responsibility until you rarely get near the bench, or the microscope.

Then, through a range of circumstances, the opportunity came to leave those professional responsibilities behind, and I was able to enrol as a full-time student at the Canberra School of Art, completing an honours degree there in 2000. Since then I have been fortunate enough to work in both fields – carrying on with the palaeontological research that interests me, and making art that is, inevitably, much informed by the view of the world inherent in geology.

The inherent poetry

What has all this to do with poetry? Poetry has always been there, sometimes in the background, but often foregrounded in the work I do. For me, geology, perhaps more than most sciences, offers a wonderful world of narrative. As a system of thought, the earth sciences make distinctive contributions to a wider culture. These include a sense of time that is beyond human perception – a sense of the sublime – as well as stories that centre on the universality of change, on the intensification of a sense of place, and a history that is based on detailed observation. Reconstructing the past demands a certain creative imagination, especially as the records we deal with are always fragmentary, tantalising. And the sweep, the range of it is enormous. In what other area could one debate the origins and behaviour of the great ice sheets that have dominated the world from time to time; or measure oceans that have been ephemeral, or lakes that have dried up, or rainforests whose spread, and retreat, across this continent we can now document?

The language to express this ever-shifting world, while it has a formality demanded by the conventions of scientific writing, often extends into the realm of the poetic. Martin Kemp, professor of art history at Oxford, who has written extensively on the relationship between the arts and the sciences, has drawn attention to this, citing a poem by Betty Roszak, 'The Crest of the East Pacific Rise', which builds, effectively, on phrases drawn from the oceanographic literature.

> Farther yet the faults
> rise up
> like giant stairways.
> Lakes of solidified lava
> hundreds of metres long
> in places
> collapsed and pitted,
> pillars and walls
> of basalt
> banded, glassy
> cooled lateral outflows.
> Mounds of minerals: sulfides of zinc, iron, copper, silver
> vented as hot fluids.

Martin Kemp describes the words as having 'an evocative richness we are not normally invited to see'. I can find the potential for this, for setting the words of the scientific literature into a different context, in my own work. For instance, I was recently reviewing publications on the history of Lake George, a large and somewhat mysterious lake north of Canberra. The lake, now in one of its periodic dry phases, is very ancient, and has, at times in the geological past, been at much higher levels – these old levels are marked by lines of pebbles – old beaches. Technically these are referred to as 'abandoned shorelines'. What could be more evocative, more melancholic, than an 'abandoned shoreline'?

Or, scanning a paper where I discussed the origins of the present Australian vegetation, I find phrases like 'slivers of continent from Australia, the leading edge of Gondwana.. embedded in southeast Asia'. There is such an incongruity of scale here – 'slivers' is not something one usually thinks of on the scale of continents. Or 'the high sea-levels ... periodically flooding the old palaeovalleys almost as far north as Kalgoorlie'; here is an evocation of contrasting seascapes and landscapes.

In a recent paper on the vegetation history of Antarctica, my co-author and I wrote of 'clasts ice-rafted to the site by freezing in the dark seasons of winter and early spring'. We use in the title of another, the phrase 'remnants of the ice-forests'. And the term 'glacial erratics' is a common one in the sedimentological literature. What does the juxtaposition of these two words evoke if you take them out of their specialist context?

And, in descriptions of fossil wood from these high latitudes, terms in common usage are 'earlywood' and 'latewood' in reference to the rows of cells added to tree trunks in these climates of seasonal extremes. At art school I made a series of paintings, abstracting these ideas, which I called 'The Winterwood Series'. In them there are sharp and sudden lines, breaks that mark the ceasing of growth in the long dark winters.

Poetry in the background

I have always been aware of poetry. Perhaps I have been lucky. My mother loved it and introduced me to it at an early age; then I have had some good teachers. And I have (or had!) a facility for remembering it easily – at least the classics. In my last year at high school the focus was on Wordsworth and Coleridge. I revelled in these, but I also enjoyed the very critical approach of a perceptive teacher, who was in fact a historian, and adept at setting contexts. When I try now to assess what it is that has stayed with me, I think it is the poets' sheer descriptive power of the natural world that lingers. This, much more than their ventures into politics and philosophy. For instance, it is the introductory section of 'Lines written a few miles above Tintern Abbey' that still gives me pleasure, so full it is of landscape detail. And on to Coleridge later. The appeal of Robert Frost remains too, perhaps again because of the simple, yet fine detail that characterises poems of his encounters with the world about him. Now, much of my work involves the remnant vegetation of high polar latitudes, and I am reminded again of his 'Birches', with their crackling ice cover – a kind of retrospective evocation.

When I eagerly went to England, at 21, to the romantic and stimulating environment of Cambridge, poetry was inevitable. T.S. Eliot's Quartets began to have meaning. I went to Ireland with a copy of Yeats in my backpack. For me then, it was Yeats's evocation of an Irish landscape, real and substantial enough in its physical presence, yet peopled with legend, that I enjoyed. I remain drawn to him, but his appeal now goes beyond his mythology and into his political references. I still find inspiring his poem 'The Second Coming', which is often quoted in globally troubled times. But I find lines from his 'To a Shade' coming into my head when I read media accounts of contemporary, confrontational politics. And 'Sailing to Byzantium' I treat as something fragile, not wanting to probe it too deeply, lest it lose its mystery, complexity and beauty.

In England in the 1960s I also discovered people like Kathleen Raine and Edwin

Muir. I think I was impressed by Kathleen Raine's coming to her work from a background in biology. There is an aptness in her delicate, often mystic, verse that may echo this. Edwin Muir's poetry is sturdier, though he was, and remains, something of an enigma. Yet, going back recently to his poem 'A difficult land', I find in it such contemporary relevance for us here in drought-ravaged Australia.

> This is a difficult land. Here things miscarry
> Whether we care, or do not care enough.
> ... Sun, rain, and frost alike conspire against us

And further:

> On dull delusive days presaging rain
> We yoke the oxen, go out harrowing,
> Walk in the middle of an ochre cloud,
> Dust rising before us and falling again behind us,
> Slowly and gently settling where it lay.
> These days the earth itself looks sad and senseless.

I think it was my daughter, in her senior years of high school, who introduced me to the poems of Seamus Heaney. It was his 'bog poems', describing the well-preserved human remains unearthed from the peat bogs of northern Europe that first drew me. Perhaps it is because I have an understanding of what goes on in swampy habitats that the poems appeal to me! But I think it goes beyond that. His 'Tollund Man' has a multi-layered quality that sustains its attraction, alluding not only to the dark earth processes acting on the body in the peat, but to the relics of Catholic saints, and identifying with the troubles in Ireland.

Science and the genesis of a classic poem

One cannot mention Coleridge without reference to the speculation that surrounds the origins of the dream-like 'The Rime of the Ancient Mariner'. This I first encountered when putting together a thesis on the art of some of the early Antarctic voyages. The art historian Bernard Smith, in his extensive discussions of the art – the visual art – produced during the voyages of Captain James Cook, has raised the possibility that the imagery of Coleridge's poem might stem from the influence of William Wales, astronomer and meteorologist on Cook's second (1772–75) voyage. That voyage saw the circumnavigation of what we now know to be the Antarctic continent, the furthest south penetration of Europeans into high southern latitudes, and the amassing of a great deal of navigational, astronomical and meteorological information. With Wales on the voyage were the naturalists Rheinhold and George Forster, the young artist William Hodges, and a second astronomer, William Bayley. All provided imagery that brought the events, and places, of the voyage to public notice.

William Wales's detailed journal of his voyage on Cook's ship *Resolution* is in the Mitchell Library in Sydney. On his return to London, Wales taught mathematics at Christ's Hospital, and taught the young Coleridge, who joined the school at the age of ten in 1782. Bernard Smith speculates that the rather jovial Wales was something of a raconteur, and, in the knowledge that he was teaching boys who would become navigators, would have drawn heavily on his experiences in high southern seas. These images, he argues, are likely to have remained with Coleridge into his adult, and fruitful years.

Smith takes some care in aligning the events of the voyage with the narrative as given in Wales's journal. He claims that the argument of the poem, as published in the 1798 version, is, in broad outline, a description of the voyage of the *Resolution.* He notes the orientation of the sun with respect to the vessel's passage, and the inclusion in the poem of descriptions of weather and other meteorological phenomena that are peculiarly Antarctic. These include details of the sight and sound of icebergs (or 'ice islands' as they were called then), the 'dismal sheen' of distant ice (was it what we now call 'ice-blink'?). Cook's own journal records the first sightings of albatross as the expedition encounters the ice islands. As the ship moves into the doldrums of the lower latitudes, even the references to the 'rotting seas' are to be found in the journals of members of the *Resolution*'s entourage, and Wales gives a vivid description of a sea snake. There are references too to the vivid colours of phosphorescent seas.

Coleridge of course makes much more of the poem than a mere exotic travelogue, imbuing it with moral significance and emotional power. But, given that it was published in 1798, and its explicit setting was that of a southern polar voyage, it is difficult to find another source for the imagery that Coleridge used, unless of course it all sprang from his own imagination. It seems too precise for that. The chronology, and the co-incidence of the imagery between Wales's journal and the poem make Bernard Smith's argument plausible. The fact that Coleridge was taught by the astronomer and mariner reinforces his claim. The link therefore between one of the most renowned voyages of the scientific enlightenment, and the origin of one of the best-known poems in the English language is an intriguing one.

Selected references

Kemp, Martin, 2000. *Visualizations: the Nature Book of Art and Science.* Oxford University Press.

Muir, Edwin, 1965. *One Foot in Eden.* Faber and Faber, London.

Raine, Kathleen, 1956. *Collected Poems.* Hamish Hamilton, London.

Smith, Bernard, 1992. *Imagining the Pacific. In the Wake of Cook's Voyages.* Melbourne University Press. (See his Chapter 6; 'Coleridge's Ancient Mariner and Cook's Second Voyage').

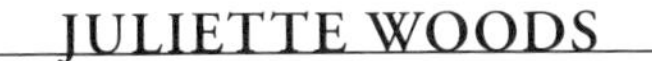

JULIETTE WOODS

Dr Juliette Woods grew up in Scotland, Florida, and South Australia. At the University of Adelaide she studied a wide range of subjects, including English, history, ecology, and geology as part of her mathematics degree; she was also publications editor for both the university's Science Fiction Association and its Literary Society. She eventually decided to specialise in the multi-disciplinary field of computational mathematics for modelling environmental systems, an area which combines many, if not all, of her scientific interests. She has worked for the state government, in the private sector, as a university researcher, and as a scholarship student with CSIRO Land and Water. During two years at the Institute for Computational Engineering and Sciences at the University of Austin, Texas, she was part of a laboratory which ran simulations for everything from nanotechnology to rocket science. She is currently Senior Groundwater Modeller at a consulting firm. She has held the position of Convenor of the Status of Women Committee for the Australian Federation of University Women. Her travel writing has been published in the UK, Australia, Finland and Sweden.

Partial truths and glimpses of light

Recently I went on a field trip to a remote part of the River Murray floodplain. In a vehicle kitted out like a mobile capsule of civilisation – with radio gear, fridge, medical equipment, GPS, spades, water and food – my colleagues and I toured the drought-stricken Chowilla floodplain. Under a grey dawn we stood eating Weeties amid a landscape of grey dust and skeletal, leafless gum trees. What was left of the bushes was tinder-dry, brittle to the touch, and the only colour we saw was a flash of orange in the distance, where graziers had left out citrus peel for their sheep. Later we lunched at a healthier part of the floodplain, sitting in dappled light under arching river red gums as we watched the pelicans splash about on the river. From time to time I'd take photographs, or would jot down our location and some notes about the geology. In the afternoon we met up with some Aboriginal Elders, to talk with them about the state of the river.

Then, once we were back in Adelaide, I described what I saw twice over. The first time, it was as a series of prose poems to friends, where I tried to succinctly convey my impressions. The second time I described the landscape in the language of mathematics, as I modified a computer model of floodplain hydrogeology. Both times, I struggled to reduce a vast, observable complexity to key details and processes; my aim was to capture a few moments in time within a wider context. I strove for precision and concision in both words and in equations.

Unlike many of the other contributors to this book, I am not particularly well-known in my field nor especially distinguished. I'm a mid-level, rank-and-file Applied Mathematics PhD, who has opted to work in the area of water resources. But I have one advantage: my hobby has always been writing. I see science and poetry as different expressions of a single human need, the urge to communicate an understanding of the world.

When I'm building a computer simulation of the environment, I always start by developing a 'conceptual model'. The world is too complicated to understand in its entirety, so I pick a few aspects to study at a time. Perhaps I pick out a single location and sketch out its geography and geology. I take my best guess about how some aspect of it works, and I codify this as equations. The properties of the location need to be simplified, without being too simple. I also need to make some assumptions about how the site interacts at the edges with the rest of the world: these are 'boundary conditions'. If I want to simulate a changing system, I need to specify the point it starts from, the 'initial conditions'. All of this is expressed as numbers and equations within the computer model. Then I can let the model run, and see if it behaves as I've seen the real world behave. Is my conceptual model a good one? Is it simple enough to understand but complicated enough to represent some part of the world we live in? Can I push it further, to predict or explain how the site might behave in the future or under other circumstances?

I think of prose and poetry in a similar way to how I think about mathematical modelling. What aspect of existence is the author trying to capture? Is it simple and succinct whilst also reflecting the complicated, interconnected depths of the universe we live in? What truths are illuminated by these bottled microcosms?

Sometimes a work will strike a false note with the reader. The reader may have an insufficient background to understand it, or the writer may have failed to provide sufficient background material. It could be one of those works which you read too young and only come to appreciate when you are older. Or perhaps the reader knows something the writer doesn't – about human nature, or fluid dynamics, or the migratory paths of a seabird – or the writer fails to communicate something that the reader doesn't know. Sometimes the work is simply wrong or reflects a narrow and inadequate viewpoint. The scientific method aims to weed those out eventually; perhaps this is harder to do with literature, given the wide variation of human experience.

There is also an element of the numinous to both poetry and science. The scientist and poet hope for a moment of inspiration while spending long hours on their crafts, spurred forward by the desire to get something just right. There's a moment of joyous clarity which one desperately wants to capture in equations or in words. Too often, that clarity is partially lost in translation from mind to symbols, but when it is captured there is great beauty in it. And someone will read it, and think, 'I never quite understood the world in that way before.'

****

Perception has its effect on the way politicians in government – who have the money for public education – reach decisions. Those decisions have their impact on the approaches of universities, the opportunities made available for reflections and pure research, the training of teachers, and the ways we decide to support learning. Recently I heard a business man calling for well-educated employees, calling for creativity and imagination and cultural awareness. His appeal suggests to me the time has come to review our approach to senior school curricula and methodology where, while interdisciplinary options get a mention, the focus is primarily on specific subjects.

To reinforce my argument I could return to the essays of Peter Doherty. Weaving together literature, personal life, films he has seen, places he has been, intricate machinery, and the science he is interested in, he offers the reader a wider, more inclusive view of our shared culture in the sciences and the humanities.

I could pick up Robyn Williams' arguments for the sciences in the twenty-first century in *Future Perfect.* He sees aspects of the different sciences as essential in every occupation. Moreover, he sees the sciences in the writing of novelists and playwrights, demonstrating how science helps with English, French translation or Latin, and shows how fiction writers use science. He refers to David Williamson's plays, Peter Carey's novel *Oscar and Lucinda*, Ian McEwan in *Saturday*, Margaret Atwood and Michael Crichton.'[51]

I could direct readers to the internet and an address, powerful in its passion and clarity, by Professor Bryan Gaensler to the Academy of Sciences. It was the Annual Symposium 'Australia's science future' 3–4 May 2000, entitled *'The universe: Looking out – looking forward.*

I could do this and more. Instead, at this stage, I suggest the writings of these contributing scientists and mathematicians are worth reading again, discussing with others, students, teachers, colleagues, lecturers, friends and parents. All of them take us into the humanity of their authors, and their points of view.

51 Robyn Williams, *Future Perfect: What Next? and Other Impossible Questions*, p. 46. Williams is pointing out that fiction writers often use science as material. He sees value in science being attached to every subject (pp. 45–47).

Chapter Three

Perspectives of American Scientists

> In *The Heart of Darkness*, Conrad writes that 'the mind is capable of anything – because everything is in it, all the past as well as all the future'. It is pleasing to think that somewhere in our minds perhaps lies a building waiting to be built, a grand unified theory of physics, the beautiful song of a hermit thrush, a sentence waiting to be written.
>
> **Alan Lightman**[1]

This quotation by Alan Lightman, astro-physicist, essayist and novelist, of those words of Joseph Conrad's in his great novel *The Heart of Darkness,* brings to mind the range possible for the human imagination and intellect. Further, his quotation of those four possibilities demonstrates our capacity, through the intellect and imagination, to make connections. For too long, in schools, the writing of scientists, except in science fiction, has not been included to explore the connections between scientists and poets, the sciences and the arts and the humanities.

In a world where mobile phones cum cameras, with their capacity to record and make contact almost instantaneously, are ubiquitous, to be suggesting that scientific essays and poems engaging with the sciences are important complementary avenues of learning might seem to be anachronistic.

I am suggesting the quiet enjoyment of beauty that brings with it a deeper level of understanding still has a place in our schools. To my knowledge, that is exactly what a number of scientists in the United States have been doing. Their writing is helping to build bridges to re-connect aspects of learning that never should have been separated in school curricula.

Not that I am suggesting that what they are writing should be swallowed whole in an uncritical way. However, I am aware of little contemporary material by Australian scientists, aside from the essays of Peter Doherty, whose writing and approach encourage the general reader in a literary way to engage with the sciences.

---

1 Alan Lightman, *A Sense of the Mysterious: Science and the Human Spirit,* Pantheon Books, New York, 2005, p. 44.

I am aware that an effort was made in the 1960s to do this very thing. Back in 1962 F.W. Cheshire Pty Ltd of Melbourne published a number of essays by scientists in *Science Speaks: A selection of English prose*, edited by Hume Dow. The editor's purpose was to remove the idea, that was already taking hold, that science might be 'some kind of black art' with, a special language and rituals known only to a select few. The authors he chose were not Australian. But one essay, 'The Creative Mind' written in 1956 by Jacob Bronowski, who later produced the television series *The Ascent of Man*, had an approach that integrated the sciences and the arts through the idea of 'unity in variety'. In this essay Dr Bronowski brought in, among others in the arts and sciences, Orpheus, Copernicus, Kepler, Newton, Blake, French novelists – Balzac and Zola – Michael Faraday and Coleridge, Shakespeare's *King Lear,* Pope, Goethe and Yeats, who all had equally valuable places in the story he was telling.

> Reality is not an exhibit for man's inspection, labelled: 'Do not touch.' There are no appearances to be photographed, no experiences to be copied, in which we do not take part. We re-make nature by the act of discovery, in the poem or in the theorem. And the great poem and the deep theorem are new to every reader, and yet are his own experiences, because he himself re-creates them. They are the marks of unity in variety; and in the instant when the mind seizes this for itself, in art or in science, the heart misses a beat.[2]

What is more exciting than the heart missing a beat? Perhaps there is a touch of fear. Perhaps one questions that moment which awakens our curiosity. That moment when something takes us in a direction we had never thought of or tells us something about ourselves that we had not realised.

The purpose of this book is similar to that of Hume Dow. It comes forty-seven years later because it would appear that we have not yet been given the chance to explore the illuminating and often entertaining writing of scientists as part of our English programs. We have science fiction, and short sharp scientific notes like those in *The Naked Scientist* by Chris Smith. We have popular science television but, even with pause buttons, these programs do not let us linger on a phrase, think about an idea, breathe in the beauty of expression, smile or laugh or grimace as a metaphor or an image takes us more deeply into a new possibility.

That is why I am concentrating on the writing of the following scientists who really speak to readers, sharing their thoughts and feelings with the general public. Each of

2 'The Creative Mind', in *Science Speaks: A Selection of English Prose*, edited by Hume Dow, F.W. Cheshire, Melbourne, 1962, p. 15.

these scientists gives us an opportunity to reflect. All of them have literary qualities acknowledged by their peers.

In the Introduction I made clear the central position of Lewis Thomas who is noted for his scientific imagination and his gift for language. In a time when there is concern that we are losing the capacity to write well, with clarity and delight, Lewis Thomas provides examples for us to explore and enjoy. For example, his essays in *The Fragile Species* offer subjects that provide such possibilities. 'Becoming a doctor' tells stories about approaches to medicine from the past to the present. The medical influence of Galen, mentioned by Ian Gibbins, probably caused the death of George Washington! 'The Life in the Mind' emphasises the role of *inner pleasure* (my italics) in 'cells alive'. He suggests that Charles Darwin might not have written *The Origin of Species* if he had not, early in life, experienced it.[3]

However, the essays in *The Fragile Species* are longer than those I have chosen to introduce Lewis Thomas, 'the poet of science'.

Lewis Thomas

Lewis Thomas (1913–1993) is considered so important in the connection between the sciences and the arts and humanities that a prize was established in his name by Rockefeller University. The Lewis Thomas Award is awarded to scientists whose writing is evocative and so clear that it enters the realm of literature, bringing together what C.P. Snow called 'the two cultures'. Established in 1993, it was first awarded to its namesake, Lewis Thomas, who died in that year.

Rockefeller University describes the purpose of the Lewis Thomas Award as follows:

> Throughout history, scientists and poets have sought to unveil the secrets of the natural world. Their methods vary: scientists use tools of rational analysis to slake their compelling thirst for knowledge; poets delve below the surface of language, and deliver urgent communiqués from its depths. The Lewis Thomas Award honors the rare individual who is fluent in the dialects of both realms – and who succeeds in spinning lush literary and philosophical tapestries from the silken threads of scientific and natural phenomena – providing not merely new information but cause for reflection, even revelation.

The writings of these prize winners provide evidence of the increasing awareness, among great scientists, of the need for the rest of us to have a feeling for and understanding of their work, its ramifications in our lives and in the lives of those who will come after us.

---

3 Lewis Thomas, *The Fragile Species*, Charles Scribner's Sons, NY, 1992; 'Becoming a Doctor' pp. 7–17, 'The Life in the Mind' pp. 28–37.

Lewis Thomas wrote very few poems that were published. Modestly he called them verses. Fourteen of them were published in a very special collection entitled *Can I Ask You Something?*

An influential medical scientist and biologist in America, he was noted for his creativity and original thinking. In the 1970s he was invited to write essays for a journal for the general reader. His style was so clear, meditative, witty and surprising that he was asked to continue to write these short essays for which he would not be paid but which would not be edited.

In the Introduction I referred to *The Medusa and the Snail.* The opening essay in that collection allowed me to understand just how inadequate was Tennyson's dramatic interpretation of 'nature red in tooth and claw'. More often than not living things have a symbiotic arrangement. They need one another in order to live. Lewis Thomas reminds us that we, as a species, are social animals. The assumption that we are just individuals without the desire or need to cooperate is false.

For potential students of the sciences, Lewis Thomas provides examples of writing that invite consideration of the point of view he offers, their literary merit and their syntax. For those of us called non-scientists, he is a breath of fresh air, inviting us to breathe a little deeper, expand our lungs and our minds to possibilities which we might never have been aware of if we had not met him.

Given the twenty-first century focus on information communication technology, first I offer for close reading Lewis Thomas's approach to computing. He wrote the accompanying essay before 1974. He was writing at a time when, in America, journalists had been investigating 'Watergate'. In 1974 President Nixon would resign as a result of that scandal. Industries around the world were being affected by the decision of the producers to massively increase and inflate the price of oil. Thoughtful people would suggest that we move away from petrol-driven vehicles to alternative energy sources. Car companies and the oil industry in USA would resist such suggestions until 2009 when bankrupted motor companies had to agree to stop producing 'gas-guzzlers'. American biologists were suggesting that genetic engineering was possible. In Australia Gough Whitlam, who would open universities to the able and interested rather than to those with money, was still Prime Minister. Australia was about to get colour television. Australians were being told that the ozone layer above the Antarctic was being affected by certain chemical propellants in aerosol sprays.

Computers have increased and are still increasing their sophistication. However, Lewis Thomas was seeing into the future. He was setting out, with a light touch, to inform the general public. At the same time he was suggesting something relevant in the twenty-first century where artificial intelligence is taking us towards robotics; that is, machines with the complexity of the human being. Questions today are being asked about consciousness and how the brain works to bring something into the realm of conscious decision-making. This is the work of neuro-scientists who are asking the questions and examining our 'circuitry'. How do we come to the decisions we make? What do we decide to do? How do we reach these decisions? Do we give a damn about their effect down the line? Do we anticipate the effect on others? Do we take into account what that decision might mean beyond our immediate self interest? What is the quality of our awareness of the world around us?

Consider Lewis Thomas's style in this essay. He is bringing to the 1974 reader possibilities of which so many were unlikely to be aware. Listen to the tone. Why does he feel the need to be reassuring about 'our software selves'?

Computers

You can make computers that are almost human. In some respects they are superhuman; they can beat most of us at chess, memorize whole telephone books at a glance, compose music of a certain kind and write obscure poetry, diagnose heart ailments, send personal invitations to vast parties, even go transiently crazy. No one has yet programmed a computer to be of two minds about a hard problem, or to burst out laughing, but that may come. Sooner or later, there will be real human hardware, great whirring, clicking cabinets intelligent enough to read magazines and vote, able to think rings around the rest of us.

Well, maybe, but not for a while anyway. Before we begin organizing sanctuaries and reservations for our software selves, lest we vanish like the whales, here is a thought to relax with.

Even when technology succeeds in manufacturing a machine as big as Texas to do everything we recognize as human, it will still be, at best, a single individual. This amounts to nothing, practically speaking. To match what we can do, there would have to be 3 billion of them[4] with more coming down the assembly line, and I doubt that anyone will put up the money, much less make room. And even so, they would all have to be wired together, intricately and delicately, as we are, communicating with each other, talking incessantly, listening. If they weren't *at* each other this way, all their waking hours, they wouldn't be anything like human, after all. I think we're safe, for a long time ahead.

It is in our collective behavior that we are most mysterious. We won't be able to construct machines like ourselves until we've understood this, and we're not even close. All we know is

4 At the time Lewis was writing, the world population was about 3 billion people (it is now approximately 6 billion). The internet, which can link computers, was not invented.

the phenomenon: we spend our time sending messages to each other, talking and trying to listen at the same time, exchanging information. This seems to be our most urgent biological function: it is what we do with our lives. By the time we reach the end, each of us has taken in a staggering store, enough to exhaust any computer, much of it incomprehensible, and we generally manage to put out even more than we take in. It has become a tremendous enterprise, a kind of energy system on its own. All 3 billion of us are being connected by telephones, radios, television sets, airplanes, satellites, harangues on public address systems, newspapers, magazines, leaflets dropped from great heights, words got in edgewise. We are becoming a grid, a circuitry around the earth. If we keep at it, we will become a computer to end all computers, capable of fusing all the thoughts of the world in a syncytium.

Already, there are no closed two-way conversations. Any word you speak this afternoon will radiate out in all directions, around town before tomorrow, out and around the world before Tuesday, accelerating to the speed of light, modulating as it goes, shaping new and unexpected messages, emerging at the end as an enormously funny Hungarian joke, a fluctuation in the money market, a poem, or simply a long pause in someone's conversation in Brazil.

We do a lot of collective thinking, probably more than any other social species, although it goes on in something like secrecy. We don't acknowledge the gift publicly, and we are not as celebrated as insects, but we do it. Effortlessly, without giving it a moment's thought, we are capable of changing our language, music, manners, morals, entertainment, even the way we dress, all around the earth in a year's turning. We seem to do this by general agreement, without voting or even polling. We simply think our way along, pass information around, exchange codes disguised as art, change our minds, transform ourselves.

Computers cannot deal with such levels of improbability, and it is just as well. Otherwise, we might be tempted to take over the control of ourselves in order to make long-range plans, and that would surely be the end of us. It would mean that some group or other, marvelously intelligent and superbly informed, undoubtedly guided by a computer, would be deciding what human society ought to be like, say, over the next five hundred years or so, and the rest of us would be persuaded, one way or another, to go along. The process of social evolution would then grind to a stand-still and we'd be stuck in today's rut for a millennium.

Much better we work our way out of it on our own, without governance. The future is too interesting and too dangerous to be entrusted to any predictable, reliable agency. We need all the fallibility we can get. Most of all, we need to preserve the absolute unpredictability and total improbability of our connected minds. That way we can keep open all the options, as we have in the past.

It would be nice to have better ways of monitoring what we're up to so that we can recognize change while it is occurring, instead of waking up as we do now to the astonished realization that the whole century just past wasn't what we thought it was, at all. Maybe computers can be used to help in this. You can make simulation models of cities, but what you learn is that they seem to be beyond the reach of intelligent analysis; if you try to use common sense to make predictions, things get more botched up than ever. This is interesting, since the city is the most concentrated aggregation of humans, all exerting whatever influence they can bring to bear. The city seems to have a life of its own. If we cannot understand how this works, we are not likely to get very far with human society at large.

Still, you'd think there would be some way in. Joined together, the great mass of human minds around the earth seems to behave like a coherent living system. The trouble is that the flow of information is mostly one-way. We are all obsessed by the need to feed information in, as fast as we can, but we lack sensing mechanisms for getting anything much back. I will confess that I have no more sense of what goes on in the mind of mankind than I have for the mind of an ant. Come to think of it, this might be a good place to start.'[5]

When he wrote 'Computers' genetic engineering was on the horizon. Six years later, in 1980 Lewis Thomas would tackle, in 'On Cloning a Human Being' published in *The Medusa and the Snail*, the fears of people who were worried about the whole notion of cloning. This subject was and remains most controversial, even more so now since we have cloned sheep and dogs and have the capacity to use stem cells in extraordinary ways. He tackled the possibility of providing 'a version of immortality for carefully, selected, especially valuable people'.

Beginning this essay with his delicate, cross-disciplinary touch, Lewis Thomas listed a number of things that we have decided to worry about. Among those things would be cloning. He would ask questions about who was worth cloning, what would happen to our 'uncloned selves' and, if we wanted to clone, for example, an expert on the Middle East, how would the scientists involved ensure that the environment remained the same. What would be the influence, for example, of relatives and strangers jostling, pushing, caressing, challenging or influencing character in one way or another?

On Cloning a Human Being

It is now theoretically possible to recreate an identical creature from any animal or plant, from the DNA contained in the nucleus of any somatic cell. A single plant root-tip can

5 Lewis Thomas, *The Lives of a Cell*, first published in 1974, Penguin Books, 1978, pp. 111–114 .

be teased and seduced into conceiving a perfect copy of the whole plant; a frog's intestinal epithelial cell possesses the complete instructions needed for a new, same frog. If the technology were further advanced, you could do this with a human being, and there are now startled predictions all over the place that this will in fact be done, some day, in order to provide a version of immortality for carefully selected, especially valuable people.

The cloning of humans is on most of the lists of things to worry about from Science, along with behaviour control, genetic engineering, transplanted heads, computer poetry, and the unrestrained growth of plastic flowers.

Cloning is the most dismaying of prospects, mandating as it does the elimination of sex with only a metaphoric elimination of death as compensation. It is almost no comfort to know that one's cloned, identical surrogate lives on, especially when the living will very likely involve edging one's real, now aging self off to the side, sooner or later. It is hard to imagine anything like filial affection or respect for a single, unmated nucleus; harder still to think of one's new, self-generated self as anything but an absolute, desolate orphan. Not to mention the complex interpersonal relationship involved in raising one's self from infancy, teaching the language, enforcing discipline, instilling good manners, and the like. How would you feel if you became an incorrigible juvenile delinquent by proxy, at the age of fifty-five?

The public questions are obvious. Who is to be selected, and on what qualifications? How to handle the risks of the misuse of technology, such as the self-determined cloning by the rich and powerful but socially objectionable, or the cloning by governments of dumb, docile masses for the world's work? What will be the effect on all the uncloned rest of us of human sameness? After all, we've accustomed ourselves through hundreds of millennia to the continual exhilaration of uniqueness; each of us is totally different, in a fundamental sense, from all the other four billion. Selfness is an essential element of life. The thought of human nonselfness, precise sameness, is terrifying, when you think about it.

Well, don't think about it, because it isn't a probable possibility, not even as a long shot for the distant future, in my opinion. I agree that you might clone some people who would look amazingly like their parental cell donors, but the odds are that they'd be almost as different as you or me, and certainly more different than any of today's identical twins.

The time required for the experiment is only one of the problems, but a formidable one. Suppose you want to clone a prominent, spectacularly successful diplomat to look after the Middle East problems of the distant future. You'd have to catch him and persuade him, probably not very hard to do, and extirpate a cell. But then you'd have to wait for him to grow up through embryonic life and then for at least forty years more, and you'd have to be sure all observers remained patient and unmeddlesome through his unpromising, ambiguous childhood and adolescence.

Moreover, you'd have to be sure of recreating his environment, perhaps down to the last detail. 'Environment' is a word which really means people, so you'd have to do a lot more cloning than just the diplomat himself.

This is a very important part of the cloning problem, largely overlooked in our excitement about the cloned individual himself. You don't have to agree all the way with B.F. Skinner to acknowledge that the environment does make a difference, and when you examine what we really mean by the word 'environment' it comes down to other human beings. We use euphemisms and jargon for this, like 'social forces', 'cultural influences', even Skinner's 'verbal community', but what it means is the dense crowd of nearby people who talk to, listen to, smile or frown at, give to, withhold from, nudge, push, caress, or flail out at the individual. No matter what the genome says, these people have a lot to do with shaping a character. Indeed, if all you had was the genome, and no other people around, you'd grow a sort of vertebrate plant, nothing more.

So, to start with, you will undoubtedly need to clone the parents. No question about this. This means the diplomat is out, even in theory, since you could not have gotten cells from both his parents at the time when he himself was just recognizable as an early social treasure. You'd have to limit the list of clones to people already certified as sufficiently valuable for the effort, with both parents still alive. The parents would need cloning and, for consistency, their parents as well. I suppose you'd also need the usual informed-consent forms, filled out and signed, not easy to get if I know parents, even harder for grandparents.

But this is only the beginning. It is the whole family that really influences the way a person turns out, not just the parents, according to current psychiatric thinking. Clone the family.

Then what? The way each member of the family develops has already been determined by the environment set around him, and this environment is more people, people outside the family, schoolmates, acquaintances, lovers, enemies, car-pool partners, even, in special circumstances, peculiar strangers across the aisle in the subway. Find them, and clone them.

But there is no end to the protocol. Each of the outer contacts has his own surrounding family, and his and their outer contacts. Clone them all.

To do things properly, with any hope of ending up with a genuine duplicate of a single person, you really have no choice. You must clone the world, no less.

We are not ready for an experiment of this size, nor, I should think, are we willing. For one thing, it would mean replacing today's world by an entirely identical world to follow immediately, and this means no new, natural, spontaneous, random, chancy children. No children at all, except for the manufactured doubles of those now on the scene. Plus all those identical adults, including all of today's politicians, all seen double. It is too much to contemplate.

Moreover, when the whole experiment is finally finished, fifty years or so from now, how could you get a responsible scientific reading on the outcome? Somewhere in there would be the original clonee, probably lost and overlooked, now well into middle age, but everyone around him would be precise duplicates of today's everyone. It would be today's world, filled to overflowing with duplicates of today's people and their same, duplicated problems, probably all resentful at having to go through our whole thing all over, sore enough at the clonee to make endless trouble for him, if they found him.

I once lived through a period when I wondered what Hell could be like, and I stretched my imagination to try to think of a perpetual sort of damnation. I have to confess I never thought of anything like this.

I have an alternative suggestion, if you're looking for a way out. Set cloning aside, and don't try it. Instead, go in the other direction. Look for ways to get mutations more quickly, new variety, different songs. Fiddle around, if you must fiddle, but never with ways to keep things the same, no matter who, not even yourself. Heaven, somewhere ahead, has got to be a change.[6]

Lewis Thomas challenged his 1980 readers to take a very different path in the future. Have we done so? However, for a non-scientist like me, it is such a pleasure to be taken beyond the abstract. He helps us to see, to expand our imaginative response. For example, he reminds readers that 'environment' means people; people doing things or not doing things, people growing things, making things, tearing things down, putting things in space, people thinking about the future or just about today, people perhaps refusing to be panicked into solutions that take into account too few long-range effects or those unintended consequences we talk about when we go 'Oops! I didn't mean that to happen'.

Four years later in 1984, the year George Orwell chose as the time for the novel that gave us 'big brother', scientists were warning about the greenhouse effect. The virus causing AIDS had been discovered. The Olympic Games would go ahead in Los Angeles without participants from the Eastern Bloc of what was then the Soviet sphere of influence. Nelson Mandela would still be imprisoned on Robben Island. Bob Hawke would win the Federal election in Australia. He and his Treasurer, Paul Keating would de-regulate the banks. The Republican candidate, Ronald Reagan, with George Bush Senior as his Vice President, would become the President of the United States of America. In England, Margaret Thatcher would be delighted to have such an ally. In December of that year Michael Jackson, the brilliant but tragic American entertainer, would bring out 'Thriller', a high point in world-wide popular culture.

6 Lewis Thomas, 'On Cloning A Human Being', *The Medusa and the Snail: Notes of a Biology Watcher*, Allen Lane, London, 1980, pp. 51–56

That same year Lewis Thomas would give us 'Humanities and Science'. He was concerned with the teaching of science in America. Was it just a matter of getting the numbers right as some people seemed to believe? Lewis Thomas did not think so. He was worried by the serious imbalance in the approach to education. He thought that science was being taught as if everything was certain, despite eighty years of knowledge gained through the work of Albert Einstein and Max Planck, despite the discovery of the uncertainty principle in that post-classical physics world. He considered that teachers of the sciences had been teaching as if scientific facts were 'somehow superior to the facts in all other scholarly disciplines'. He would point out in classroom practice that science was being taught as 'an unambiguous, unalterable, and endlessly useful display of data needing only to be packaged and installed somewhere in one's temporal lobe in order to achieve an understanding of the natural world'.

He insisted that this was wrong. In this essay he set out to show that such an approach was bogus. Looking to the future once again he spelt it out. 'For getting a full grasp, for perceiving real significance when significance is at hand, we shall need minds at work from all kinds of brains outside the fields of science, most of all the brains of poets, of course, but also those of artists, musicians, philosophers, historians, writers in general.'[7] And he went further. Science would need to be taught in a thoughtful way, considering the quality of evidence, the element of uncertainty, the different interpretations put upon information and the motivation of the interpreters, to 'those who [would be] needing to think about it'. That meant, and means, us; we who will vote on issues, influence directions and need to have the knowledge to counter the 'spin' paid for by whichever industry, ideology, or political party that might not want us to have access to and examine the evidence.

He would face the problem of 'the two cultures' in an essay entitled, 'On Matters of Doubt'. In 2009, the fiftieth anniversary of C.P. Snow's polemic, it is worthwhile listening to Lewis Thomas's views on that notion of the 'chasm'. He wrote that 'we would be better off if we had never invented the terms "science" and "humanities" and then set them up as if they represented two different kinds of intellectual enterprise.'

He could not see why we ever did this. 'Now to make matters worse, we have had these two encampments not only at odds but trying to swipe problems from each other'. The examples he gives include a description of the literary 'deconstructionists' as wanting to be the scientists of poetry, 'looking at every word in every line with

---

7 Lewis Thomas, 'Humanities and Science', *Late Night Thoughts on Listening to Mahler's Ninth Symphony*, Bantam Books, Toronto, 1984 p. 143.

essentially the reductionist attitude of particle physicists in the presence of atoms, but still unaware of the uncertainty principle that governs any good poem: not only can the observer change the thing observed, he can even destroy it'.[8]

By this time Lewis Thomas was worried about the future for the young. He wrote: 'I do admit to worrying, late at night, about that matter of time: obviously we will have to get rid of modern warfare and quickly, or else we will end up, with luck, throwing spears and stones at each other. We could, without luck, run out of time in what is left in this century and then, by mistake, finish the whole game off by upheaving the table, ending life for everything except the bacteria, maybe – with enough radiation, even them. If you are given to fretting about what is going on in the minds of the young people in our schools, or on the streets of Zurich or Paris or Sydney or Tokyo or wherever, give a thought to the idea of impermanence for a whole species – *ours* – and the risk of earthly incandescence; it is a brand-new idea, never before confronted as a reality by any rising generation of human beings.'[9]

I hope these examples of his writing will encourage teachers, students, lecturers and general readers to find other essays. In his essay 'The Lives of a Cell' you can feel his concern for us and his concern for language. In fact he names one collection, *The Fragile Species*, for us. We are the fragile species, so quick to denude and destroy, so slow to revive and restore. This collection, published in 1992, a year before his death, contains a wonderful essay which reminds me why he is at the heart of this book. 'Comprehending My Cat Jeoffry' demonstrates his approach to knowledge. He detests the way it is split up into self-contained subject divisions and most particularly the decision to separate the 'two cultures'. He brings the English eighteenth-century poet, Christopher Smart, into an essay where, he tells us, 'I shall instead stay very close to the surface of things, mostly on thin ice, playing light hunches all the way'.[10]

Coming at the end of his life, it does not surprise me that Lewis Thomas brings together so much of what he considers important. He concludes *The Fragile Species* with the three 'C's – 'Cooperation, Communication, Connections'. In his inimitable way, he encourages us to explore the idea of the 'comity *of* nations', rather than conflict *among* nations. He takes us to the Indo-European root of the word 'comity', which means to

---

8 Lewis Thomas 'On Matters of Doubt', *Late Night Thoughts on Listening to Mahler's Ninth Symphony*, Bantam Books, Toronto, 1984, pp. 156–163.

9 Lewis Thomas 'On Matters of Doubt', *Late Night Thoughts on Listening to Mahler's Ninth Symphony*, Bantam Books, Toronto, 1984, pp. 156–163.

10 Lewis Thomas, *Et Cetera, Et Cetera; Notes of a Word-Watcher*, Little, Brown and Company, Boston, 1990, pp. 77–78.

smile on one another, and he suggests that such friendly cooperation is 'not beyond imagining'.[11]

His delight in language, evident in that reference to 'comity', with the adventures possible through the exploration of words was given its own collection, *Et Cetera, Et Cetera: Notes of a Word-Watcher*. And he was not afraid of including that Anglo-Saxon four-letter word. In Chapter 19 'SCRUTINY, FRENETIC, BOTHER, STOP etc' he offers the information that 'Each everyday word that we choose, every day, to fit properly in a string of other words is, in itself, a tiny language'. In the process, he provides a different avenue of learning, Exploring 'friend' in an etymology dictionary, I find that 'friend', connected to comity, comes from Old English and describes 'one joined to another in mutual benevolence and intimacy'. In Chapter 23 'Children and Language' he offers insights into the way children learn language, taking us to those 'new, natural, spontaneous, random, chancy children' he loves.

I think, when we are about to set up a national curriculum binding everyone into the processes, skills, problem solving approaches and technology that will be considered useful to build the 'knowledge economy' that the Commonwealth Minister for Education talks about, we should make room for the great writing of scientists who might think 'outside the square' and give us interdisciplinary options that we might not have considered.

Lewis Thomas's prose has a rhythm and engaging lilt that carries the reader along. His knowledge is matched by his wit and the power of his imagination to envisage future possibilities. His poems were collected in a special edition, *Can I Ask You Something?*, by the Library Fellows of the Whitney Museum of American Art. This prose poem completes his collection of verse.

And Did You Know

And did you know that you can take a cell (handle it gently now; bathe it in a warm buffer, have some respect, it is a living thing) and crack it open like an egg and all the things that spill out are alive? Did you know this about a cell?

The little oval things are ribosomes. They spin and weave out strands of silk. No hand is needed. It is automated, done with something like the circuits of computers but of course much smaller, and soft and warm. The ribosomes have gatherings of cousins, link chains of peptides into intricate antique designs for coils and mats, and they believe that cells are theirs to use and occupy as given places, like walled gardens.

11 Lewis Thomas, *The Fragile Species*, Charles Scribner's Sons, New York, 1992.

The mitochondria are all the source of power. They sweat, complain, take in and burn the fuel, make heat, swarm angrily to the far places where the other parts of cells have work to do, and there provide the energy. They were created separately, swam into cells before the time of lamprey eels or fossil ferns or any brown dry land. They have adapted and like Welsh miners in the western hills of Pennsylvania they keep their ways. God is a carbohydrate. They make their own nucleic acids, code themselves in dialects, breed privately and in dark mystery off at the edges of dividing cells, replicate while the great celebration of division and the dancing and the music and the assembling of the strands of spindles, and the pulling apart, are going on.

The centrioles hold the spindles, call the dances, govern the distribution of all estates, read out all wills and shout aloft the orders for division. They are alien creatures, invaders from another continent, carrying information from unremembered places. The cilia are oarsmen singing other songs.

The nucleus is heavy, drowsy, sodden, choked with unspeakable stores of knowledge always needing looking up. It has its own pulsating membrane, breeds its young, lives its life. Be careful how you handle it.

And there are all the other things, smaller, breathing, listening. When the time comes and the signal sounds for swarming, molecules cluster quickly in the dark, form particles in tanks, make crystal corridors, and then construct from nothing but themselves long microtubules for the skeleton of cells, extending bony legs, protrusions, fingers, all alive.

You could farm these creatures, feed them, breed them on acres of glass surfaces. If someone placed a teapot cover over them, the life inside would make it rattle. You could send trains up Everest, lift trolleys out to Jupiter. You could make cells, I think, as big as Brooklyn if you had the funds and glass enough, or even plastic. It would be complicated and costly but I have not the slightest doubt that it would work.

Except, of course, for the mitotic business and the dividing. Imagine centrioles erecting gleaming silvery spindles from Coney Island all the way to Ozone Park, and then the sound of the splitting.

But I had something else in mind. I started out to make another point. I did not mean to change the topic. It is this: these parts, these swimming things split from the broken cells, touching, swarming, living inside each other, are little animals.

So many things are changing. There is no cause to worry. Do not weep. I am not weeping. See. I am a world of secret fauna, an earth of tiny ecosystems, a confusion of other animals. Am I in charge? I could not possibly arrange it. For one thing I do not have the time. And anyway they seem to get along. I have other things to do, and anyway for all I know it is the other way around. When they are sensing me, hearing my music, listening me deep in the park, thinking me, they have a certain claim.

I only hope they realize that I am here, that when I die it may be hours or even days before the news can reach them all, and there are some who never will be told.'[12]

'We Live Inside Each Other' – an example of Lewis Thomas's poetry

For me, Thomas's recognition of our interconnectedness is the reason I want people to read his work. It is my conviction that the essence of his mind and heart has significance for everyone in the century ahead. He shows us in language that excites while it challenges what we fail to recognise, that is, the intensity and presence of life. And sometimes we are afraid of it. And he is afraid that we might not value it.

We Live Inside Each Other

An oak tree and my grandfather are parents
Of certain plankton in the sea. The genes
Encased in chromosomes of some Sargasso eels
Can code the enzymes needed for high Norway pines
Or transform hillside cornflowers to bees.

The tissues of the earth adhere, stream over hills,
Stream under slabs of concrete, touch and lock together.
New embryonic shapes are cast from continents of swarming cells.
Moulded and multiplied astonished, flowered in different parts
No more alike
Than startled eyes resemble beating hearts.
We live inside each other.

---

12 *Can I Ask You Something?* Verse by Lewis Thomas, Etchings by Alfonso Ossorio, published by The Library Fellows of the Whitney Museum of American Art, New York, 1984, p. 30.

If I should touch your fingertips and we were then
To touch by accident the pollen in an exhalation
Of a gulf breeze blown to England, we would feel
The shock of surging current, the leaping linked pulsation
Of Oriental children, giant calling birds, and maple leaves.

Cicadas, running men, and nesting gannets ride the same
Upwelling tides, drift with the goats in olive groves,
Bask in the sun together, walled by the membrane
Grown into every where in a continuum,
Pulsed by the sun,
Joined in asymmetry, fused in a syncytium.
We live inside each other.

The cytoplasm, drummed to life by moonrise, is the soil. Deep currents
In the tidal waters, rivers, lakes, and all of the springs that run
Beneath the seas, are blood. The brain is a circuitry of woven filaments
Strung from receptors in the forest trees, out to the sea beasts,
Up to the midges in the sun, down with cascades of meditation
to the wax-white
Shrimps blind in the pools of caverns under the hill. The bone
Is coral, limestone, shells in shale, chalk cliffs,
Walled in the membrane, fastened to basalt.

Plumes, sibilant drafts of air are blown
Out from the chloroplasts, breathing the warm, moist breath
Over the breathing membrane,
Opaque to probability, impermeable to death.
We live inside each other. [13]

We are in the twenty-first century and it is time that the writing of this 'poet of science' should be on offer to students and teachers in the humanities. In addition to Lewis Thomas, and lauded as his successor as a writer of science, is Natalie Angier whose book, *The Canon: A Whirligig Tour of the Beautiful Basics of Science*, was published in

13 *Can I Ask You Something?*, The Library Fellows of the Whitney Museum of American Art, New York, 1984.

2007. She is seen as an inheritor of his genius, acknowledged as such by the award of the Lewis Thomas Award, and she too offers new insights in sparkling prose to the general reader.

Winners of the Lewis Thomas Award, and their writing

Among the science writers awarded the Lewis Thomas prize is Freeman Dyson who makes close connections between the sciences and poetry. For example, the first chapter of his book, *Disturbing the Universe,* is entitled 'The Magic City'. It is a reminder of how significant our early childhood experiences can be. As an eight-year-old Freeman Dyson read *The Magic City*, a fairy story by Edith Nesbit, that late-nineteenth century writer of children's stories with unexpected technological elements.

Explaining why this book stayed in his mind as 'somehow special' Dyson wrote '*The Magic City* is not just a story about some crazy kid. It is a story about a crazy universe. What I see now, and did not see as an eight-year-old, is that Nesbit's crazy universe bears a strong resemblance to the one we live in.'[14] Then he takes us into the world that has been created in the twentieth century.

> That we live in a world of overgrown toys is too obvious to need explaining. Nikolaus Otto plays for a few years with a toy gasoline engine and – bingo! – we all find ourselves driving cars. Wallace Carothers gets interested in condensation polymers and – zing! – every working-class girl is wearing nylon stockings that are as fancy as the open-work silk that was for Nesbit in 1910 the hated symbol of upper-class privilege. Otto Hahn and Fritz Strassmann amuse themselves with radiochemistry and – boom! – a hundred thousand people in Hiroshima are dead. The same examples also illustrate Nesbit's rule about the consequences of wishing for machinery. Once you have wished for cars, nylon or nuclear weapons, you are stuck with them in a very permanent fashion … When Otto Hahn stumbled upon the discovery of nuclear fission in 1938 he had no inkling of nuclear weapons, no premonition that he was treading on dangerous ground. When the news of Hiroshima came to him seven years later, he was overcome with such grief that his friends were afraid he would kill himself. … Scientists are not the only people who play with intellectual toys that suddenly explode and cause the crash of empires. Philosophers, prophets and poets do it too. [15]

That last sentence 'Philosophers, prophets and poets do it too', brings to mind a connection between scientists and poets that Simon Armitage, an English poet, will take up in his contribution to *Contemporary Poetry and Contemporary Science.*

---

14 Freeman Dyson, *Disturbing the Universe*, Harper & Row, New York, 1979, p. 3.

15 Freeman Dyson, *Disturbing the Universe,* Harper & Row, New York, 1979, pp. 6–7.

Freeman Dyson won the Lewis Thomas Award in 1996. In 1984 he published *Weapons and Hope*, taking us through the impact of technology in both World Wars on scientists, particularly J.B.S. Haldane in World War I and J. Robert Oppenheimer in World War II, and on poets, from Rupert Brooke to Wilfred Owen in 1918, and from C. Day Lewis at the beginning of the World War II to Jimmy Porter in John Osborne's play *Look Back in Anger* in 1956.

Probably Rachel Carson's writing in *The Silent Spring* appeared too soon for her to win this prize and, until recently, the prize winners have been men. The first woman awarded the Lewis Thomas Award was Natalie Angier who won the Pulitzer Prize for *Woman: An Intimate Geography,* considered 'an essential read for anyone interested in how biology affects who we are'.

Every paragraph of Natalie Angier's that I have read in *The Canon: A Whirligig Tour through the Beautiful Basics of Science* has made me want to stop and enjoy the way she takes me into the science she is describing. Consider these sentences about the Earth in her geology section. 'Most of the Earth's girth is taken up by the mantle, a word that comes from the German term for "cloak", as the mantle cloaks the core. And though the cloak is much less dense than the core, do not mistake it for gossamer.' [16]

Another scientist, Max Perutz, remarkable for his discoveries in Cambridge where he was supported by Sir Lawrence Bragg, is also important for his role in the omission of Rosalind Franklin from recognition as a key figure in the discovery of DNA. (The Braggs are honoured in the adjunct to the Royal Institution – RiAus – established in Adelaide in 2009.)

Lists of the winners of the Lewis Thomas Award are to be found on the Internet. All are there because their writing is of the quality that gives their books recognition as literary works of art. We see their authors as human beings not 'laboratory men'.

Consider Abraham Pais. Born in Holland, he managed to complete his PhD in physics just before the Nazis, occupying the Netherlands, refused Jews the right to study. He tells this story of his education in his autobiography. He knew English and writes of how he filled in his time in hiding. Unlike Anne Frank, he survived. Here is his description of how he spent time.

> What I remember most particularly about that period is an enormous amount of reading. Tineke knew a man who lived nearby who had quite a decent private library, and who had been kind enough to make a list of his books at Tineke's request. That list was for me; I would select books, Tineke would fetch them for me. My recollection of what books I

---

16 Natalie Angier, *The Canon: A Whirligig tour through the Beautiful Basics of Science*, Houghton Mifflin Company, Boston, New York 2007, p. 220.

read those days is poor. All I remember are wonderful hours with Tolstoi's *War and Peace* and with many of the writings of Dostoyevsky. The library also contained a four-volume German edition of the complete plays of Ibsen. In one week I read all of these.[17]

Abraham Pais would become a Professor of Physics at Rockefeller University.

Dr Steven Weinberg of the University of Texas was awarded the Lewis Thomas Award in 1999. He has been described as a one of the Renaissance men of our time, the 'Einstein' of our day. He won the Nobel Prize for uniting the electromagnetic and the weak nuclear forces into a single force. It is said that nobody since Loren Eiseley and Lewis Thomas has written so beautifully, turning science into poetry.

In his essay Scoresby Shepherd refers to Edward O. Wilson who was awarded the Lewis Thomas Award in 2000. This American biologist uses the word 'consilience' to emphasise the need for the unity of knowledge. It was first coined by Professor Whelwell of Cambridge. (Whelwell also coined the words that Michael Faraday needed to describe what happened when electromagnetism occurred – anode and cathode.)

In 2001 an emigrant from Britain, Oliver Sacks, won this award. His autobiography, *Uncle Tungsten: Memoirs of a Chemical Boyhood,* gave me an understanding of how the periodic table was created. In this autobiography one feels the significance of family. In particular I learnt about the role played by the mother of Dimitri Mendeleev (who worked out the periodic table), who made sure her son received the education he needed to fulfil his potential.

For Lewis Thomas ignorance was not an end. It was a beginning. When one asked a question or read a book that brought new knowledge to light, one was – and is – able to contribute more fully to the life around us.

For Roald Hoffmann, the Nobel Prize-winning quantum chemist, it is a journey of discovery and creativity. That creativity is equally evident in the writing of Alan Lightman.

An astro-physicist, essayist and novelist – Alan Lightman

This American scientist, an astro-physicist, I discovered through the third volume of Joy Hakim's book for American students, *The Story of Science: Einstein Adds a New Dimension.* He has been said to have 'a graceful style, dazzling imagination, and a talent for clarifying scientific issues that place him alongside Lewis Thomas and Stephen Jay Gould'.

17 Abraham Pais, *A Tale of Two Continents*, Princeton University Press, Princeton, New Jersey, 1997, pp. 108–109. Born in 1918, a theoretical physicist, Abraham Pais wrote an acclaimed biography of Albert Einstein.

Alan Lightman began publishing essays about science and the human side of science in 1981. In 1989 he was appointed Professor of Science and Writing and senior lecturer in physics at the Massachusetts Institute of Technology. He was the first professor at MIT to receive a joint professorship in the sciences and the humanities. That decision to make such a connection shows the increasing awareness in the USA of the need to get rid of the notion of 'the great divide'.

Alan Lightman understands the role of theatre in helping people consider ideas and feelings that challenge the way we interpret human behaviour and human actions. Students of the humanities may know the play by Bertolt Brecht, *Galileo*, which explores that scientist's dilemma. Does he tell the truth and possibly be condemned to death for heresy or does he decide to survive? The play embraces his humanity and his moral dilemma. In Sydney, in 2008, a play presenting the ideas of Richard Feynman was staged. That one-man drama, written by Peter Parnell, is called *Richard Feynman, Q.E.D.* Michael Frayn has brought to the stage one of the big issues of the twentieth century in *Copenhagen,* using the conversation between Niels Bohr and Werner Heisenberg. Alan Lightman has co-founded the Catalyst Collaborative at MIT, which is a collaboration between MIT and the Underground Railway Theatre of Boston. *CC@MIT* commissions new plays and produces existing plays that involve science or scientists.

In 1984 he published *Time Travel & Papa Joe's Pipe: Essays on the Human Side of Science.* While I should prefer to include his essay 'A Visit by Mr Newton', 'Pas de Deux' picks up, in a delicate way, the role physics has in dance.

Pas de Deux

In soft blue light, the ballerina glides across the stage and takes to the air, her toes touching Earth imperceptibly. *Sauté, batterie, sauté.* Legs cross and flutter, arms unfold into an open arch. The ballerina knows that the easiest way to ruin a good performance is to think too much about what her body is doing. Better to trust in the years of daily exercises, the muscles' own understanding of force and balance.

While she dances, Nature is playing its own part, flawlessly and with absolute reliability. On *pointe*, the ballerina's weight is precisely balanced by the push of floor against shoe, the molecules in contact squeezed just the right amount to counter force with equal force. Gravity balanced with electricity.

An invisible line runs from the center of the Earth through the ballerina's point of contact and upward. If her own center should drift a centimeter from this line, gravitational torques will topple her. She knows nothing of mechanics, but she can hover on her toes for minutes at a time, and her body is continuously making the tiny corrections that reveal an intimacy with torque and inertia.

Gravity has the elegant property that it accelerates everything equally. As a result, astronauts become weight-less, orbiting Earth on exactly the same trajectories as their spaceships and thus seeming to float within. Einstein understood this better than anyone and described gravity with a theory more geometry than physics, more curves than forces. The ballerina, leaping upward lightly, hangs weightless for a moment amid flowers she has dropped midair, all falling on the same trajectory.

Now she prepares for a *pirouette*, right leg moving back to fourth position, pushing off one foot, arms coming in to speed the turn. Before losing balance she gets four rotations. Male dancers, on *demi-pointe* and with greater contact area, can sometimes go six or eight. The ballerina recovers well, giving her spin smoothly back to Earth and remembering to land in fifth position smiling. Briefly her feet come to rest, caught between the passage of spin and the friction of the floor. Friction is important. Every body persists in its state of rest or of uniform motion unless acted upon by outside forces. Every action requires a reaction.

The ballerina depends on the constancy of the laws of physics, even though she herself is slightly unpredictable. In this same performance last night she went only three-and-a-half turns through her first *pirouette*, and then took the *arabesque* several feet from where she takes it now. Regardless of these discrepancies, the atoms in the floor, wherever she happens to touch and at one millisecond's notice, must be prepared to respond with faithful accuracy. Newton's laws, Coulomb's force, and the charge of electrons must be identical night after night – otherwise, the ballerina will misjudge the resiliency of the floor or the needed moment of inertia. Her art is more beautiful in its uncertainty. Nature's art comes in its certainty.

The ballerina assumes one pose after another, each fragile and symmetrical. In the physics of solids, crystal structures can be found that appear identical after rotation by one-half, one-third, one-quarter, and one-sixth of a circle. Crystals with one-fifth and one-seventh symmetries do not exist because space cannot be filled with touching pentagons or septagons. The ballerina reflects a series of natural forms. She is first ethereal, then lyrical. She has struggled for years to develop a personal style, embellished with fragments from the great dancers. As she dances, Nature, in the mirror, pursues its own style effortlessly. It is the ultimate in classic technique, unaltered since the universe began.

For an ending, the ballerina does a *demi-plié* and jumps two feet into the air. The Earth, balancing her momentum, responds with its own *sauté* and changes orbit by one ten-trillionth of an atom's width. No one notices, but it is exactly right.[18]

18 Alan Lightman, 'Pas de Deux', *Dance for Two: Selected Essays*, Pantheon Books, New York, 1996, pp. 3–5.

In *A Sense of the Mysterious: Science and the Human Spirit*, Alan Lightman has published another collection of essays. 'Metaphor in Science' is worth consideration. There was a time when the lateral thinking evident in the use of metaphor appeared to have limited place in school-based science courses, except in the hands of science teachers who refused to see the sciences and other areas of study as separate areas of learning. Here is his essay 'Words'.

Words

As a member of two communities, physicists and novelists, I've been fascinated by the different ways in which they work, the different ways in which they think, and their different approaches to truth.

One important distinction that can be made between physicists and novelists, and between the scientific and artistic communities in general, is in what I call 'naming'. Roughly speaking, the scientist tries to name things and artists try to avoid naming things.

To name a thing, one needs to have gathered it, distilled and purified it, in order to identify it with clarity and precision. One puts a box around the thing and says what's in the box is the thing and what's not is not. Consider, for example, the word *electron.* As far as we know, all the zillions of electrons in the universe are identical. There is only a single kind of electron. And to a modern physicist, the word *electron* represents a particular equation – the Dirac equation with field operators.[19]

That equation summarizes, in precise mathematical and quantitative terms, everything we know about electrons – every interaction, the precise deflections and twists of electrons by particular magnetic and electric fields, the tiny effects of electrons and their antiparticles materializing out of nothing and then disappearing again. In a real sense, the name *electron* refers to the Dirac equation. For scientists it is a great comfort, a feeling of power to be able to name things in this way.

The objects and concepts of the novelist cannot be named. The novelist might use the words *love* and *fear*, but these names do not summarize or convey much to the reader. For one thing, there are a thousand different kinds of love. There's the love you feel for a mother who writes to you every day during your first month away from home, and the love you feel for a mother who, when you stumble into the house drunk after driving home from the prom, slaps you and then embraces you. There's the love you feel for a man or a woman

19 Joy Hakim tells the story of Paul Dirac, the British physicist, in *Einstein Adds a New Dimension.* 'Dirac, whom Niels Bohr said had "the purest soul", figured out that every charged particle, like the negative electron, must have a twin, an antiparticle, with an opposite charge (like the positron).' His ideas influenced what is called 'string theory' (p. 165).

you've just made love to. There's the love you feel for a friend who calls to give you support after you've just split up with your spouse. But it's not just the many different kinds of love that prevents the novelist from truly naming the thing. It's also that the idea of love – the particular sensation out of the thousands of different kinds of love – must be shown to the reader not by naming it, but through the actions of the characters.

And if love is shown, rather than named, each reader will experience it and, what's more, will understand it in his or her own way. Each reader will draw on his or her own adventures and misadventures with love. Every electron is identical, but every love is different.

The novelist does not want to eliminate these differences, doesn't want to clarify and distil the meaning of love so that there is only a single meaning, like the Dirac equation, because no such distillation exists. And any attempt at such distillation would undermine the authenticity of readers' reactions, destroying the delicate, participatory creative experience of a good reader reading a good book. In a sense, a novel is not complete until it has been read. And each reader completes the novel in a different way.

I'll give another illustration of the difference between naming and not naming. Let me represent science by expository writing. Like science, a piece of expository writing takes a reductionist and reasoned approach to the world. You have a position or argument, you structure this argument in logical steps, amassing facts and evidence to convince your reader of each assertion. We all learn that in expository writing it is good form to begin each paragraph with a topic sentence. A topic sentence, in effect names the idea of the paragraph at the outset. You thus begin by telling your readers what they are going to learn in the paragraph and how to organize their thoughts so as to gain as ordered and structured an understanding as possible.

But in fiction, a topic sentence is usually fatal. Because the power of fiction is emotional and sensual. You want your reader to feel what you are saying, to smell it and hear it, to be part of the scene you are creating. You want your reader to be blindsided, to let go and be carried off into a magical place. Every reader will travel differently, depending upon his or her own experiences of life. With a topic sentence, you don't leave room for your reader's own imagination and creativity. The difference can be stated in terms of the body. In expository writing, you want to go first to your reader's brain. In creative writing, you want to bypass the brain and go straight for the stomach, or the heart.[20]

Now to Roald Hoffmann who insists that scientists need to connect with 'their friends in the humanities' and who argued that Fritz Haber's approach to science was wrong.

---

20 Alan Lightman, 'Words', in *A Sense of the Mysterious: Science and the Human Spirit,* Pantheon Books, New York, 2005, pp. 45–48.

Roald Hoffmann – Nobel prize-winning quantum chemist and poet

Born in Poland, Hoffmann came from a happy Jewish family but grew up in the dark days of 1937 Europe. He and his mother were hidden in a schoolhouse from the Nazis by a Ukrainian family. His father, Hillel Safran, was caught by the Nazis when he tried to organise a breakout from the Polish ghetto in June 1943. Most of the rest of his family suffered the same fate. He was brought up by his second father, Paul Hoffmann, a kind and gentle man.

All that time he was learning new languages. As displaced persons in Europe after the end of the war, his family emigrated to America where he went to a selective school. His fascination with chemistry grew. He gained his PhD from Harvard in 1962.

In 1981 he shared the Nobel Prize for Chemistry with Kenichi Fukui. I invite you to find out more about this man, an acknowledged poet and scientist who, as the book cover of *The Same and Not the Same* says, 'puts the creative activity of chemists in its rich human context'. In 1990 Roald Hoffmann was the host of a twenty-six segment television documentary on the US Public Broadcasting Service entitled *The World of Chemistry.*[21] Roald Hoffmann does not hesitate to pick up the question that Fritz Haber would have said was irrelevant for the scientist.

The Social Responsibility of Scientists

> There are no bad molecules, only negligent or evil human beings. Thalidomide seems as harmful as they come, in the first trimester of pregnancy. But there have been persistent hints of its utility in treating inflammation associated with leprosy. And there are recent studies claiming that thalidomide can inhibit the replication of HIV-1 (the virus that causes AIDS). Nitric oxide, NO, is an air pollutant but also an absolutely natural neurotransmitter. Ozone serves an essential (to us) function in the stratosphere, a thin layer of it absorbing much of the sun's harmful ultraviolet radiation. At sea level the very same molecule is a bad actor in photochemical smog, the atmospheric pollution caused mainly by automotive exhausts. Ozone destroys automobile tyres (weak vengeance), plant life and our tissues.
>
> Molecules are molecules. Chemists and engineers make new ones, transform old ones. Still others in the economic chain sell them, and we all want them and use them. Each of us

21 His most recent collection of poems is *Soliton* published by Truman State University Press, 2002. An essay 'Science, Language, Poetry' can be found at http://www.pantanto.co.uk/issue6/Hoffmann.htm. For more information about him and his work see http://nobelprize.org/chemistry/laureates/1981/hoffmann-autobio.html. This information comes from the Liverpool University Centre for Poetry and Science (LUPAS) which 'is a forum to facilitate discussion about the relationship between those two traditionally opposed subjects, poetry and science.' Roald Hoffmann's poem 'Monolayer' is on their website.

has a role in the use and misuse of chemicals. Here is what I see as our social responsibility as scientists to our fellow human beings.

I see scientists as actors in a classical tragedy. They (we) are sentenced by their nature to create. There is no way to avoid investigating what is in or around us. There is no way to close one's eyes to creation or discovery. If you don't find that molecule, someone else will. At the same time I believe that scientists have absolute responsibility for thinking about the uses of their creation, even the abuses by others. And they must do everything possible to bring those dangers and abuses before the public. If not I, then who? At the risk of losing their livelihood, at the risk of humiliation, they must live with the consequences of their actions. It is this duty that makes them actors in a tragedy and not comic heroes on a pedestal. It is this responsibility to humanity that makes them human.'[22]

Chemistry, Education and Democracy

Roald Hoffmann, has shown again and again how closely he sees the connections between chemistry, the humanities and, in particular literature. Now he comes to education. I include this essay because it speaks to us as present and future citizens with responsibilities in Australia and around the globe, as well as the citizens to whom he is most closely connected in the USA.

To me the Alar controversy was humbling, educational, and instructive, an opportunity to learn rather than a chance to blow off some steam against environmentalists. I learned some chemistry from it; I learned some from Bhopal, and I intend to learn some from the next chemical disaster. People's minds open up when knowledge is accompanied by a relationship to something critical – a disaster, one's body, even the prurient and scandalous. One can use ill events in an educational sense.

I have come to education. I view education as a crucial part of the democratic process, a privilege and a duty of the citizen. In fact I'm not concerned about scientific illiteracy (and this is my opinion only, I remind you) so much from the point of view of its limiting our man-or-woman-power base or affecting our global economic competitiveness. What worries me about the prevalent chemical illiteracy – a failure of the educational process – are two other matters.

First, if we do not know the basic workings of the world around us, especially those components that human beings themselves have added to the world, then we become

22 Roald Hoffmann, Part 4, 28 'The Social Responsibility of Scientists', *The Same and not the Same*, Columbia University Press, New York, 1995, pp. 139–140. In 'Cheiron' Roald Hoffmann takes us to Prometheus as interpreted by the classical Greek playwright Aeschylus.

alienated. Alienation, due to lack of knowledge, is impoverishing. It makes us feel impotent, unable to act. Not understanding the world we invent mysteries or new gods, much as people did around lightning and eclipses, around St Elmo's fire and volcanic sulfur emissions a long time ago.

My second point of concern about the chemical illiteracy returns me to democracy. Ignorance of chemistry poses a barrier to the democratic process. I believe deeply, as must be clear by now, that 'ordinary people' must be empowered to make decisions – on genetic engineering or on waste disposal sites, on dangerous and safe factories or on which addictive drugs should or should not be controlled. Citizens can call on experts to explain the advantages and disadvantages, the options, the benefits and risks. But experts do not have the mandate; the people and their representatives do. The people have also a responsibility – they need to learn enough chemistry to be able to resist the seductive words of, yes, chemical experts who can be assembled to support any nefarious activity you please.

Here then is the importance of constructing primary and secondary school chemistry courses that reach out to a wider audience. And of training and rewarding teachers that can teach these classes. Chemistry of course must be faithful to the intellectual core of the subject. But they also need to be attractive, stimulating, intriguing. They must be aimed primarily at the non-science student, at the informed citizen, not toward the professional. New chemists, brilliant transformers of matter, will come from among these youngsters. Of this I'm sure. But they will not be able to do what they are capable of doing unless we teach their friends and neighbours, the 99.9 percent who are *not* chemists, what it is that chemists do.[23]

In his short essays for American students Roald Hoffmann considers the role of creativity in chemistry. He sees creativity in chemistry, the science of molecules, as well as discovery. He sees discovery in the process of the writing of poetry, and in the other arts. As a scientist he is always aware of the ethical issues. He is also, in the view of Miroslav Holub, a gifted poet as well as a gifted scientist.

I have ended this section with this essay in which he connects the need for chemists to reach a wider audience if we are to have an electorate that is not bamboozled by 'spin doctors' of whatever persuasion, paid to promote whatever interest.

His collection *Chemistry Imagined: Reflections on Science,* offers plenty for the general reader.

23 Roald Hoffmann, 'Value, Harm and Democracy', p. 45, 'Chemistry, Education and Democracy', in *The Same and not the Same*, Columbia University Press, New York, 1995, pp. 227–228.

'It is Lewis Carroll meets Lewis Thomas'

I cannot leave the contributions of American scientists and writers about science without returning to the latest winner of the Lewis Thomas Award and Pulitzer Prize winner – Natalie Angier. While her purpose is to bring the sciences to all of us, she has room for William Blake, paraphrasing his image of earth as a grain of sand to 'gain a richer sense of cosmic proportions'.

She keeps her readers connected with the wider culture of our times. For example, in Chapter 4, 'Physics', Natalie Angier brings in the song 'And Nothing's Plenty for Me', from George Gershwin's *Porgy and Bess*. She brings Roald Hoffmann, scientist and poet into Chapter 5 'Chemistry', and admits that Walt Whitman had something when he saw the universe in a blade of grass.

The Nobel Prize winner Leon Lederman says of her book: 'Her command of language shames the poets; her grasp of how science works exposes the joy and beauty of discovery, which I thought belonged only to scientists. How dare she write so artfully, explain so brilliantly, rendering us scientists simultaneously proud and inarticulate.'

That praise alone for *The Canon: A Whirligig Tour of the Beautiful Basics of Science* should encourage teachers and students to explore what Richard Dawkins sees as her 'sentences that sparkle with wit and charm'. On the blurb inside the front cover, her book is described as 'a joyride through the major scientific disciplines: physics, chemistry, biology, geology and astronomy. Along the way, we learn what is actually happening when our icecream melts or our coffee gets cold, what our liver cells do when we eat a caramel, why the horse is an example of evolution at work and how we're all made of stardust. It's Lewis Carroll meets Lewis Thomas – a book that will enrapture, inspire and enlighten.'[24] And I, a student of the humanities, found that the claim was not extravagant. I laughed, held my breath at some times when she startled me and delighted me by the connection she was making, and I longed to share lines that stayed with me with everyone I met. In fact I will share this one now. Dealing with the spurious argument about nature or nurture – one of those simplistic either/or questions that this book wants to discourage – she writes 'Nature needs nurture and nurture kneads nature …'.[25] So simple, so direct, so complete. We need more scientific writing of this calibre for students of English.

---

24 Natalie Angier, *The Canon: A Whirligig Tour of the Beautiful Basics of Science*, Houghton Mifflin Company, Boston, New York, 2007.

25 Natalie Angier, *The Canon: A Whirligig Tour of the Beautiful Basics of Science.* Referring to Stephen Jay Gould she writes, 'you can't uncouple nature from nurture, he and other scientists insist, any more than you can uncouple a rectangle's length from its width.' p. 210.

Concluding her book, the final chapter is, 'Astronomy: heavenly creatures'. In it Natalie Angier explores the idea of other civilisations that might exist and she reminds us, as Lewis Thomas does, of the dangers we face.

> Admittedly, the terrible distances between galaxies could well preclude any communication beyond the science fictional, but it's good to think they're out there, those probabilistic star-flecked partners in space-time. And who knows? They may be better off than we are and have found the perfect intergalactic wormhole and are steadily heading our way. Please, please, stop by, any time, any stardate. We can't promise, but we will try, with all our heart and haemoglobin and everyone of our 90 trillion body cells and our bacterial symbionts too, to hang on, and dodge our own bullets, and be here when you arrive.[26]

26 Natalie Angier, *The Canon: A Whirligig Tour of the Beautiful Basics of Science*, Houghton Mifflin Company, p. 264

Chapter Four

Perspectives on the Sciences in Australian Poets

'Unravelling the secrets of nature is stimulated as much by the imagination as by writing or reading poetry.'

Scoresby Shepherd

'The arts and sciences are two sides of the one coin.'

Elizabeth Truswell

'There is an element of the numinous in both poetry and science.'

Juliette Woods

Challenging the Divide is a project that tries to remove the stereotype that poets and scientists belong on different sides of an impassable chasm. That oversimplification of the differences in approach of specific subjects has had its impact in schools. We have seen evidence of that in the biographical details about Janine Baker who was told that, with a background in the arts and humanities, it would be too difficult for her to move into an area of scientific study. In my forty years of experience as a teacher in the humanities, I have been aware of the subtle and not so subtle ways in which a dividing line has been laid down to keep students – and often staff – on one side of that divide or the other.

In the twenty-first century those making decisions about the national curricula have been giving the nod to interdisciplinary approaches, and to cross-curricular cooperation, and they are encouraging senior students to explore independently what are being called 'external learning initiatives'. The curriculum advisers appear, at this early stage of development, to be encouraging students and teachers to make connections in new ways. I could not be happier. Part of that exploration has to be the acquisition of knowledge. With that knowledge, we can begin to grow intellectually.

In my approach to this project that independent exploration is what I have been doing. My focus has been on English because, as an area of study, it need have no boundaries. However, we have tended to make assumptions about what belongs in its domain and what does not. We have been told that poetry belongs in its domain and science does not. I hope that the examples of writing by Australian scientists reveal where they see the connections which can begin to bring about a broader approach to language in prose and poetry. We have had glimpses and sometimes more than glimpses of the personal behind what has been considered the 'impersonal' in science. We have shared their delights and concerns in such a way, I hope, that the stereotypes have disappeared. We have been learning, as Juliette Woods and John Lowke in particular have revealed, where the language of mathematics has been paramount. We have heard the reasons for the different ways language is used, and value the beauty, clarity and elegance wherever we find it.

I have added information through examples of writing by scientists beyond Australian shores, writing aimed at the general reader, not for a peer-reviewed journal. I have hoped, in this process, to suggest gateways, doors, windows of opportunity, avenues, pathways, by-roads, tracks, super-highways that students of any age can explore. I have hoped that, as is my experience, these explorers will be open to ideas, possibilities, new information, have pleasure in the finding, wherever it may be, on radio, on television, in a book shop, in a garden, at the beach, in a desert, on or under the sea, on a slide beneath a microscope, in conversations with neighbours, in critical appraisal by friends; wherever the senses are alive to possibilities, the mind is awake and the heart is open to the life of the world.

Scientists have spoken of language, of imagination and the significance of reason as they explore connections. That is the trinity at the heart of English studies in language and literature. It is there in prose and poetry. What I am doing here is revealing where that exploration has taken me in the realm of non-fiction scientific writing. I hope now to give clues about what I think I have found through such exploration to make clear where writers, primarily poets, have engaged with the sciences in their writing.

So much has come to me through unexpected connections simply because I have been open to the possibility that they exist. I still call it 'the magic hand of chance'. So, do not expect a precise, well-ordered linear approach. To give the following chapters some semblance of order I am beginning with Australian poets, as I began with the contributions of Australian scientists. And I am taking as my theme these words of Judith Wright, 'the feeling world of ideas', because in that phrase thought and feeling come together in the mind and heart of a fine Australian poet.

Karen Lamb wrote of Judith Wright:

> Wright lived a life in simpatico with those ideas, demonstrating whenever she could a belief in 'the feeling world of ideas', where love might compete equally with logic and where feeling would not simply be accorded its customary hiding place in art.[1]

Judith Wright – 'the feeling world of ideas'

In her 1993 Foreword to *Collected Poems 1942–1985* Judith Wright deals with rationalism, one of the abstractions affecting our lives. She says: 'I doubt whether literary critics and teachers take it on themselves to explain the context of poems; and no historian is likely to provide the necessary emotional background of the times during which the poems were written. Much has to be left to the readers' own response in imaginative terms – and that is no bad thing, provided that the reader has been encouraged to use her or his imagination. But imagination and feeling are now devalued in favour of the harder values of so-called rationalism.'[2]

In that statement Judith Wright reveals the subject-oriented boundaries that traditionally have undermined the way we have considered poetry in school. She believes that the teachers and academics in the disciplines of literature and history might be unwilling to treat the poem as a whole, remembering that poems do not come out of a vacuum. She wants the reader to be free to explore the poem 'provided the reader has been encouraged to use his or her imagination'.

How did Judith Wright feel when she wrote *Australia 1970?* The date provides a clue. But I must be careful now. I want to say why I believe Judith Wright did not want her poetry just to be 'visceral'. I want to reveal my pleasure in her passion and my view of the reason for her passion in this poem. If I did I would be doing exactly what she did not want to happen. I would be taking from the reader the right to his or her imaginative response in their reading of it.

However, I will allow myself to provide this 'emotional background of the times'. In the name of the economy, and profit, shareholders were making huge profits in a nickel boom, a boom that would crash, leaving many shareholders destitute. In 2009, the emotional impact of speculation in the price of oil and on the stock market might strike a chord in the reader, so that understanding of the reason behind her passion can be felt.

In the late 1960s there appeared to be plans to permit mining on the Great Barrier

---

1 Karen Lamb, review of *With Love and Fury: Selected Letters of Judith Wright*, *Weekend Australian*, 10–11 March 2007.

2 Judith Wright, *Collected Poems, 1942–1985,* Angus and Robertson, Sydney, NSW, 1994.

Reef. Judith Wright led the campaign for the protection of this world heritage reef. In 1969 Concorde had taken off from Heathrow and flown to New York. Some business interests wanted this supersonic jet to fly to Sydney. She was appalled by our lack of concern for our environment. Explore the poem for yourselves and see what I mean about the evidence in it of her sense of 'the feeling world of ideas'.

This is not the place for a detailed consideration of her poetry but I include these poems to show the connection she makes with science The first explores what she sees as the 'upside-down' approach, that she thinks is taken too often in this country.

Swamp plant

I have seen those very seldom-seen plants;
small earth-hugging rosette,
stem like a thread and downward-turning bell
of meditative blue. Half-size to a grasshopper,
what insect is small enough
to drink from you? *Mazus,*
Mazus pumila, somebody saw and named you.

Only science, then, has noticed you,
not poetry.
It's that way round in this country,
upside-down as ever.
Living on swamp-edges
turning your face to the ground, shyer than
Wordsworth's violet,
no words but dog-Latin
have tagged you.

But for your colour –
such a colour as old sea-goddesses chose
(Mediterranean goddesses)
I would not have stooped to look.

But there are no flowers here
Persephone could have gathered;
nor do our people go

down on their knees at swamp-edges
or shorten their range of sight
to your less-than-finger's height.

Leaving you there, I take you home with me,
one tiny image
of still untouched unknown tranquillity.[3]

In the second poem 'Words, Roses, Stars', everything is connected: language, imagination and reason.

Words, Roses, Stars

(for John Béchervaise, answering a Christmas poem)

A rose, my friend, a rose –
and what's a rose?
A swirl of atoms bodied in a word.
And words are human; language comes and goes
with us, and lives among us. Not absurd
to think the human spans the Milky Way.

Baiame bends beside his crystal stream
shaded beneath his darker cypress-tree
and gives the gift of life, the endless dream,
to Koori people, and to you and me.
Astronomers and physicists compute
a mathematic glory in the sky.
But all those calculations, let's admit,
are filtered through a human brain and eye.

If I could give a rose to you, and you,
it would be language; sight and touch and scent
join in the symbol. Yet the word is true,
plucked by a path where human vision went.[4]

---

3 Judith Wright, *Collected Poems,* p. 367.
4 Judith Wright, *Collected Poems,* p. 410.

'If I could give a rose to you, and you/it would be language'

That is the gift being given to us by scientists and poets. We have met Alan Lightman who writes of the different ways words are used in his essay with that title. If we consider the words of Niels Bohr we would find his belief that the language of poetry was entering the world of the atom.

Earlier, in *The Weather Makers* the scientist Tim Flannery has quoted the poet Bill Neidjie. So, it is appropriate to follow Judith Wright's concern for the felt life of the land with Bill Neidjie's poem breathing the spirit of the land and, with it, this 'feeling world of ideas'.

I feel it with my body
with my blood.
Feeling all these trees,
all this country.
When the wind blow you can feel it.
Same for country,
You feel it
You can look.
But feeling …
that make you.[5]

What I have found here is the aspect of human wisdom discounted by the traditional separation of mind from matter, mind from body, thought from feeling, the intellect from the emotions that grew out of the Cartesian separation of mind from body. In my view it is, perhaps, the loss of this aspect of imaginative understanding of the spiritual and historical aspect of land that puts extractive mining interests before the aeons-old petroglyphs on the Burrup Peninsula.

This is one of the aspects of life in Australia that worried Judith Wright when she published her first collection of poetry, *The Moving Image*, in 1946. In that collection her poem 'Bora Ring' expresses her concern for this Aboriginal loss 'in an alien tale'. The bora ring was and still can be a teaching and learning ring, so different from desks in rows with the authority figure up at the front on a dais.[6] What distresses her might

5 Bill Neidjie, *Gagudju Man*, JB Books, Marleston, South Australia, 2002, p. 39.

6 In *Stradbroke Dreamtime*, illustrated by Bronwyn Bancroft, Angus & Robertson, Australia, 1993, Oodgeroo describes the bora ring – Burr-Nong with the details of that educational process for boys and girls in her community (p. 71).

be called the failure of the imagination.

Another Australian poet, Gwen Harwood, brings a different imaginative perspective to a specific scientific topic, Schrödinger's thought experiment.[7] The footnote to Gwen Harwood's poem makes the story clear. 'His famous thought experiment hinges on the random nature of radioactive decay. A cat is sealed in a box with an ampoule of cyanide which is released when a single radioactive particle is emitted. There is an equal opportunity at any time that the particle will or will not have been emitted. Until we open the box the cat is considered to be both dead and alive. Opening the box makes up its mind for it.'

Schrödinger's Cat Preaches to the Mice

Silk-whispering of knife on stone,
due sacrifice, and my meat came.
Caressing whispers, then my own
choice among laps by leaping flame.
What shape is space? Space will put on
the shape of a cat. Know this:
my servant Schrödinger is gone
before me to prepare a place.

So worship me. The Chosen One
in the great thought-experiment.
As in a grave I will lie down
and wait for the Divine Event.

The lid will close. I will retire
from sight, curl up and say Amen
to geiger counter, amplifier,
and a cylinder of HCN.

When will the geiger counter feel
decay, its pulse amplified
to a current that removes the seal

---

7 Erwin Schrödinger, whose book *What is life?* played a part in the entry of physics into biology and into the story of the discovery of DNA, undertook this thought experiment in 1935. He published a three-part essay on *The present situation in quantum mechanics* in which his famous cat paradox appears.

from the cylinder of cyanide?
Dead or alive? The case defies
all questions. Let the lid be locked.
Truth, from your little beady eyes,
is hidden. I will not be mocked.

Quantum mechanics has no place
for what's there without observation.
Classical physicists cannot trace
spontaneous disintegration.

If the box holds a living cat
no scientist on earth can tell.
But I'll be waiting, sleek and fat.
Verily, all will not be well
if, to the peril of your souls,
you think me gone. Know that this house
is mine, that kittens by mouse-holes
wait, who have never seen a mouse.[8]

There is a playful cat-and-mouse element in this poem. Science-minded students might like to experiment, taking on the adventure of exploring this poem by a poet who dares to play with Schrödinger's thought experiment.

Gwen Harwood had dedicated this poem to A.D. Hope, an Australian poet noted for his love of the classics and for his fondness for the Augustan poets. A.D. Hope was also a satirist. Why not research other Australian poets who were classicists and satirists? There was nothing accidental about the way I went about finding an example of a poet able, like Hope in some of his poems, to tackle aspects of the sciences.

Pursuit with a purpose

The poet I found was John Bray, Chief Justice of the Supreme Court of South Australia, Chancellor of the University of Adelaide. A founding member of Friendly Street, the open-reading poetry group established in Adelaide the day Gough Whitlam was sacked by the Governor General, Bray was a lover of the classics. The breadth of his knowledge,

8 Gwen Harwood, *Collected Poems 1943–1995*, University of Queensland Press, St Lucia, 2003, pp. 392–393.

ranging from a Goddess of Roman mythology to the 'modern Magi', 'the lords of the laboratories', showed a capacity for lateral thinking that was able to continually surprise and delight his readers.

Hymn to Chance

Madam, from time to time you are accosted
By poets, clamorous solicitors,
Seeking with invocations sugar-frosted
To lure into their hovels heavenly visitors.

Sometimes they turn quite rude and call you strumpet,
Abusing you in language far from solemn.
Sometimes they sing your fame with fife and trumpet:
So Horace sang you, kicking down the column.

Your name is greatly honoured in this nation,
Save by a few sour prigs or earnest crackpots.
Witness the race track's weekly salutation
And those loud clangs that vomit up the jackpots.

Now by new worshippers your praise is spoken.
The modern Magi, lords of the laboratories,
Lay on your shrine their enigmatic token,
And chant your anthems in their plastic oratories.

Predicability, it seems, you shatter
When at your whim the lively atoms crackle,
And from the cramped and rigid limbs of matter
The links of logic at your nod unshackle.

Astronomy as well for you goes paging –
No wonder Romans thought you a divinity –
When from some unseen catapult or staging
You hurtle galaxies towards infinity.

Well may these triumphs cause to gasp and falter
That pince-nez prude, your sister, prim Causation,
Disconsolate by her deserted altar
That barely rates a soda-pop libation.

Save when some faithful lawyer or philosopher
With premise, enthymeme, or what-not subtler
Essays the scantness of her state to gloss over.
(I grant I stole that rhyme from Samuel Butler.)

Felicitations, madam, on your conquest.
I know these verses cog with too much friction.
But if I decked them for the Muses' contest
I'd get arrested for poetic diction.

I hardly like to ask you a great favour.
I've heard your followers complain and mutter
That when your bounty they begin to savour
You turn your wheel and toss them in the gutter.

So if you find these verses, madam, pleasing –
Where physics leads can poets make resistance? –
I only ask that you forbear your teasing
And spin the world ignoring my existence.[9]

Speaking of 'lively atoms', one poet throws light on Lord Rutherford

Though born in New Zealand in 1913, Douglas Stewart has been claimed as an Australian poet for his influence on Australian literature as the literary editor of *The Bulletin.*

In Stewart's poem 'Rutherford' Lord Rutherford appears to be meditating. He knows one cannot predict the future but he knows, just as his work has been built on the genius of his predecessors, that others will surpass him. And he knows the splitting of the atom has resulted in 'a dangerous toy'.

9 John Bray, *Satura, Selected Poetry and Prose,* Wakefield Press, Adelaide, 1988, p. 85.

From **'Rutherford'**

So much they would surpass him, those who came after,
What was he now but that small lump of a boy
Who made his own miniature wheel to splash in the water
Such ages ago, working all day in the joy
Of pure and bubbling creation, copying his father!
Just so it was small and would work, just so it sparkled,
And yet the truth was, this was a dangerous toy:
The lightning swam where those electrons circled.

Look at it this way, that way, face the thing squarely,
Could some fool in a laboratory, he'd ask his assistant,
Blow up the world with this? You could pay dearly
For probing too deeply into that dark resistance
Where light lay coiled in stone. He had seen clearly
In flashes of the mind each atom exploding the next
To the end of the world, and the light came out of the distance
Like a wave upon him, towering ... They were perplexed

Whether he was joking or not. Well, he was joking,
There was no need to cower, and what was more,
Though sometimes he touched these things with his hands shaking
He did not propose to; he'd carry the load he bore,
Which was no light one, till his broad shoulders were aching
But need not, except as precaution, think the unthinkable:
There was no chain reaction could go so far;
The force must die out; the good old world was unsinkable.
So let his atoms be used to do man good
And nothing but good – pierce the cancer cell
As the Curies were doing, bring him more health, more food,
Drive the turbine, the dynamo, turn the wheel,
Blow a mountain up if it got in his road,
Let him be master of air and earth and ocean,
The whole wide world and the stars if he liked as well.

> He had not given his lifetime's skill and devotion
> To bring man harm. And yet this thing was force;
> And when could you give poor man and his five wits
> Any new force but he would use it in his war.
> And blow himself, if not the whole world to bits? [10]

Another way I discovered other poems by Australian poets that have taken aspects of the sciences as their starting point, was through a process of discussion that led to the research by members of the science and poetry group of the Port Adelaide chapter of the University of the Third Age (U3A). That is the way we found Les Murray's poem 'Infra Red – For Prof. Fred Hoyle and the *IRAS* Telescope'.[11]

The U3A group contained people from all walks of life. One watched *Red Dwarf.* Another was fascinated by the stories of the stars. The reference to Fred Hoyle was a clue. One of our members searched the internet for 'brown dwarfs'. What did the metaphor of 'brown dwarfs' as 'cannon-fodder' suggest? Did Les Murray want us to look beyond 'the peak nodes of fury'? Why was he taking us to 'the dim, the cannon fodder of stardom'? Astronomy and poetry were being brought together in a thought-provoking way.

Astronomy and poetry was coming in a very different way through 'Poetica' *Gateway to the Sphinx* by Tony Page

Among recently published Australian poets, my greatest surprise has come through the work of Tony Page who is exploring so many different sciences in *Gateway to the Sphinx*. He has dared to range from astronomy, through evolution, to chemistry, physics, and the Big Bang.

In the Introduction Phillip Adams refers to popularisers of science who include Paul Davies, Carl Sagan, Stephen J. Gould and the late Jacob Bronowski. Phillip Adams sees Tony Page's poems as 'simply wonderful'. He finds the writing 'exhilarating' and suggests that Blaise Pascal, the seventeenth century French mathematician and one of the world's great natural philosophers, would have been delighted by them. Pascal had

---

10 Douglas Stewart, *Rutherford and Other Poems*, published by Angus and Robertson Ltd, 1962 pp. 75–85. Responses of Australian writers to the nuclear age are included in *Imagining the Real: Australian Writing in the nuclear age*, published by ABC Enterprises, Sydney, 1987.

11 Les Murray, *Collected Poems*, Black Inc, Melbourne, Victoria, 2006, pp. 264–265.

insisted that 'we know the truth not only through our reason but also through our heart.'[12]

For a student of the humanities, Tony Page's passionate, and occasionally ironic, engagement with the scientific aspects of our world is certainly a gateway. It became a gateway to ideas so new to me, bringing with them feelings of awe at the magnitude of all these discoveries in the sciences. The following poem put the twinkling of stars in a different perspective.

One hundred million years ABT (10^{15} sec)

Almost everywhere, darkness:
Sooty hydrogen murk,
A stellar nursery swamp.

Gravity grinds the ooze,
Huffing and puffing to ignite.

Darkness still ... Wait ...
There – an uncertain fire,
A smouldering beacon.

Ah, the morass twinkles
Its first little star.[13]

In the work of Tony Page I found passion, knowledge, excitement and, now and again, rueful expressions of concern about how we, as human beings, might behave as we go further into the twenty-first century in what Paul Davies has called the 'Goldilocks world'.[14] In 'Tutorial with flowers and light' Tony Page has caught the exhilaration scientists must feel.

Tutorial with flowers and light

Today's subject, the speed of light –
300 000 kilometres per second.
In one year a pilgrimage of

12 Blaise Pascal, *Pensées*, translated A.J. Krailsheimer, Penguin Books, London, revised 1995, p. 28.

13 Tony Page, *Gateway to the Sphinx* published by Five Island Press, Wollongong University, NSW, 2004, p. 79. ABT is the acronym for After the Beginning of Time.

14 Paul Davies, *The Goldilocks Enigma*, Penguin, 2006.

9 500 000 000 kilometres:
The bench mark of time.

Write out all the zeros.
Glue them on a mirror each morning,
On your lamp the last view before sleep.
Digest this speed. Every breath,
Another epoch absorbed.

Look at the flowers on my windowsill –
Notice how light makes their petals shake?
The sun glows on our fingertips,
Sparks flying here in eight minutes
To set these buds on fire.

Behind our backs, Alpha Proxima
The next star, 4.3 light years
Through that fragile opening.
My branches turn towards the southern sky
Thirsty for its splendour.

Rubbing shoulders with us
Andromeda the next galaxy
(Wispy-haired spiral)
Flaming its radiance towards this vase
Across our neighbourhood of two million years.

Then quasars – the most far-flung
Objects yet observed. Feel it,
Twelve billion years before their
Radiance comes to rest on my flowers.
Their rays, exhausted, surrender
Energy to the petals in this room.

If light did not override the emptiness
We could not see ourselves.
Prepare for the epic,
Swallow the zeros –
May we have strength enough.

'Feel it' the poet said. For me, this is more than an intellectual exercise. 'Feel it' he says and I do. I enter 'the feeling world of ideas'. It opens my eyes. I have another way to see and feel the dawn light through the young red leaves of my Lorraine Lee rose. The feeling of wonder expands and the desire to know and learn increases.

The first section of his collection concentrates on astronomy. The poem 'Mapping the Galaxy Blind' is in three parts. Moving from the young boy who 'scouted the evening sky',

> Trying to clutch stars
> Before they floated away;

to

> The child and I …
> Standing puzzled on this rock,
> Clutching the blueprint
> Matching symbol to star;
> Grateful there were others
> Who learnt how to look
> Beyond their eyes –
> And where to leap.'[15]

In so much of Tony Page's poetry[16] I have been encouraged to look out into space, just as so much of Judith Wright's poetry has reminded me of the world beneath my feet and the spiritual quality of my engagement with it.

A second reference to 'Poetica' came through conversation at a dinner

As part of a conversation about poetry and science I had been talking about doctors as poets and poets who were doctors. I was told that Mike Ladd, the producer of ABC Radio National's 'Poetica' program, had presented a program on clinician poets. I had no idea that a collection of poems by contemporary clinician-poets of Australia and New Zealand had been published.

Edited by Tim Metcalf, *Verbal Medicine*, with the poems of twenty-one clinician–poets, was published by Ginninderra Press, Canberra, in 2006. Tim Metcalf was concerned with changes in our society, and in his Introduction wrote:

---

15 *Gateway to the Sphinx,* pp. 13–15. Other poems in this section include 'Hunting the edge of the universe', 'What NCC 628 may never see', and 'The Door'.

16 See, for example, Tony Page, *Gateway to the Sphinx*, Five Island Press, Wollongong University, NSW, 2004, pp 18–19.

> Our universe, say the astrophysicists, burst into light from the void. Eurynome, said the ancient Greeks, was the Goddess of All things who arose from this furious chaos. Later there was Apollo, God of both Medicine and Poetry. Finally there came science, which for the first time insisted the twin roles of Apollo should be separated.[17]

Tim Metcalf felt that 'the Number, as statistics, the clock, computational power and money [was imposing] a comforting new order' that was challenging the Word. He feared its loss and insisted that in the poet was the empathetic voice which 'requires experience to become capable of transformation into poetry ... Every day this voice warns us to attend to the numinous universe beyond the files of personal detail.'[18]

Among the contributors to *Verbal Medicine* was Peter Goldsworthy. Tim Metcalf provided readers with the background to the work of these contemporary clinicians by the inclusion of brief biographies of earlier medical men who wrote poetry. He makes particular reference to Grace Perry who graduated as a doctor in the early 1950s. She founded *Poetry Australia,* a literary journal of great significance in the encouragement of Australian poets.[19]

That discovery made me to go browsing to find Peter Goldsworthy's poems

Peter Goldsworthy is a prize-winning Australian poet with an international reputation and a novelist whose work has been translated into most major Asian and European languages. He wrote the libretto for Richard Mills' opera *Batavia*. His novel *Maestro,* now a play, is also being made into a film.

In his latest collection, *New Selected Poems,* it becomes clear that Peter Goldsworthy has been thinking about the sciences; about mathematics, chemistry, rainbows and the Cartesian principle.

The very title of one poem, 'Descartes on Bell's Beach', alerts a reader to the problem I have been writing about, the relationship between mind and body. In a series 'A Brief Introduction to Philosophy', the fifth poem asks the question 'Is the mind or the body

---

17 Tim Metcalf (ed.), *Verbal Medicine: Twenty-one Contemporary Clinician-Poets of Australia & New Zealand with introduction, historical sketch and select bibliography,* Ginninderra Press, ACT, 2006.

18 Tim Metcalf, p. 10.

19 It is worth noting that since the publication of *Verbal Medicine* an Australian poet has brought Number into the realm of poetry. He is π.o, a Melbourne poet whose collection, *Big Numbers: new and selected poems,* was published in 2008 by Collective Effort Press. By chance, on Radio National, I heard him interviewed about his work. π.o told the listeners of the connection between his inheritance and Pythagoras.

the problem?' That question tells me that the either/or problem, that insistence on one alternative or the other, that has been at the heart of this project, is unresolved in his mind.

The temptation to comment on the poems is very great indeed but that is not the purpose of this section of *Challenging the Divide*. But I can say which poems make me want to come back to them. Of his other poems in this section I like best 'What comes next?' He is asking about that unknown future and wonders if there might be 'a fair and even redistribution of matter.'[20] His next section is 'Chemistry' and we have '1 Glass', '2 The Still', '3 Water', '4 Alcohol', '5 Bromine' – which is his favourite element – '6 Ether', and '7 Acid'.

Then, in 'Roy G. Biv' Peter Goldsworthy brings Keats's rainbow of the imagination and Faraday's candle of knowledge together in his response to each of the colours of the rainbow, all Newtonian seven of them; red, orange, yellow, green, blue, indigo, and violet.[21] Each does what a poem does best. They take the reader further. In my estimation, they awake thought and feeling, sometimes synthesise senses, perhaps bring a smile to the lips and light to the eye and mind. They waken taste buds, take an everyday image and transform it or bring the extraordinary within reach. For instance in '3 Yellow'

> High in the blue is a big Yellow Page
> advertising summer …

Another poem might take you to childhood and the 'first set of Derwents'

> The blues in their flat tin box
> were a rainbow of blue themselves:
> smalt- and sky-, cobalt- and Prussian-

One colour becomes a sound, another a taste, another 'a hazard-lamp' and so much more comes in his last poem in this series.

---

20 Peter Goldsworthy, *New Selected Poems*, Duffy and Snellgrove, Sydney, 2001, p. 79. The extracts following are from 'Roy G. Biv', pp. 87–93.

21 In Goethe's colour wheel there were six colours.

7 Violet

More cello-coloured than viola,
More iodine than violin, violet
Is the bloom of the double bass
Wavelength; light at largo pace,
Eyes set at widest aperture,
So wide they are really ears.
Beyond here, everything is ultra.

I love the musical connections of 'Violet'. Peter Goldsworthy is bringing us the gift of wonder. He is making connections, in one way or another, with the complex and often invisible worlds that have been brought into our ken by twentieth-century scientists in so many different disciplines. And I would have readers return to the surprise, clarity and interconnectedness of Peter Goldsworthy's poems, and to re-read 'Roy G. Biv', the mnemonic for the colours of the spectrum.

Besides such presents, gifts came in other ways

Poems by an Australian earth scientist were sent to me by Professor Fenner.

Timewarp

Time is a silver wing in the rain
A railway station bench
Will I ever see you again
Will my thirst ever quench?

Future's recess to memories
Can't cease my headlong quest
Wind blows out candles, trees
Will grow where I rest.[22]

Through poems and photographs, Andrew Glikson has brought together so many aspects of our universe, the past through myths or earlier poems, the present and the

22 Andrew Glikson, *Dreaming a UniVerse: Gondwanaland Flower: A poetic & photographic journey through time*, 2nd edition, Fyshwick, ACT, 1992, p. 145.

future. In 'Red Rocks', for example, to warn us, he first quotes from Shelley's poem, 'Ozymandias'.[23]

Other gifts have come through sharing readings with other poets. At Friendly Street, Adelaide, I heard 'Bright Morning' by Paul Wilkins.

Bright morning

From inner space
I stepped out
Into the milky way,
Myriad stars
Fallen to earth
From soft velvet night.

Festooned jewels,
Diamonds of light,
King Solomon's glory,
Fabergé's silver birds,
Singing in paradise.

'Hibiscus' by Jean Groome, with its evocation of the circadian rhythm, grew out of reflections on poetry and science by our University of the Third Age group.

Hibiscus

Standing tall
in a carpet of yesterday's fallen blooms.
Today's buds follow the Circadian rhythm
awaiting the sunshine's touch
before bursting forth
flush with deep red-throated full pink blooms.
Night comes again.
Flowers fold following the timeless call
to fall away and make way.
The cycle begins again.

---

23 Andrew Glikson, *Dreaming a UniVerse: Gondwanaland Flower: A poetic & photographic journey through time,* 1992, p. 49.

The candle and the rainbow – knowledge and imagination

Concluding this chapter, I feel I must return to these images. Peter Goldsworthy's seven poems reveal that John Keats's fears that the rainbow would become a 'dull catalogue' were unfounded. The poet had the knowledge and the imagination that I did not have. Initially I thought Roy G. Biv was a person. In my schooling I had never been exposed to this mnemonic for the spectrum of colours that form the visible light from the sun. It would have remained a mystery except for the fact that I wanted to understand and I had a reference to which I could go. Joy Hakim alerted me to the truth. 'In the visible light of the spectrum, each colour has a different wave length.'

Joy Hakim explained in scientific terms how we get the blue of the sky and the red of the sunset.[24] Discovering the science increased the wonder once I became aware of the significance of the molecules that are 'dancing and scattering' in the shorter wavelength of the blue. The knowledge gained only added to my pleasure in Peter Goldsworthy's poems. Poetry and science were enhancing one another.

And, when I look up at a rainbow, my spirit does lift. It is more than just a 'bow or arch exhibiting the prismatic colours in their order, formed in the sky by reflection, double refraction, and dispersion of the sun's rays in falling drops of rain'. And recently, flying above the clouds, I saw a rainbow that seemed to be lying flat on the clouds as a circle. As I gaze up at the rainbow lorikeets feasting on blossoms high in the lemon-scented gum in my backyard in the suburbs I feel this is part of my everyday connection with poetry and science.

Part of this world, as Judith Wright makes clear, from the beginning of the Dreaming, is Baiame, created by the rainbow serpent, one of the wise men bringing the 'gift of life, the endless dream to Koori people and to you and me', as Wright says. We still have Iris, messenger of the Greek gods in her multi-coloured cloak, now part of the eye. We have Newton's refractive law and James Thomson's praise of this 'philosopher sun'. We have through the study of optics, the discovery of the different wavelengths of colours. And here, through optics, and the telescopes, are 'the twinkles in a galaxy's eye'.[25] So, here is the answer to Keats's fears.

Besides Wordsworth's insistence on the role of the rainbow in lifting the spirit of humanity, we have the work of the Braggs, father and son, in X-ray crystallography

---

24 Joy Hakim, *The Story of Science: Einstein adds a new dimension,* Smithsonian Books, Washington and New York, 2007, pp. 96 and 97.

25 In *The Advertiser* 4 September 2006, was a photograph, 'a dazzling image from a nearby dwarf galaxy from NASA's Spitzer Space telescope' providing the wonder in an article by Lucy Hood and Richard Ingham, p. 7.

making it possible to see inside of us. We have the electron microscope and so much more. We have Peter Goldsworthy's exploration of synaesthesia in the seven colours of the rainbow. And we have this personal experience of another Australian poet, Graham Rowlands.

Once in a lifetime: a perfect rainbow

On the very same day my wife tossed out
my mother's wedding photograph
with my agreement
but without my
last look

while I was weeding easy to weed soursobs
my fork, as if a divining of water,
struck a weed's greening out of
an empty shell once
a snail.

It was as if all green through pine & grass & vine
had coiled into the one swirling &
swivelled out of not only
the earth but
the sea

& the sky's mist caught the sun in a rainbow
arched so far that my wife & I
had to turn our heads to
find the sky divided
into halves –

once in a lifetime,
a perfect rainbow. [26]

26 Graham Rowlands, *Collected Poems*, Lythrum Press, Adelaide, 2009, p. 93.

Chapter Five

Perspectives from American, English and European Poets and Scientists

... many of the poets were learning their science from the *Scientific American*

Peter Middleton[1]

The arts and the sciences hang together. Any conception which does not see them together in their interrelation belittles them both.
What is good for one is good for the other.

I.F.A. Bell[2]

I should not have been surprised that I would find more poets in America engaged with the sciences, in one way or another, in their work. After all, it was in America that I found the beginning of this recognition, through the Rockefeller University's establishment of the Lewis Thomas Awards, of writing by scientists that had a quality of literary excellence.

I should not have been surprised by the engagement of poets with the sciences since, in an essay by Peter Middleton entitled 'Poets and Scientists', in the words quoted at the beginning of this chapter, I would find this statement about the role of the *Scientific American* in spreading understanding of the sciences to the general public and poets.

> ... for much of the century the title of this magazine would have appeared to them to be a tautology: to be American was to be scientific and to be scientific was to be American in spirit.[3]

1 Peter Middleton, Chapter 11, 'Poets and Scientists' in *A Concise Companion to Twentieth-Century American Poetry*, edited by Stephen Fredman, Blackwell Publishing, Malden, MA USA, Oxford UK, and Carlton, Victoria, 2005, p. 227

2 Peter Middleton is quoting from I.F.A. Bell's *Critic as Scientist: The Modernist Poetics of Ezra Pound*, London, Methuen, 1981, p. 83.

3 Peter Middleton, p. 227.

My process of exploration remains the same in this chapter as it has been throughout my search for the connections that I have felt sure exist. By listening, often to Radio National, by searching in the library for poems with titles that suggest such a link with aspects of the sciences, by browsing, reading, and even finding references that take me off on a most productive tangent.

A dramatic moment, however, influenced my approach to this interdisciplinary study. It came through the work of an American poet. At a meeting of the University of the Third Age seven years ago, when I introduced connections between the sciences and the arts and humanities through poetry, I outraged one member of the group. It was the poem 'Who Do You Think You Are' by Carl Sandburg that provoked her reaction.

In the poem Sandburg points out some of the chemical constituents of the body – including oxygen, hydrogen, nitrogen, carbon, iron, phosphorus, sulphur, and so on – elements that are found in the earth and in the air, and which have prosaic uses – phosphorus is used in matches, for example – but which he notes also have their mystical beauty – 'compounds equal to the burning gold and amethyst lights' of the mountains near Santa Fe.

Given my humanities background, what I found invigorating, she found appalling. Was she angry about the reduction of who we are to these elements? Was she angry about the reference to the 'laboratory man [taking] you apart'? She was a very fine science teacher. I had always admired her capacity to engage students in the life of the scientist, the questioning, the desire to find ways to ease the lives of people, the challenging to intellectual effort of girls considered 'non-academic' in a girls technical school. She was admired for her belief in the role of the sciences in the improvement of humanity. However, she saw the arts and humanities as cultures separate from the sciences. The sciences would build a better world. The arts would just be there for pleasure. Perhaps Carl Sandburg's emphasis offended her.

However, her explosive reaction made me decide that, when I took the program further, I would do my best, given the level of my ignorance of the sciences, to bring in the ideas and achievements of the scientists as well as the poems that incorporated aspects of the sciences in their themes and imagery. Furthering this aim was made possible by the discovery of the three volumes of Joy Hakim's *Story of Science* and the stories of where the sciences, the arts and the humanities came together whenever they enhanced the understanding of the scientific achievements of their time. And the members of our group with their different backgrounds, schooling, education and experiences would bring their knowledge and our common humanity to the exploration of whatever happened to be our topic of study.

Considering 'Poets and scientists' by Peter Middleton

So, when I came to this section of *Challenging the Divide* I was delighted to find, in the opening to Peter Middleton's essay, the emphasis he placed on Ezra Pound's role in the early twentieth century dilemma, that went back into the nineteenth century, about 'a poet who feels out of place in this modern world'.[4] Ezra Pound did not hold this view: he saw such a refusal to be engaged as 'self-destructive'. Instead, according to I.F.A Bell, Pound was convinced that '[t]he arts and the sciences hang together. Any conception which does not see them together in their interrelation belittles them both. What is good for one is good for the other.'

Middleton posed the question, 'But why did science and technology seem so important to Pound and later American poets'? He quotes Douglas Bush, an American critic, who had written in 1950 that 'all poetry has been conditioned by science, even those areas that seem farthest removed from it.'[5]

Even a student of the humanities such as myself, whose only formal engagement with science was Leaving Botany, and whose informal connection with science had been membership of the Field Naturalists Society in primary school years, would be aware of the impact of science in so many aspects of life.

There was the dynamic power of it all, in its capacity to change how we saw the world. For example, the sheer explosion in communications technology, wireless, telephone, telegrams before World War II, television and satellites after 1945 and now all kinds of information coming from cyberspace. In medicine so much has happened, with the possibility of vaccines to prevent epidemics, improvements in surgery and the implanting of artificial parts into the anatomy; even the notion of artificial intelligence. In transport cars, aeroplanes, in space travel, in every sphere – domestic, local, national, international and now inter-planetary. Then there is the expansion of areas of scientific investigation, ecology being one of the more recent developments. These changes might have ignored the impact on the natural world, and it would take a while for Nature to be seen as an integral part of the sciences, arts and humanities interaction, even though an important scientific journal is called *Nature.*

Peter Middleton's essay is useful, providing as it does an entry into the stories of American poets who, in one way or another, took up the challenge of the dynamism, the energy in the sciences. However, that is all it is. I will be only making reference to

4 Peter Middleton, 'Poets and Scientists', p. 212. Middleton is referring to Pound's poem 'Hugh Selwyn Mauberley'. That feeling of being out of place had been evident in the work of the Pre-Raphaelites.

5 Peter Middleton, 'Poets and Scientists', p. 213.

a few of the major American poets and their reactions to the sciences but I expect that, if these themes cannot be part of a class English program, students can take up the challenge to investigate these connections in non-fiction and in poetry independently.

William Carlos Williams

First among these American poets is William Carlos Williams. In 1902 he began medical studies at Pennsylvania Medical School where he met Ezra Pound. Of Williams's approach, Peter Middleton writes: 'No single poet could cover all aspects of the changes brought about by science and technology, but Williams certainly tried.'[6] After World War I when Einstein visited America, William Carlos Williams wrote a poem connecting Einstein and April 'in which the scientist's new knowledge brings the same joy as the arrival of daffodils in spring'.[7]

Writing an introduction to a volume of his poems published during World War II, Williams would describe the poem as a 'machine'. That war had such a major impact on the sciences and the way poets saw them. Middleton goes into the details about the division in American history brought about by that war. Before 1939, 'no one science dominated public perceptions of its activities, and technology was the visible sign of science's achievements ... As a result of World War II the entire way science was organised altered. Now science was big. Small laboratories and individual researchers were increasingly replaced by large teams of scientists working with massive equipment such as linear accelerators and later, DNA sequencers'.[8]

Other approaches before and after World War II

Middleton makes clear how the approaches of poets to the sciences differed before and after World War II. Before the war Hart Crane would be awed by it and wonder 'what it was doing to the human world', but he would believe that it is possible to integrate scientific materialism and imagination. By contrast, Wallace Stevens would want to ignore the impact of science and technology. However, Middleton sees ignoring science and technology in an age when their dominance is obvious as 'still a poetics of science and technology'. What mattered to Wallace Stevens was the failure of scientists 'to *imagine* (my italics) the botany in the rose among the iron filings.'[9]

---

6 Peter Middleton, 'Poets and Scientists', p. 218

7 Peter Middleton, 'Poets and Scientists', p. 215

8 Peter Middleton, 'Poets and Scientists', p. 218

9 Peter Middleton, 'Poets and Scientists', p. 220. Peter Middleton quotes from a literary essay by Ezra Pound in which the poet demonstrates why scientists needed poets. 'The rose that

Among the post-war American poets, Middleton says Charles Olson 'probably had a deeper understanding of the transformations of knowledge brought about by science than any other poet of his time'.[10] Writing of poets of the late twentieth century, Middleton concentrates on the scientific developments in molecular biology and genetics. He sees new connections happening 'because DNA is now treated as a language, and poets are usually quick to respond to any new understanding of language'.[11] He writes of Gary Snyder who sees poetry as a 'manifestation of biology'. He refers to Alice Fulton and Denise Levertov, and comments on Ron Silliman who composed what he called 'new sentences'.[12]

Middleton returns to the significance of *Scientific American* because 'poets might read scientific accounts of the city or race in a prestigious journal like *Scientific American* and challenge the assumptions, as did George Oppen in his poem *Of Being Numerous*, which is a rejoinder to studies of the city published in *Scientific American* and elsewhere that treated the metropolis as a scientific problem to be solved rather than a political and cultural challenge'.[13] It is clear that the role of American poets could be to challenge scientific assumptions as well as to imbue their poems with their delight in the new possibilities offered by the sciences for their craft.

I cannot leave this American section without mention of an unexpected link that was made for me. In the bookshop of the Adelaide Botanical Gardens, engaged in my perennial search for books for children, I found a book of verses by Joy N. Hulme of California. Entitled *Wild Fibonacci: Nature's Secret Code Revealed,* her collection of verses offered a connection between that mathematical code and the interests of children in the natural world. Her verses embraced the tusks of walrus, elephants and hippos, the beaks of parrots, the teeth of crocodiles and alligators, the talons of eagles, the claws of tigers and leopards, the horns of Rocky Mountain sheep, the tails of sea horses, the bills of ibises and the twists of sundial shells.[14] Delighted as I was to find these connections

---

his magnet makes in the iron filings, does not lead him to think of the force in botanic terms' p. 213. Wallace Stevens, referring to this statement, is picking up a concern that Shelley expressed a century earlier, the problem of the lack of imagination as science made its way influencing human life.

10 Peter Middleton, 'Poets and Scientists' p. 221. See Charles Olson's *Archaeologist of Morning.*

11 Peter Middleton, 'Poets and Scientists' p. 222.

12 See Ron Silliman, *The New Sentence,* New York, Roof Books, 1987.

13 Peter Middleton, 'Poets and Scientists' p. 224. See G. Oppen, *New Collected Poems*, edited by Michael Davidson, New Directions, New York, 2002.

14 Joy N. Hulme, *Wild Fibonacci: Nature's Secret Code Revealed,* illus. Carol Schwartz, Tricycle Press, Berkeley, California, 2005.

being made for children, I was surprised by Peter Middleton's mention of the Fibonacci code. The poet Ron Silliman in *Tjanting* had begun to construct 'paragraphs whose sentence count follow[ed] the Fibonacci series (in which each number is the sum of the two preceding ones, a progression found widely in nature).'[15]

This topic might be an avenue of exploration for students interested in these issues. As students of English, they might seek out examples of where writers and poets are bringing the sciences and poetry together for children.

There is an old saying, 'As the twig is bent, so grows the tree'. If children feel the pleasure in these connections early in their lives, they might be strong enough to resist those who, later on, decide to tell them that a background in the arts and humanities is not appropriate for the study of the sciences.[16]

Across the Atlantic – first to England

The Lewis Thomas Award helps me to bridge the Atlantic, since its recipients include English and European scientists. The connection of poetry and science through the work of poets, whose work is either written in English or translated into English, now offers evidence of the interest in the sciences and technologies being taken by poets.

Miriam Rothschild, a naturalist

On ABC Radio National's Science Show[17] Robyn Williams introduced the work of the British naturalist, Miriam Rothschild who lived from 1908–2005. She undertook studies in Australia: her focus was fleas. She was the world's leading authority on them. In her taped interview with Sharon Carlton Miriam Rothschild made this fascinating comparison between the propulsion of fleas and that of rockets.

> We were all very curious to know how fleas jumped. And then we discovered that they had in their legs, rather like the joints above their legs really, it was a rubber-like substance rather like sorba rubber, which when it was compressed and then suddenly released it shot the flea up into the air and the acceleration rate was so enormous – it developed an acceleration of 129*g*, which is greater – *twenty times* greater – than that of a moon rocket re-entering the earth's atmosphere.

Miriam Rothschild was educated at home because her father hated schools and

15 Peter Middleton, 'Poets and Scientists' p. 223

16 One place students might begin if they are interested is *The Puffin Treasury of Verse*, edited by Brian Patten, Puffin Books, London, 2006

17 Science Show, ABC Radio National, 26 March 2005.

public examinations, so she never took any. However, 'at home natural history and science were part of everyday life: it wasn't a subject, we just lived it, and the first thing I can remember is having a bird as a pet and having white mice to look after and I grew up as a naturalist from the word go'. Then listeners heard this poem, reminding us of the unexpected ways that children might find their way through the world. It is taken from the letters and poetry in Dr Rothschild's book, *Butterfly Cooing Like a Dove.*

Child

I dreamt, and in my dream
I was a butterfly.
I woke: or is it simply that,
Weary of the sky,
Some butterfly is sleeping
And dreams that it is I.[18]

The discovery of her book *Butterfly Cooing Like a Dove* is one of the unexpected delights of my research. I have never known what I might find and where it might lead. Her brief essays bring together prose, poetry, the visual arts and her love and understanding of nature in a way that excites the imagination and connects the spirit, the heart and mind in a most delicate way.

A useful introductory anthology

Peter Forbes, the editor of *Scanning the Century: the Penguin Book of the Twentieth Century in Poetry* provides an entry to the exploration of and engagement with the impact of the sciences on twentieth-century poets. Published in 2000, his anthology combines a chronological and thematic approach to the work of poets of many different nationalities, among them American, Australian, Czech, English, Italian, Polish and Russian. Peter Forbes has knowledge of history and he brings us examples of poetic responses that might be seen to coincide with different historical stages in the last century. In the process, for example, he introduces part of a poem by Joseph Brodsky that brings scientific achievements of all kinds into a long, clever, sometimes ironic examination of the twentieth century. Brodsky, a Russian who migrated to USA, won the Nobel Prize for his poetry.

18 *Butterfly Cooing Like a Dove,* Doubleday, New York, 1991, p. 150.

However, where the connections with the sciences is concerned, Peter Forbes's purpose is simple. In his brief introduction to the section 'New Things under the Sun: Science and Technology', he writes: 'The sciences in [their] exploration of micro-worlds and conceptual landscapes' are providing 'an enlargement of poetry's subject matter'.[19]

It is in the spirit of that 'enlargement of poetry's subject matter' that I am making reference to only a few of the poets included in this anthology. However, as I ended with mathematics in the American section, I wish to begin with mathematics here. First there is Howard Nemerov's poem 'Figures of Thought' which takes the reader to 'the logarithmic spiral on/sea-shell and leaf alike'. Next, a poem by the Polish Nobel Prize winning poet, Wisława Szymborska, whose wonder-filled, playful poem π has been translated by Adam Czerniawski. In it she makes a connection with Shelley's skylark. It is the first poem in which I have found such delight in that mathematical symbol.

π

π deserves our full admiration
three point one four one.
All its following digits are also non-recurring,
five nine two because it never ends.
It cannot be grasped *six five three five* at a glance,
eight nine in a calculus
seven nine in imagination,
or even *three two three eight* in a conceit, that is, a comparison
four six with anything else
two six four three in the world.
The longest snake on earth breaks off after several metres.
Likewise, though at a greater length, do fabled snakes.

The series comprising π
doesn't stop at the edge of the sheet,
it can stretch across the table, through the air,
through the wall, leaf, bird's nest, clouds, straight to heaven,
through all the heaven's chasms and distensions.
How short, how mouse-like, is the comet's tail!

19 Peter Forbes, *Scanning the Century; the Penguin Book of Twentieth Century Poetry,* 2000. p. 446.

> How frail a star's ray, that it bends in any bit of space!
> Meanwhile *two three fifteen three hundred nineteen*
> *my telephone number the size of your shirt*
> *the year nineteen hundred and seventy three sixth floor*
> *the number of inhabitants sixty-five pennies*
> *the waist measurement two fingers* a charade a code,
> in which *singing still dost soar, and soaring ever singest*
> and *please be calm*
> and also *heaven and earth shall pass away,*
> but not π, no, certainly not,
> she's still on with her passable *five*
> above-average *eight*
> the not-final *seven*
> urging, yes, urging a sluggish eternity
> to persevere.[20]

I do not know how mathematicians might respond to her poem but I found in it so much more than ways of measuring aspects of the circle.

The poem 'The Life and Life of Henrietta Lacks' by Carole Satyamurti tells the story of a woman who went on contributing to life, in a special scientific way, after her death. The poet brings to life the woman behind this development in science. There are two other sections that have themes that focus on relationships between the sciences and poetry. They are 'The Way We Live: Existence' and 'By the Light of Orion: Sci-Fi & Space'. The anthology concludes with 'Unfinished Business', a good starting point for us so early in the twenty-first century.

Dialogues between scientists and poets

The following collection of dialogues, *Contemporary Poetry and Contemporary Science* was published by Oxford University Press.[21] It was the initiative of Robert Crawford of the University of St Andrew's. It is called a 'crossover volume', and is seen as 'the first book of its kind'. Robert Crawford decided that poets and scientists should have the opportunity to share ideas and attitudes with one another. In 2006, as a result of his

---

20 *Scanning the Century,* pp. 448–449. The Melbourne poet, Peter Bakowski has written a poem for Wisława Szymborska. It is 'I prefer' in *Wagtail – 26,* 2003, p. 8.

21 Edited by Robert Crawford, *Contemporary Poetry and Contemporary Science,* Oxford University Press, Oxford, 2006.

invitation, poets and scientists took time to express their views of their relationships with one another. One of the scientists, also a great poet, Miroslav Holub, opens the collection with his essay 'Rampage, or Science in Poetry'.[22]

Born in Plzin, Western Bohemia in 1923, he was a practising immunologist as well as a fine poet. His poetry is 'intellectual, hard hitting and precise'.[23] In his contribution to *Contemporary Poetry and Contemporary Science,* Holub throws out a challenge to poets, a challenge that is worth taking up. He insists that 'the poetry of a practising scientist is basically a dialogue; consequently it should be clear enough to be understood and strong enough to lead somewhere in human terms. Science in poetry should shed some relatively new light. It is definitely not the post-romantic and post-modern poetic way of wearing dark glasses on a moonless night.'[24]

I do not intend to paraphrase the dialogues in Robert Crawford's collection of essays. However, I should be able to show where I find interaction that I find equally significant. For that reason I have chosen, as the poet, Simon Armitage, who came to the Adelaide Writers' Festival in 2006.[25] From among the scientists I have chosen Jocelyn Bell Burnell, the Cambridge astronomer who discovered pulsars.

Simon Armitage's contribution to a dialogue between poets and scientists

In *Contemporary Poetry and Contemporary Science* the poet Simon Armitage's essay 'Modelling the Universe: Poetry, Science, and the Art of Metaphor' provides a number of challenges. He begins on the defensive with his anecdote about a course in a university where he taught creative writing called *Astronomy for Poets.* It was an elective for people who could not add up. *Astronomy for Poets,* or *Physics 1141 Unravelling the Universe* as it was more properly known, was a hitch-hiker's guide to suit all students with no knowledge of calculation. In the top left-hand corner of the hand-out came the all-important tag line, 'electives without maths'.[26]

After enjoying himself exploding myths such as one that suggests poets cannot drive, Armitage returns to his theme and says, 'Presumably, not all scientists think of poetry as ineffectual, effete, and useless'. His style reminds me of the 'attack is the best form of

---

22 Miroslav Holub, in *Contemporary Poetry and Contemporary Science*, pp. 11–24.

23 Dr Jan Culik, essay on Miroslav Holub on the Internet.

24 Miroslav Holub, 'Rampage, or Science in Poetry' in *Contemporary Poetry and Contemporary Science,* Oxford University Press, 2006, p. 24.

25 See Simon Armitage, *Selected Poems,* Faber and Faber, London, 2001.

26 Simon Armitage, 'Modelling the Universe: Poetry, Science, and the Art of Metaphor' in *Contemporary Poetry and Contemporary Science*, Robert Crawford (ed.), OUP, 2006, p. 111.

defence' approach some people take when they feel threatened. But once he has relieved himself of that level of irritation, he goes on in a way I find challenging. He writes:

> And although I've begun with anecdotes that suggest friction between science and the arts, what I want to go on to suggest is that poetry and science, for all their perceived differences, might well be attempting to accomplish the same thing and through remarkably similar means. And because I'm a writer, I want to do this by drawing on further parables from personal history.[27]

Simon Armitage recalls the story of a mystery. He takes us into an event in his childhood. What had happened to the tyre he and his ten-year old gang rolled down a hill to burn on a village bonfire? It had disappeared. That uncertainty was an opportunity for the young. He includes part of his poem about the experience and uses the example to make a plea for that early time of life. He writes:

> I'm not advocating a belief in fairy stories, mumbo jumbo, or even magic, but I am carrying a torch for that time of life when instinct and intuition still hold sway over logic, reason, and law. And I'm putting my faith in a way of describing events in terms of how they feel, metaphorically, rather than giving an incident its scientific sub-title. Science, it seems to me, is besotted with the issue of prediction. The possibility of an event happening again on the grounds that it has happened before in the same circumstances. Poetry might seem in conflict with that position, since it goes out of its way to describe every occasion in a new and fresh and surprising way. But, in fact, it attempts the same thing, albeit through sensation rather than understanding. The reaction a poem provokes is presumably a response by chemical and electrical components within the body to a set of external stimuli. There are, presumably, an infinite number of ways of describing how a large inanimate object such as a tyre can go missing, and presumably an infinite number of reactions. But a successful poem brings about a kind of animal comprehension rather than its theoretical explanation, and comprehension comes from a common pool of experience. Some of us hope to remain open to that kind of perception.[28]

Armitage then tells the story of his eccentric science teacher who asked him and another boy to go outside and measure the size of the human voice. The difference between the narrative in prose and his poem 'The Shout' is a comparison worth making. Next he describes his experience with his O level Physics teacher who was not impressed by his independent thinking when Armitage chose to measure the 'swing' of a cricket

27 Armitage, *Selected Poems,* p. 112

28 Armitage, *Selected Poems,* p. 113

ball. The confusion between scientific investigation and cricket folklore is mentioned, his ultimate failure in physics and, at the age of twenty-one, writing his first poem about science which had something to do with an electric fence, electric shocks and kissing the Van de Graaff generator. His poem 'Newton's Third Law' follows this explanation.

We follow his history and its connection with the poetry he would write. Instead of pursuing that, despite his interest in astronomy and its possible comparison with Jocelyn Bell Burnell's essay, I prefer to focus on a comment he made about the role of poetry in the history of the twentieth century. His view of those events is one that some of us might never have imagined.

> Life, as we know, imitates art, and science I believe imitates life. I don't suggest that as a hierarchy of importance, but to reinforce the interconnectedness of the two disciplines through the intermediary of the human presence. In placing this kind of importance on poetry, I'm asking it to come forward and be congratulated for its achievements, but also to take responsibility for the error of its ways.
>
> Science did not take man to the moon. It might have worked out the trigonometry, but it was a poetic dream that propelled us into the heavens to set foot on the lunar mass which has pushed and pulled at us before we had eyes to see it. But science did not drop the bomb on Hiroshima either. It was a poetic nightmare-vision of hell-fire discharged into the infrastructure and flesh of an unsuspecting city that opened the bomb-hatch over the Ota river delta on 6 August 1945, even if science guided it down to its target. And the ego of poetry erected the World Trade Centre, just as a suicidal glimpse of poetic paradise brought it down again.
>
> Poetry proposed the existence of the DNA double helix with its eye for detail, and poetry postulated the theory of relativity with its penchant for cryptic crosswords, and poetry produced the first light bulb because of its fear of the dark, and poetry learned how to create fire from friction because of its grumbling dislike of the cold and its fascination with the supernatural effects of combustion.
>
> By the same token, poetry's mean-streak designed the rack and the whip and the cattle prod and the stun-gun, and the devil in it pumped poison gas into the Tokyo underground, and its rhetoric took a million people into the killing fields, and its sense of worth went about slaughtering indigenous populations across massive proportions of the globe. Wondering if there could be any more poetry after Auschwitz doesn't take into account the part poetry played in the visualizing of a holocaust. Genocide is not simply a meeting place between biology and calculus, it is a conceptual art of a kind we would prefer not to think about.

I had never thought of poetry in this light: Simon Armitage places the emotions, the dreams, the nightmares at the forefront of decisions. Dreams of Aryan supremacy, the desire to demonstrate the power at one's command, the determination to fulfil one's dreams of destiny regardless of human cost. The absence of any consideration of the impact on people's lives. Simon Armitage's interpretation of the part poetry can play in human catastrophes is most provocative. But where is he placing science? Is he seeing the sciences as Fritz Haber did? Are they there, with their knowledge of physics, mathematics, chemistry and biology to provide the means of fulfilling whatever the vision might be?

There is so much more to this essay. Simon Armitage's reference to Ted Hughes, the great English poet, could send me off on a tangent to explore Hughes's view of anthropomorphism and its impact on the way poets began to approach the description of animals after his influence was felt among younger poets. Personally, I doubt whether Ted Hughes would have liked Robert Burns's 'poor wee timorous beastie'. Hughes was against sentimentality. He insisted that giving human attributes to animals was denying them respect for what they are. He helped to establish a taboo, in the writing of poetry, on anthropomorphism.[29] This might have been a result of the scientific study he undertook at Cambridge.

In conclusion, bringing us into our contemporary technological world, Simon Armitage suggests that there are plenty of reasons for poetry to keep watch and ensure that language is not lost in this digital binary world. 'Language can provide a bridge with the vitality of the world, keep open that channel of communication when double glazing, central heating, screen savers and pot-noodles conspire to disconnect us from it. Poetry can be part of the campaign to stop reality becoming entirely virtual.'[30] There is such a contrast between his style and that of Jocelyn Bell Burnell.

'Astronomy and Poetry' in *Contemporary Poetry and Contemporary Science*[31]

Here is no feeling of defensiveness. Jocelyn Bell Burnell begins with these lines from the poem 'Delay' by Elizabeth Jennings, 'The radiance of that star that leans on me/ Was shining years ago.'[32] There is gentleness. She speaks to us, telling us when and how

29 In *The Human Nature of Birds: A Scientific Discovery with Startling Implications*, (Bookman Press, Melbourne, Victoria, 1993) Theodore Xenophon Barber argues that 'the hoary taboo against anthropomorphism has prevented any detailed consideration of intelligence in the animal kingdom'. p. 113. He quotes James Lovelock 'To survive we face the hard task of … learning again to be part of the Earth and not separate from it.' p. 158.

30 Simon Armitage, *Selected Poems,* p. 122.

31 Jocelyn Bell Burnell, 'Astronomy and Poetry' in *Contemporary Poetry and Contemporary Science,* Robert Crawford (ed.), Oxford University Press, 2006, p. 125–140

32 Elizabeth Jennings, *New Collected Poems*, Carcanet, 2002

she came to appreciate music and poetry later in life. She describes the approach she uses to 'lay audiences'. Speaking of her desire 'to draw others, especially women, into science,' she says, 'I would like to give fair space to the human side of science, but lack vehicles with which to do so in these talks. So, I have been left a little unsatisfied by the exclusively scientific content of my own talks.'[33]

Elizabeth Jennings's poem was a catalyst. It added a 'new dimension to her life'. Burnell started 'collecting' poetry with an astronomical theme to use in her talks and she found it was speaking to something in her. Jocelyn Bell Burnell has always loved words and has 'appreciated the richness and diversity of English vocabulary'. I must confess I have come back again and again to her essay. She argues her case calmly. She appreciates poetry for 'its healing properties' and comments on the ways that people turned to it after September 11. She sees poetry in that circumstance bringing 'comfort' 'closer to the original meaning of comfort – making strong. It strengthens because it recognises and articulates hurt that many of us experience but may not be able to express. That recognition, that confirmation that others have similar experience, is reassuring. This is the start of the healing'.[34]

She recognises where 'behind the complementary nature of science and poetry, there is of course a divide' and takes us to the spell-check on her computer to describe it. And she says, 'Poetry addresses the heart as well as the head, the emotional as well as the rational, and seems to me to do so better than prose. It reaches where no other words can reach; and the assiduous spell checker is blind to its nuances.'[35]

She takes us into the history of modern astronomy and reveals, from 1950 onwards, what has been developed while considering the connections between poets and astronomers. Some poets had relatives who were astronomers. Others, like Thomas Hardy in England and Robert Frost in America were amateur astronomers. And she brings us to Rebecca Elson, who is rare in that she is a poet and an astronomer.

It is a long essay offering access to the work of many poets who write about astronomy. One is Diane Ackerman whose poem 'We are listening' she quotes. Miroslav Holub's poem 'Night at the Observatory' is noted for 'one of the earliest references to radio astronomy'. In Patric Dickinson's 'Jodrell Bank' she finds a confrontational tone. Adrienne Rich's 'Planetarium' has a long subtitle 'Thinking of Caroline Herschel' (1750 –1848, astronomer sister of William and others). That poem was written in 1968 when Jocelyn Bell Burnell discovered pulsars and the astronomer tells the story of how and

33 Jocelyn Bell Burnell, 'Astronomy and Poetry', p. 126

34 Jocelyn Bell Burnell, 'Astronomy and Poetry', p. 127

35 Jocelyn Bell Burnell, 'Astronomy and Poetry', p. 127.

why Caroline Herschel was left out of a series of lectures about famous astronomers.

Jocelyn Bell Burnell has collected over a hundred poems about astronomy and is constructively critical, given her detailed knowledge of the themes that poets have chosen.

The 2003 Columbia Space Shuttle accident gives her pause. Had astronomers and space scientists become too confident? In the poem by Rebecca Elson 'When You Wish upon a Star' she quotes the lines that reveal 'the troubled yet lyrical imagery of stellar lights juxtaposed with space debris.' [36] It disappoints her that, too often, the poetry does not engage with the wider world that astronomy is opening up to us. In her conclusion she brings us to the question of dark matter and tells us that 'the amount of dark matter in the universe [will determine] its future' and she brings us again to a poem by Rebecca Elson 'Let there Always be Light (Searching for Dark Matter)'.[37]

Examples of scientists as poets

Rebecca Elson – astronomer and poet

Rebecca Elson was born in Montreal, and undertook her PhD at Cambridge where she won an Isaac Newton Studentship. Her research was concerned with 'dark matter', that part of space that is at this time hypothesised but undetectable.

Among its collection of Oxford Poets, Carcanet Press has published her work entitled *A Responsibility to Awe*. Her poems have that sense of reverence, sublimity, inspiration and respect in the face of mystery that has been mentioned by Australian contributors John Lowke and Ian Plimer. Rebecca Elson recognises the significance of this feeling as poet and scientist. Her collection includes not only her poems but also journal entries in which she explores ideas for poems. Her essay 'From Stones to Stars' is autobiographical. In 1999 Rebecca Elson died of cancer, aged only 39. But in her poems, she brings us both her love and understanding of the sciences and poetic illumination. Consider this four line poem which, to my mind, encapsulates us.

36 Jocelyn Bell Burnell, 'Astronomy and Poetry', p. 136.

37 Jocelyn Bell Burnell, 'Astronomy and Poetry', pp. 139–140.

Evolution

We are survivors of immeasurable events,
Flung upon some reach of land,
Small, wet miracles without instructions,
Only the imperative of change.[38]

Rebecca Elson speaks of her kind in 'We Astronomers', takes us to the Big Bang through the simple pleasure of 'Girl with a Balloon', gives us a different way of seeing it in 'Dark Matter', asks a question in 'What if there were no moon?' and draws our attention 'To the Fig Tree in the Garden'. Considering problems in cosmology, she writes in her journal (31 October 1993) of 'Origins'

As a flower might invent
Some memory of the smooth
Husk of seedhood
So we imagine seeds of galaxies
Shaken in the dark soil of space.[39]

To conclude this brief acquaintance with Rebecca Elson, here are:

Some Thoughts about the Ocean and the Universe

If the ocean is like the universe
Then waves are stars.

If space is like the ocean,
Then matter is the waves,
Dictating the rise and fall
Of floating things.

If being is like ocean
We are waves,
Swelling, travelling, breaking
On some shore.

---

38 Rebecca Elson, *A Responsibility of Awe*, Anne Berkeley, Angelo di Cintio and Bernard O'Donoghue (eds), Carcenet Press Ltd, Manchester, 2001, p. 31.

39 Rebecca Elson, *A Responsibility of Awe*, p. 87.

If ocean is like the universe then waves
Are the dark gravity
Where stars will grow.

All waves run shorewards
But there is no centre to the ocean
Where they all rise.[40]

Rebecca Elson's essay 'From Stones to Stars' reveals how her early education in science began. Out with her family, 'it was a natural process of assimilation, like a child learning to speak her native tongue'. Writing of her interests she says, 'It was never the facts that interested me so much as the possibilities they opened up to the imagination'. And all the time she was writing poems. While science was part of her formal education 'rarely was school science an opportunity for real exploration'. She says 'the subject may have been science, but the process wasn't'. She refers to the comparison someone once made between astronomy and a big circus tent – 'there's room for everyone' – and we learn that she feels 'privileged indeed to be able to spend [her] days inside a tent with such a dazzling roof'.[41]

I cannot give the same amount of space to other scientists who are poets but I felt, as a result of her significance in Jocelyn Bell Burnell's essay, it was important to make readers aware of her work.

Another scientist and poet, in this case a physicist, came to my attention through radio, as Miriam Rothschild had done.

A contemporary Irish physicist and poet – Iggy McGovern

I discovered Iggy McGovern through ABC Radio National.[42] He was lecturing at Latrobe University about 'Science and Poetry'. He referred to Miroslav Holub's essay in 'The Dimension of the Present Moment' and gave me another reason to look for the work of that scientist and poet.

Iggy McGovern explained that science and poetry are not so different, insisting that there must be some common ground. He saw, as John Lowke and Alan Lightman emphasise, that there are differences in the way they use words. One conveys a single idea, the other as many ideas as possible.

40 Rebecca Elson, *A Responsibility of Awe*, p. 25.

41 Rebecca Elson, 'From Stones to Stars', pp. 149–159.

42 The Book Show, ABC Radio National, 24 October 2006.

Comparing the making of the poem and the doing of the experiment, he told his audience that you have to decide what you are going to do, and that there must be enthusiasm. Next, doing it, you must have discipline and be prepared to lose. But the Eureka moments that we know from Archimedes' story, for both scientist and poet are beautiful. One can be involved in both exercises.

This poet and physicist took for his subject, in the poem below, the air-pump invented in eighteenth-century England. This invention was the subject of a painting by Joseph Wright, one of the eighteenth-century painters, entranced by the prospects of the Enlightenment, who did not believe that these scientific discoveries were undermining the quality of English life.

Writing in 2005 about the most famous of Joseph Wright's paintings, Iggy McGovern provides an unusual perspective on this experiment.

An Experiment on a Bird in the Air Pump

After the painting by Joseph Wright of Derby, 1768

An after-dinner port and snuff diversion.
This century of 'the scientificate'
is seriously right-in-front-of-the-children:
even a daughter must remark the fate

of the dove (is it?) perhaps a family pet.
What rare conclusions might the magus draw,
his fingers God-like on the air inlet,
enunciating one more Sacred Law?

The others play at minor parts, the job
of cranking up the vacuum takes the breath
from one son; the assistant with the fob
watch later writes a poem about Death.

Let's not forget, stage right, the courting pair:
eyes only for each other, left alone
they'd set some feathers flying through the air
and make a fine snuff-movie of their own.[43]

43 Iggy McGovern, *The King of Suburbia*, The Dedalus Press, Dublin, 2005, p. 54.

Universities show an interest in poetry and science

Liverpool University

The dialogues published by Robert Crawford reveal that more scientists and poets are finding that they have something to say to one another. All this indicated that the notion of two incompatible cultures is being undermined. It is important to recognise that those dialogues are going on via the Internet.

For example, the Liverpool University has established a Centre for Poetry and Science which has a website on the Internet under the acronym LUPAS. Each month there is a new poet. One was Roald Hoffmann. Another who is interested in the connections of these disciplines is Lavinia Greenlaw. One of her poems appeared on the LUPAS website in 2007, and she says: 'Poetic freedom can be used to express scientific ideas in a more broadly comprehensible manner and can locate them within the cultural, historical and ultimately human context by which science is driven and defined'.[44] She enters the story because of the dialogue between poets and scientists increasingly taking place in the United Kingdom.

University of Warwick

David Morley's poem 'Mathematics of Light' appeared on the on-line LUPAS site but I discovered his work at the University of Warwick as a result of the collaboration of members of the University of the Third Age group at Port Adelaide.[45]

With a degree in zoology from Bristol University behind him as well as research into acid rain in the Lake District, he became the Director of the Writing School at the University of Warwick. A scientist and a poet, he wrote about his experiences in the on-line publication of LUPAS.

David Morley opened his essay, 'Creative Recognitions: Science, Writing and the Creative Academy', with quotations from John Keats, referring to the capacity in people for 'negative capability', and from Niels Bohr, who wrote, 'when it comes to atoms, language can be used only as in poetry'. He began by seeing an empty page as

44 Lavinia Greenlaw, in 'Unstable Regions: Poetry and Science' in Francis Spufford and Jenny Uglow (eds) *Cultural Babbage, Technology, Time and Invention,* Faber and Faber, London. 1996, p. 217 quoted in *Contemporary Poetry and Contemporary Science* in the essay 'Wit and the Cambridge Science Park' by Drew Milne, p. 176.

45 David Morley's poems appear in *Scientific Papers* and *The Invisible Kings* published by Carcanet Press. Cambridge University Press is currently publishing David Morley's work *The Cambridge Introduction to Creative Writing.*

open space and took us to the space-time aspect of the theory of relativity. He said, 'Writing a poem, a story, or a piece of creative nonfiction, is to catalyse the creation of a four-dimensional fabric, that is the result when space and time become one'.

His essay might be as much for those engaged in higher education courses for creative writing as for students and teachers of English at senior school level. In it he ranges from icebergs and space; to hedgerows and trees, then to midges and bees. In the second section he raids the language of science. In the first section he explores the submerged part of the iceberg, where 'the brain interacts with itself: *hearing* words, *seeing* words, *speaking* words and generating *verbs*'.

David Morley tells us:

> These functions occur in widely spaced sections of the brain. Creative writing 'commands' these different departments of self to start co-operating, and they will, by stretching out synapses over relatively huge neural distances, wiring up. What else are they going to connect with along the way? What monsters or angels might be imagined into being? This is how writers are made, how the nanotechnology of your imagination is intricately (and provisionally) constructed.

His very thorough essay describes how neurologically 'we are *changed* (his italics) by our experience of writing as much as by reading'. He explains that:

> Scientific, philosophical and artistic breakthroughs often go through four stages of cognitive and creative process: attention to detail (of a problem), translation to metaphor, defamiliarisation, receiving something at a different angle, perceiving it anew as a child does. We now know a little more about the physiological and neural states that certain types of creativity take, as well as those phases which acts of creativity and metaphor engender in readers.

David Morley explores the writing of poets. For instance, he writes about the American poet Marianne Moore, whose notes 'illuminate the extent of her library, the compendiousness and open-mindedness of her reading [and] … they throw light on not only the subject of the poem, but also the geometrical design of her work'. He concentrates not only on the precision evident in her work but precision and science. He tells us that 'the right names and terms give your writing greater power and shows you have done your work. Precise language wakes or re-wakes the world and replicates it more immediately than a film could'. His example from poetry comes from 'A Cold Spring' by Elizabeth Bishop, another American poet.

In his contribution to Chapter 2, Peter Doherty bemoans the fact that outstanding young Australian scientists do not write clearly. David Morley takes on the whole problem that has made it more difficult to write well. Those students, he argues, who have been denied the literary aspects of learning have been cut off from an important source of clarity. In Part III 'Midges, Bees' Morley deals with the division of the supposed 'two cultures'.

> I began my working life as a scientist, one who also wrote creatively, and I would say that if what you do requires you at best to write clearly, then we are all writers. The Two Cultures, the division of knowledge systems into Arts and Science, was a splintering of the processes by which knowledge and language move and grow. There are no Two Cultures, and there never were. The debate between science and arts was based largely on prejudice, fear and a kind of snobbery – a class war between disciplines, their teachers and their students. We might as well say there are a Million Cultures for all the illumination such a debate brings. Creative writing as a discipline may help to shift the debate into a more constructive set of engagements.

He describes the process his students undertake at the University of Warwick. Most of the enthusiastic students at the University of Warwick come from physics, computing and mathematics. 'They borrow the concision and play of poetic technique to understand the concision and play of the languages of their own subjects. They use narrative fiction to tell science-based stories.'

In the section 'Creative Writing and Science' David Morley refers to some of the writers in the sciences. He concentrates on English writers, of whom Max Perutz is one and Richard Dawkins another, both recipients of the Lewis Thomas award. In addition he mentions Margaret Boden, Steven Rose and Steven Pinker.[46] That is another avenue that readers of this book can pursue. He calls them *creative* writers because 'they prize imagination, energy of expression, style and understand their own process of creativity'.

Scientists and poets in Europe

Before I move into contemporary twentieth-century Europe, I want to introduce a great mathematician. Her name is Sofia Vasilyevna Kovalevskaya (also known as Kovalevsky). She is so admired by scientists today that a crater on the Moon has been named for her. Born in Russia, in 1850, of a Russian father and German mother, she loved mathematics. On her family's country estate, on the wall of a room was unusual wallpaper: the lecture notes of Mikhail Ostrogradsky on differential and integral calculus. She was entranced.

46 *The Oxford Book of Modern Science Writing*, Richard Dawkins (ed.), Oxford University Press in 2008, has useful brief introductions to each scientist and their work.

In addition, while her grandparents had been mathematicians, she had an uncle who was not but who was fascinated by science and fed her interest.

Like so many European academies, Russia had no place for women in its universities. There is not enough room here for her story but she was a woman who would not be defeated by the conventions and restrictions of her time. She married to get out of Russia. Enough to say here that she was so outstanding that, when she was denied access to classes at the University of Berlin, she had private lessons from Karl Weierstrass, another of Europe's exceptional mathematicians. Aware of her brilliance, he supported her and taught her privately.

Her PhD was so outstanding she did not have to sit for an examination. Back in Russia, she was denied a teaching role at a university. She turned to writing for a journal to earn a living and wrote a novella, *Vera Barantzova*, which was translated into other languages. Later she would collaborate in writing a play with Anna Konstantinova, *The Struggle for Happiness*. She wrote another novel, *A Nihilist Girl,* at the time when nihilism was growing in Czarist Russia because the intelligentsia was fighting against the tyrannical control of the autocratic Czarist government.

But mathematics was her passion. She returned to Europe, was accepted as a Professor of Mechanics at a university in Sweden. In 1888 Sophia Kovalevsky, as she has become known, was awarded the Prix Bordin from the French Academie Royale des Sciences. She had discovered what became called the 'Kovalevsky top' because she had worked out how Saturn's rings rotated around that planet. She died of influenza in 1891.[47]

Mention has been made of the work of Miroslav Holub that comes to us in translation. Miroslav Holub's collection *Vanishing Lung Syndrome,* from which Peter Doherty quoted 'Animal Rights', also contains 'Landscape with Poets'. His poem 'Zito the Magician', translated from the Czech by George Theiner, in the section 'New Things under the Sun: Science & Technology' in *Scanning the Century,* shows what happens when magic comes face to face with mathematics.[48]

Another Czech poet was Vítězslav Nezval. One of the Czech avantgarde, he influenced the approach of Miroslav Holub. He wrote a major poem about Edison. Considering all the possibilities brought to life by electric switches turning on electric lights, he enters the lives of the scientists and inventors, finding poetry in the work

47 The literary life of Sophia Kovalevsky is explored in *Little Sparrow: A Portrait of Sophia Kovalevsky* by Don H. Kennedy, Ohio University Press, Athens, Ohio, 1983. She had known Dostoyevsky.

48 *Scanning the Century; the Penguin Book of Twentieth Century Poetry,* p. 450.

they do. In particular, he concentrates on the American inventor who made so many inventions, including the phonograph, the electric lamp and the microphone.[49]

A Russian poet, Boris Slutsky, was born in 1919 and lived until 1986. He thinks he has worked out 'why physics is in honour' and 'poetry is not'. In a derisive tone he seems to find it 'amusing'

> ... to watch how greatness
> staidly
> Retreats into logarithms.[50]

There are poems by a Serbo-Croatian poet and by another Russian poet who was a Zionist and emigrated to Israel. Abba Kovner suggests a reason why 'The Scientists are Wrong', but the poem that matters most to me in this section is by the Polish winner of the Nobel Prize for literature in 1996. Her name is Wisława Szymborska. Her poem that explores the possibilities of the mathematical expression π is one of the most exhilarating poems I have read, even though I must read it in translation. (Quoted on page 163.)

Primo Levi – industrial chemist, novelist, essayist and poet

Primo Levi is considered one of the great literary figures of the twentieth century. *The Monkey's Wrench* was so important to Roald Hoffmann that I quote the connection he made with engineering in 'The Chemist' in *Chemistry Imagined,*

> Chemistry is the science of molecules ... so many molecules are made by us, in the laboratory ... The synthesis of molecules puts chemistry very close to the arts. We create the objects that we or others then study or appreciate. That's exactly what writers, composers, visual artists, all working within their areas, working perhaps closer to the soul, do. I believe that, in fact, the creative capacity is exceptionally strong in chemistry. Mathematicians also study the objects of their own construction, but those objects, not to take anything away from their uniqueness, are mental concepts rather than real structures. Some branches of engineering are actually closer to chemistry in this matter of synthesis. Perhaps this is a factor in the kinship the chemist-narrator feels for the builder Faussone, who is the main character in Primo Levi's novel *The Monkey's Wrench*.[51]

49 *Scanning the Century,* pp. 458–461.

50 *Scanning the Century,* 'Physics and Poetry' translated from the Russian by Vladimir Markov and Merrill Sparks, pp. 447–448.

51 Roald Hoffmann, *Chemistry Imagined*, pp. 68–71.

Peter Doherty makes mention of Primo Levi's essays in *The Periodic Table* where Levi explores the elements in an unusual way, giving them a connection that takes them out of the realm of abstraction. I felt that his stories gave me access to those elements, gave me a way to approach Mendeleev's discovery of the periodic table and to take on the formulae as far as I need them as a member of our twenty-first century society.

Primo Levi was an industrial chemist, an Italian Jew, a survivor of the Holocaust who often felt guilty for surviving when so many had been murdered in gas chambers in Auschwitz. His experiences made him pessimistic. This poem, translated by Ruth Feldman, is an example of his fears for our future.

Almanac

The indifferent rivers
Will keep on flowing to the sea
Or ruinously overflowing dykes,
Ancient handiwork of determined men.
The glaciers will continue to grate,
Smoothing what's under them
Or suddenly fall headlong,
Cutting short fir trees' lives.
The sea, captive between
Two continents, will go on struggling,
Always miserly with its riches.
Sun stars planets and comets
Will continue on their course.
Earth too will fear the immutable
Laws of the universe.
Not us. We, rebellious progeny
With great brainpower, little sense,
Will destroy, defile
Always more feverishly.
Very soon we'll extend the desert
Into the Amazon forests,
Into the living heart of our cities,
Into our very hearts.[52]

52 Primo Levi, 'Almanac', trans. Ruth Feldman, *Collected Poems*, Faber & Faber, 1988.

Miroslav Holub – immunologist and poet

When he died in 1998, a eulogy by Sarah Boxer was published in the on-line *New York Times*, 22 July 1998. Ted Hughes has called him 'one of the half dozen most important poets writing anywhere'. In a book called *The Government of the Tongue* (1988), Seamus Heaney praised Holub as a poet who could lay things bare, 'not so much the skull beneath the skin, more the brain beneath the skull'. Holub's poetry, he wrote, is 'too compassionate to be vindictive, too skeptical to be entranced'.

Miroslav Holub's ironic poem about animal rights was referred to by Peter Doherty. I found more about his essays and poems on the Internet. While we have his work in translation, like so many other scientists, he has a feeling for the history of where the sciences have come from, in a way that non-scientists – thanks to that divisive approach to the curriculum – too often do not. His essays, brought together in *The Dimension of the Present Moment and Other Essays* by the translator David Young, are likely to have a more ironic twist than essays by Lewis Thomas.

He was, after all, born in Czechoslovakia, formed from the Austro-Hungarian empire broken up after 1918. In its brief period of freedom, he attended a gymnasium (high school), concentrating on Latin and Greek, but also enjoying poetry, such as the work of Goethe, and Romain Rolland and French poetry in general. He lived through the Nazi occupation, and after 1945 studied medicine and science, and wrote poetry. I discovered when and how luck enters the story. We know him because his work was widely translated *before* he became a 'non-person' between 1970 and 1980.[53]

The essays in this collection are often brief. One such is 'Windmills'. In 'Growing Up', writing of the problems of the popularisation of science he acknowledges the writing of Lewis Thomas when he says:

> In many fields, the beauty of a thought or experimental operation is impossible to communicate in popular ways, yet at least some approximate generalisations can be endowed with the beauty of elegant and imaginative language. In this sense real popularisation requires the same talent as a real poem. It should not become the domain of writers who simply cannot do anything else. The best form of writing about science is the essay, by Lewis Thomas, say, which presents selected problems and the scientific way of thinking in a refined literary form.[54]

53 Miroslav Holub, *The Dimension of the Present Moment,* David Young (ed.), Faber & Faber, London, 1990.

54 Miroslav Holub, 'Growing Up', pp. 89–90.

Holub's views on science and the arts come together in the longest essay in the collection, with his own poems, in 'Poetry and Science – The Science of Poetry/The Poetry of Science'. He writes of 'the lab in the mind', of the First Science of the Greeks. His examination of the Second Science takes us back to Matthew Arnold and culture as 'the best that had been thought and said in the world' and forward to explore the writing of scientists and poets and to examine his own process as a poet when he 'is doing it'.

'Finding it', he says 'is one of the few real joys in life.' And he reaches the point that I would hope might, one day, be reached in education. 'Yes, there is a common root to all so-called creativity; there is the same experience of fulfilment and inner reward.'[55] Readers might enjoy his poem 'Brief Reflection on the Test Tube', which completes the essay.

In that collection, and in a later collection, *Shedding Life: Disease, Politics and Other Human Conditions* is the essay 'Shedding Life', which begins with the reduction of a muskrat to a 'shapeless soggy ball of fur with webbed hind feet and bared teeth' by a wanton killer.[56] Holub takes us further into the desire in the cells to go on fulfilling their functions.

For a taste of what is in this collection, there is 'Kidneys and History' which takes us into the lives of significant figures in a way that those who write history from ideological standpoints will not fathom. This essay is, therefore, a valuable antidote to what might be termed 'mainstream' history. 'The Experiment of 1688' – how life might arise through non-life – 'Off-the-wall Inventions', 'A Journey to Jupiter' and 'Eureka' – the last essay a challenge to movie directors. And so much more.

Miroslav Holub intersects the scientific with the everyday in a way that is an antidote to what is dull and pretentious. And that is just his prose. What of his poetry?

In 'The Clock' Miroslav Holub wrote a poem that helps us see how the certainty of classical physics has been modified in the twentieth century. He goes back further in Western history to the first mechanical clock. That resonates with the eighteenth-century metaphor for God as the Divine Watchmaker who set us all ticking. Holub takes us through the history, moving from the past to the present.

55 'Poetry and Science', p. 145.

56 Miroslav Holub, *Shedding Life: Disease, Politics, and Other Human Conditions* translated by David Young, Milkweed Editions, Minneapolis, 1997. Lewis Thomas is quoted at the beginning. 'Essays are short, carefully organised avenues into understanding in ways that present ideas, feelings, amusement, delight, and, in a relatively short space, take a long view. If short stories are said to be harder to write than novels, in the realm of non-fiction, the essay has that special gem-like quality as each different facet is turned to the light.'

The Clock

In the tenth century
a monk named Gilbert
put together the first
mechanical clock:
the human spirit's yearning
towards the Eternal Infinite
needed to be marked off
by a regular sound.
It needed a balance wheel
an acrobat hanging on a bar
coming loose.

The regular sound begot bells
the sychronised bells
begot towns,
the towns begot cities,
the cities begot more hours
the hours begot
minutes
the minutes begot
seconds,
a second begot a moment.

And there is no nature in a moment.
No town. No bells, no tick.
No monk. No ash.

The acrobat in the cupola
reaches for a bar
which isn't there.[57]

Miroslav Holub is fascinated by the ironies of history. He has a way of seeing that takes

57 Miroslav Holub, *Vanishing Lung Syndrome,* translated by David Young and Dana Hábová, Oberlin College Press, Field Translation Series 16, Ohio, 1990, pp. 78–79.

us beneath any surface – not surprising in an immunologist – in ways we might never have imagined. I would invite readers to explore 'The British Museum'. It can be found in *The Rampage*. That poem gives us a new way to see ourselves because:

> The British Museum is in us,
> in our very hearts,
> in our very depths.[58]

Undoubtedly there are other scientists who are poets and who do not allow themselves to exist on one side of a 'chasm' with no way of connecting with the other side. The best example of the human capacity for connection came to me when, in 2007, I was invited to speak to the students at the Australian Science and Mathematics School. The result of that invitation constitutes the next chapter 'Comets, Conical Flasks and Conundrums'.

58 Miroslav Holub, *The Rampage,* translated by David Young with Dana Hábová, Rebekah Bloyd and the author, Faber and Faber, 1997, pp. 45–46.

Chapter Six

Comets, Conical Flasks & Conundrums

Poetry and Science at the Australian Science and Mathematics School
An anthology written and produced by students

In June 2007 I wrote to Associate Professor Jim Davies, Principal of the Australian Science and Mathematics School (ASMS). I felt that if I could interest such a school in this project, I would be able to show its validity for all senior students. After meeting Professor Davies, he passed on my letter to Terry O'Reilly, the Coordinator for Interdisciplinary Curriculum: English and the Humanities. He rang me to arrange a meeting.

The Australian Science and Mathematics School is an initiative shared between the South Australian Department of Education and Children's Services and the Flinders University. It was designed to create workshop areas rather than classrooms, enabling the cultivation of innovative learning environments where the flow of ideas across the curriculum and discussion of their interaction could be fostered. The approach to curriculum is holistic. It was not established as a selective high school. Students come from Years 10 to 12, from Australian schools and from overseas. Those who wish to enrol are interviewed and their interest in the sciences and mathematics explored.

In the foyer, as I waited to be collected, I saw a television screen reminding students of the imminent close of a poetry competition. That seemed promising. I was taken to the teachers' area, not a separate room away from students, a place apart and yet available, with room for four teachers with their computers. No fourth wall. It was an interdisciplinary space where teachers working in different disciplines could talk, encourage enquiry, examine alternative ways of interpreting information, respond to students and share ideas with one another, all in the cause of expanding the students' and their own understanding of one another's fields of study.

In Terry O'Reilly's corner of this teachers' alcove, we spoke of the inter-connectedness I believed essential, if science in the twenty-first century was not to continue to be separated from the humanities and the arts as had been the case too often and for too long in the last century. I spoke of the poetry competition. Only a few had so far chosen to enter. We spoke of Coleridge.

A month later Terry O'Reilly rang. Would I like to come and see what the students had done, and would I like to speak to them? He would like me to see the ways in which students had connected poetry and science. Moreover, he would like me to speak to the whole school!

On 14 August 2007 I went to the school to be overwhelmed by the range of ideas and interpretations of aspects of the sciences by Year 10 students. There were multi-media avenues for presentations of poems visually, videos, laminated posters of poems they had found by poets, and work of their own.

The arts provided a range of ways to express the thoughts and feelings about this or that aspect of one or more of the sciences. And, on a big stand, with the posters for all coming past to stop and consider, was the sign POETRY *and* SCIENCE. I could not have been happier. But to speak to a whole school dedicated to the sciences and mathematics, to some degree, caught up in past assumptions about the 'soft' nature of the humanities and the arts, was a challenge.

Address to the Australian Science and Mathematics School
14 August 2007

Students of ASMS may be like a student I had at Marion High School although it does not seem like sixteen years ago. He wrote this poem about independence. He was in Year 11:

> Safety constrains me
> like a strait-jacket.
> My sheltered life
> like an asphyxiating shroud.
> When shall I be released
> from my prison of liabilities
> and rise up
> as if on the wings of eagles
> into the bliss of independence?
>
> Michael Brown

On the subject of old age, back in 1991, before we had the idea of 'grey nomads' gadding about, and others graduating with higher degrees in their 80s and 90s, another student wrote this poem.

A skeletal frame, fragile, frail and weak
With hands covered by the markings of age
Folded and blemished, wrinkled and flaccid.
Veins like rivers and eyes cloudy like mist.
Independence ignored by the impatience
Of a patronising society.
Trapped by circumstances and frustration.
Just another old man resigned to fate
Left, confined to a life of memories.

Allyson Grout

Why am I here talking to you about connecting poetry and science as one aspect of the study of English when the convention has been that poetry and science are the antithesis – at the extreme opposites – of one another? 'Science and poetry are,' as Elizabeth Truswell says, 'Two sides of the one coin'.

I'm here because it is not true to see them as 'two separate cultures'. Imagination does not belong in one area and reason in the other. Both belong in both. Discovery does not belong in one area and creativity in the other. Both belong in both. That rather convenient separation of the sciences from poetry has been part of the separation of the mind from matter, the intellect from emotion, the mind from the body, in what has been called the Cartesian principle. It placed abstraction and the realm of intellectual endeavour above all else. It ignored the structure of the human being and the fact that we are beings feeling, laughing, crying, learning, questioning, experimenting – one way and another – from the moment we are born.

How many of you, in the course of your lives have been labelled? Recently the journalist father of a girl who won an English prize wondered why she valued it because, at university, she was going to study science. He had 'pigeon-holed' his own daughter apparently unaware of the concerns expressed by top scientists that brilliant young scientists cannot write well enough to be understood. (Oxford University now has a Chair for the Public Understanding of the Sciences.)

Over half a century ago, as a humanities student, my friend who was a mathematical physicist called me 'one of the clawless tigers'. He was not afraid of using metaphors when he wanted to make me feel inadequate. But gradually, from 1966 onwards, I have been discovering the truth, helped most recently by the writing of wonderful scientists whose work has been acknowledged internationally for its literary quality. I want students to have access to their writing as part of their English course. I want students to have access to the dialogue going on between scientists and poets. I want students to have access to the poetry of scientists and poetry that tackles aspects of both the wonder and worry of engagement in the sciences. Some of it is the best writing I have come across in the realm of non-fiction.

We know now that the kind of labelling that made some people 'non-scientists' or 'non-academics', 'heads' not 'hands' – notice the absence of 'heart' – came out of a way of thinking that was convenient for the followers of René Descartes, the French philosopher. His phrase 'Cogito ergo sum', translated as 'I think, therefore I am', enabled Descartes to develop this idea of the separation of mind and the world of abstractions from the messy, complex world of body-mind. It explained his existence in a way that satisfied him and it satisfied others until now.[1]

But we know the mind cannot work without the body, without the brain, without the nervous system, without the senses that alert the consciousness to problems or possibilities, without the blood vessels that take the oxygen to the brain. But it has taken us two centuries to go back to the connections and scientists are helping us to do it. Therefore their writing should be part of the study of English in a world where ignorance of what is happening is dangerous. Our school curricula, in my view, have not yet caught up with the need for this balance.

If you listen to the poems, Michael Brown could not have written his poem effectively without that technical term 'asphyxiation'. You feel the intensity. Listen to the sounds in the word as they shut off life. He needed the image of the eagles to help the reader to feel the sense of freedom, the soaring glory of those majestic predators that represented for him the 'bliss' of independence. 'Bliss' is an old-fashioned word that takes me to Wordsworth who thought it was 'bliss' to be alive at the dawn of the French Revolution which was supposed to usher in the age of Reason, of 'Liberté, Egalité, Fraternité'. Consider the quality of observation in Allyson Grout's poem, the clarity of imagery, the

1 In 1953, the 'father of the atom bomb', J. Robert Oppenheimer, gave a talk entitled 'The Scientist in Society'. Oppenheimer had had time to realise fully the impact of the dropping of the atomic bombs. It dismayed him. He had seen the Cartesian principle at work and made the following comment on the approach to education fostered by the separation of the mind from the body. He wrote: 'I think that whatever may have been thought of Cartesian and Newtonian reforms in the intellectual life of Europe, the time when these were what the doctor ordered – all that the doctor ordered – is long past.' J. Robert Oppenheimer, 'The Scientist in Society', *The Open Mind*, Simon and Schuster, New York, 1955, p. 129.

recognition of the impatience of a 'patronising society', the intelligence in the awareness of attitudes in society. Look at the connection of discovery, thought and feeling. Clarity and compassion. If I were a science teacher, I would be delighted to have a student with her capacity to be exact.

That is one of the reasons I came to the Australian Science and Mathematics School to see whether students here would accept the challenge to be aware of the connections. I met your Principal who is now concerned with approaches to education to meet 'the new era'. I was invited to meet Mr O'Reilly who was interested enough to see whether students would take up the challenge to explore science in poetry and write poems that embraced the sciences, perhaps complemented them, or approached them in what Simon Armitage – an English poet – would call an adversarial way. You have done so and I congratulate you for taking the plunge.

[I told the students about the scientists who had contributed to this project, named the American, European and English scientists, examples of whose work is in the previous chapters. I wanted to make them aware of the evidence of those, in the disciplines for which the ASMS is named, who are challenging the divide. I wanted the students and staff to be aware of what the presence of scientists who are poets means for assumptions about the supposed 'chasm' separating the sciences from the humanities and the arts.

Where, often was the poetry? If we should look at the 1816 changes to the *Shorter Oxford Dictionary* definition, we would find it was to 'lift the spirit, express emotional qualities, to please' and I would add 'to challenge' as Miroslav Holub does. Wonder and awe are part of the sciences as they are in other aspects of life. Anxiety, fear, concern are part of the sciences as they are part of the other elements of life. So I concluded my address with the following words.]

We are human beings with all the possibilities that entails before we are anything else. We are more than machines. Our spirits need to be lifted. Sometimes it happens through music, through art, through the beauty of the world available through the electron microscope, some times through the mystery. We are social and as such have codes of conduct. We have characters and we cannot separate any of that. Our education has, in the past, encouraged us to think in a different way. We are 'one' yet we are 'many' inside ourselves. So the holistic approach which recognises the significance of connections is the way to go.

Flinders University is setting up a Centre for Science Education in the Twenty-first Century. Its Director is from a multi-disciplinary background. The University of South Australia has an Eco Centre at Mawson Lakes where the emphasis is on the quality of thinking and feeling. Adelaide University is setting up a Research Institute on Climate Change which is multi-disciplinary and states clearly that it intends to make connections with the humanities. Politicians, ideologues of different kinds may prefer division but that is not the intelligent, open-minded, thoughtful way to go into the uncertainties of the future.'

****

I could not know how that address would be received. In November the phone rang. Would I like to come and see the anthology that the Year 10 and 11 students had produced of the poetry of science? In that interim, with all the other demands on their time, students had produced *Comets, Conical Flasks & Conundrums: The Poetry of Science*, an anthology by the students of the ASMS. A copy of it was in the post. Students were involved in editing it, the front cover was by a student. Would I launch it the following Tuesday?

Their anthology was divided into a number of different sections: Scientific Ponderings, Time Thoughts, Mathematical Meanderings, Technology Meditations, Sustainable Questionings, Haiku – 5,7,5, Science and Art, Biological Banter, Odes to Space and the Atomic Muse. Forty-five students had contributed. How could I do justice to the range? Here, was 'the feeling world of ideas'.

One student, Sammantha Bamber, felt so strongly the absence of political will, with its depressing impact on the attitudes of people, in 'Waiting'.

> I watch as the polar ice melts and the seas rise,
> As the sea currents change and the coral dies,
> As humans pollute the waters,
> As the marine animals are slaughtered.

She watches and waits and concludes

> I watch and hope that they all realize what they have done.
> I wait for the rebirth, a new beginning …
> I wait …

Sammantha was not alone. A number of young poets expressed their fears and hopes for the future. Until I read Tom Heinrich's poem I did not know that the atomic bomb dropped on Hiroshima had been called 'Little Boy'. So often the poems were asking questions about the world we have created or allowed to be created. On the question of prolonging life, Grace Hill, asked in 'Miracle or Immoral?':

> Should humans have the power,
> To keep a shell,
> A body with no soul, the brain long dead,
> Suspended in life when there is no hope of recovery?
> Prolonging the agony of kin?

Another poet let everyone understand what it means to live with 'D', diabetes. Cassie White helped us to walk in her shoes, to develop the capacity for empathy. In 'Borrowed Breaths' Selina Ahktar expressed her appreciation for the donation of organs that have allowed a loved one to be reunited with her family. There was the joy as she realised:

> Sensory inputs,
> The chest rises
> The diaphragm relaxes
> Air crawls up the nasal cavities.
> Realisation wrenches open the eyelids.
> She is alive!

Michelle Grixti personified the innate immune system in 'My Osmosis Jones'. The science was good, the understanding was there. For a student of the humanities, this became a humorous way to find out how the immune system, that can never rest, works.

Dennis Grauel explored inventions – the wheel, the fork, glasses, parachutes, Morse Code, the refrigerator, dynamite, computers and X-rays.

> Being able to see inside
> Brought a new era of medical pride
> No scalpel incision
> Of doubtful precision
> Indeed a valuable guide.

Rory Stokes's poem 'Frontiers of the Mind' took me to 'the marvels of maths, like glistening gems'. Luke Wilkinson-Turner saw time as:

… bliss, – is caring,
She is everywhere.

For Joshua Renfrey 'Time is as a God'. We had the wonder of gravity in Rachael Cottam's poem. Luke Victor was teaching us the forms of 'Energy'. He hoped we '[had] learned each of them'.

Clearly the teachers of the sciences and mathematics had cooperated with the humanities teachers and, in particular the teachers of English. That willingness to collaborate had contributed to the quality of the anthology. Excitement, a sense of purpose, questions about where science might be taking us as well as a feeling of awe filled some of the poems. Finn Stokes told the reader that each line in his poem 'Molecular Blueprint' begins with the letter A,T, C or G, the letters representing the bases of a DNA codon. 'Codons are sequences of three bases that stand for a single amino acid. The amino acids represented by the verses are (in order) Histidine, Lysine, Arginine, Threonine, Leucine, Proline, Stop Codon.'

Nicholas Camac asked and answered the question:

What is science?

Science is a religion,
That knows no boundaries.
Science is a wave,
Constantly crashing against the ship of discovery.
Breakthrough after breakthrough,
We evolve from basic life forms into complex beings of immense power.
Science is a pulse,
One that pumps through people with a passion that is hard to resist.
Science is a lifestyle,
A choice that engulfs one's life as if it were thrust upon them.
Science is strong,
It has the power to unite and to detach.
Science is secretive,
Undiscovered information is held within like a grain of sand trapped in an hour glass.

And there was so much more in his extensive series of metaphors: Science 'is a doctor'. 'is infinite', 'an imaginary friend'. 'a playhouse', 'a boxer', 'a flower', 'a rollercoaster', 'a doorway', 'is justice', 'the sun', 'a teenager' –

One that rebels against all beliefs.
'a key' and 'a playground'.

Daniel del Pilar answered the same question. Among the stanzas in 'What is Science?' were the connections I had hoped to be finding. While:

Science is a jigsaw puzzle;
Complicated but simple,
Hard but attainable,
Separated but unified

At the same time:

Science is literature
A simile, a metaphor.
Science is art
A painting, a sculpture.

and
Science is a story,
With plots unique themselves.
Science is a chapter,
With each new beginning.

So much was encompassed in this anthology and it was done so well with invigorating visuals. The poetic styles ranged through different forms. In content, there were paradoxes, the wonder of gravity, energy in its many forms as well as challenges about whether science is helping or not.

There were no easy answers here, particularly for a 'non-scientist' like me. Many poems here made me reflect on, think about and explore ideas with which I am not familiar. I felt the intellectual challenge, enjoyed humour grounded in knowledge when I met 'the ninja cell', felt the intense appreciation of the role of organ donors in 'Borrowed Breaths'. I felt the depth of concern in 'Miracle or Immoral?'

Every reader of the poems in this collection would be encouraged to empathise with the student living with diabetes. Reading it, I told the school, 'We are thinking *and* feeling, learning *and* increasing in sympathetic understanding. We recognise, as those who separated the intellect from the body did not, the significance of the senses. The concern of the young with the future we are creating is here in poems under the heading of 'Sustainable questionings'. I heard 'Earth's Sigh', delighted in 'The Sunrise', smiled wrily at 'Five Ways to Control a Woman', learnt more through 'Odes to Space', found beauty in 'Inspiration', took in 'Celestial Relationships', while 'Atoms' connected me with love and life.'

Concluding the launch I told the school a story about the first American Nobel prize winner (in 1907), Albert Michelson. The story of how he gained the education he wanted is instructive. He was a brilliant experimenter and Einstein said, 'I always think of Michelson as the artist in Science'. In his book, *Light Waves and Their Uses* Albert Michelson had written: 'If a poet could at the same time be a physicist, he might convey to others the pleasure, the satisfaction, almost the reverence, which the subject inspires. The aesthetic side of the subject is, I confess, by no means the least attractive to me. Especially is its fascination felt in the branch which deals with light.'[2]

The achievement of these students lights the way to future possibilities

I see the students of this school as being at the beginning of a change, a change that will expand the understanding of the sciences to humanities students. That understanding should make the sciences more accessible. In a civilised society, where ethical issues matter, the sciences cannot be separated from other areas of study. Interdisciplinary approaches and multi-disciplinary approaches will help to get rid of the prejudices 'the two cultures' notion has fostered in schools. Instead we will value, as Judith Wright does, 'the feeling world of ideas' in all its complexity.

The students and staff of the Australian Science and Mathematics School have demonstrated what is possible. They have turned a dream of connections into a reality. Their work sheds new light on what is possible where collaboration within and between schools is fostered. This school has been built on this connected approach, recognising the individual strength of their disciplines as well as the ways they interact, into the hearts and minds of students. Nothing has been lost. Much has been gained.

I commend the work of these students and the ideas expressed by the contributors to this book to all who are interested in fostering an approach to education that has the broader vision that Peter Doherty urged us to develop. Finally, I must emphasise how heartening I have found the generosity of spirit in the writing of the scientists and poets who have contributed to and made possible the publication of *Challenging the Divide.*

2 Joy Hakim, *The Story of Science: Einstein Adds a New Dimension*, Smithsonian Books, Washington and New York, 2007, p. 35.

Afterword

I was dreaming, as I often do, about aspects of this book. The conversation in my head took me to a phrase 'passions of the mind'. Assumptions that the intellect was cold and separate ignored the passionate views of so many who cling to this or that idea. And *Passions of the Mind* was also the title of a collection of essays by A.S. Byatt.

I took her book from the shelf the following morning. It opened at a page where Coleridge was quoted – I had obviously been here before. In 1797, thinking about the ideal great poem that a poet could aspire to write, Coleridge wrote:

> I should not think of devoting less than 20 years to an Epic Poem. Ten to collect materials and warm my mind with universal science. I would be a tolerable Mathematician. I would thoroughly know Mechanics and Hydrostatics, Optics and Astronomy, Botany, Metallurgy, Fossilism, Chemistry, Geology, Anatomy, Medicine – then the *mind of man*, then *the minds of men* – in all Travels, Voyages and Histories. So I would spend ten years – the next five for the composition of the poem – and the last five to the correction of it.[1]

There was that wonderful line 'warm my mind with universal science'. Coleridge believed in the 'interrelated unity of all human knowledge'. I laughed with delight when I read his words. I was determined to share with those who might be interested in this project Coleridge's description of what he believed essential in the preparation needed to write a great epic poem. A Romantic poet, he was aware of the need to engage with the sciences without losing the warmth of love, of beauty, and human compassion.

I was just as delighted when I found the references that David Morley had made to John Keats and Niels Bohr that I have referred to in Chapter 5. David Morley had been describing the 'Writing across the curriculum' approach that was introduced in England in the 1980s. (It had been part of our process in schools in the 1970s but was not accepted by a number of subject-oriented disciplines.) This movement in England had grown in response to a perceived deficiency in literacy among university students in the 1980s. In South Australia the Writing-based Literacy Assessment – WBLA – was put in place to try to make teachers of all disciplines recognise the importance of

1 A.S.Byatt, 'Coleridge: An Archangel a Little Damaged', *Passions of the Mind: Selected Writings*, Chatto & Windus, London, 1991, p. 282.

the writing component in their subject, now replaced by another requirement that is expected to foster concern for the quality of one's writing.

David Morley opened his essay, *Creative Recognitions: Science, Writing and the Creative Academy,* with quotations from John Keats, referring to the capacity in people for 'negative capability' and from Niels Bohr, who says, 'when it comes to atoms, language can be used only as in poetry'.

His very thorough essay described how neurologically 'we are *changed* (his italics) by our experience of writing as much as by reading'. That explanation has been extensively quoted in Chapter Five. He said that 'Writing in Disciplines' is part of the movement of 'Writing Across the Curriculum'; 'At my own university [the University of Warwick], we experimented with using many creative writers and creative Writing Games to deliver these parts of the curriculum, and to do so with creative panache, teaching them as though they were performance art. *External teaching tests have shown real progress, and a side-benefit of increased recruitment when science is suffering in this respect*. [my italics.]'

In his reference to Keats, David Morley approached what the young poet considered necessary for the growth of 'Men of Achievement'. He referred to a letter that John wrote to his brothers. Keats was exploring the idea he called 'negative capability'. When I spoke of my excitement in discovering what this capability entailed, a friend suggested that surely in the twenty-first century, we needed 'positive' capabilities. What Keats was describing in this phrase was a quality of mind that he found 'enormously' in Shakespeare.

In a letter to his brothers, George and Thomas Keats, in December 1817, he wrote:

> I had not a dispute but a disquisition with Dilke, on various subjects; several things dovetailed in my mind, & at once it struck me, what quality went to form a Man of Achievement especially in Literature & which Shakespeare possessed enormously – I mean *Negative Capability,* that is when man is capable of being in uncertainties, Mysteries, doubts, without any irritable reaching after fact & reason – Coleridge, for instance, would let go by a fine isolated verisimilitude caught from the Penetralium of mystery, from being incapable of being content with half knowledge. This pursued through Volumes would perhaps take us no further than this, that with a great poet the sense of Beauty overcomes all other consideration, or rather obliterates all consideration.

This capacity to be at rest in uncertainty, to muse on the question, to wait, let something come, is as important in the sciences as it is in the arts. This capacity is undermined by governments that insist on discoveries being able to be applied commercially for profit. This capacity to question, to allow curiosity to take one somewhere is now being fostered in primary schools. Whether it has room in senior school study is another question. Hopefully, it is there at least in the 'external learning initiative' that students will be undertaking.

Hopefully, it is there in the Independent Research Project that is an essential part of the new South Australian Certificate of Education (SACE). That external learning initiative, reminiscent of the 'independent cross-disciplinary study' that I experienced at Marion High School, should enable students to cross boundaries and develop the capacity to make connections they might not have realised are there.

This capacity may be just as evident in men and women who have never been to university. It is a human capacity and might be strong when one is passionate about some aspect of life. As Marcello Costa makes clear the brain is working even when we appear to be doing nothing.

In his sonnet, 'When I have fears that I may cease to be', Keats refers to 'the magic hand of chance' that I have found so valuable during the time I have worked on this project. Keats's concept of 'negative capability' has been reinforced for me, by 'the magic hand of chance' in a most unexpected way.

In 2008 I listened to a conversation between Robert Hannaford, visual artist, and Professor Tanya Monro, an expert in photonics at the University of Adelaide. The artist spoke of 'defocusing', taking his eye from the direct observation of the object and looking into a middle distance to concentrate on the structure he wanted to capture in his painting. It might give him a different perspective to enable him get to the heart of his painting.

I took that term, 'defocusing', and Keats's concept of 'negative capability', to the University of the Third Age at Port Adelaide, asking what this process did to over-simplified notions of 'subjective' and 'objective' since Keats recognised, in Shakespeare, the capacity to be objective.

Among the responses from members of the group was the following mind map produced by Howard Groome, a former lecturer in Aboriginal Education at the University of South Australia. Concerned as a trainer of teachers, he was interested in the process of 'negative capability' and what it could mean for the process of learning. His interpretation as a mind map, part of current curriculum practice, is meant to alert readers to the process going on as the brain reflects on an idea.

And chance brought me Stephen Lawrence, at the time poetry editor of *Wet Ink*, whose interest in poetry about science became evident at Friendly Street. His essay 'The Sounds of Science', which forms the Appendix, introduces readers to a number of contemporary Australian poets exploring the sciences.

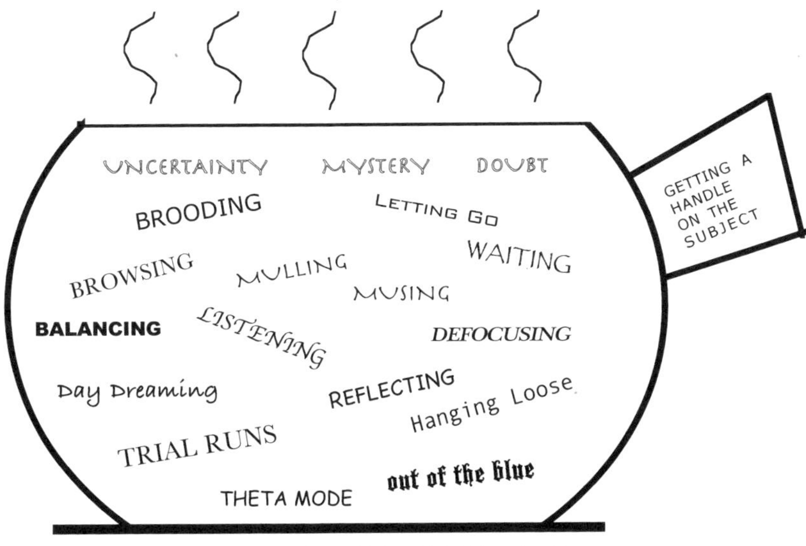

THE NEGATIVE CAPABILITY COOK POT

I intend to add other connections that I keep finding to the website to be developed to complement *Challenging the Divide*. It is to be hoped that the national curricula, with which all schools will soon be expected to comply, will have recognised that treating subjects as 'silos' did not help us to think through and feel the impact of the major concerns that influenced our lives in the twentieth century. The collaborative connections between different disciplines and the possibilities for cross-over, being recognised in universities, need to be an part of pre-tertiary education. May Coleridge's understanding of the inter-relationship between all human knowledge replace that divisive notion of 'two cultures'.

Appendix

'The Sounds of Science'

a contribution by Stephen Lawrence

Stephen Lawrence is a poet, and has been the poetry editor for *Wet Ink*. His interest in contemporary science is evident in his poetry. His involvement with contemporary science-oriented poetry is of value here, since the chances are that, in Schools of Education where integrating and interdisciplinary approaches are being encouraged, there is limited information of this kind. His series of poems about quantum gravity begins his essay.

What Quantum Gravity Looks Like

Time keeps everything from
happening at once.

Countless dimensions
will be needed to survive
the four we're lost in.

The universe duplicates
every time we look.

Time does not exist;
there is only more likely
and less likely.

There is not single now, now.
And there never was.

We feel a river.
In reality there is
only the ocean.

In the following essay Stephen introduces the work of contemporary Australian poets.

The Sounds of Science – Science in Poetry

Imagination is the basis of all science.

(Einstein)

Nothing gets right in Love because
Of Time, and Motion; poetry touches that.

(Luke Davies, '(Hell)')

Creative writers and artists are uniquely placed to contend with scientific subjects. As Niels Bohr wrote, 'When it comes to atoms, language can be used only as in poetry'.

The Surrealist manifesto claims, 'Poets have as much right to do research as scientists'. And the key figure of this twentieth-century art movement, Salvador Dali, to whom science was a lifelong passion, said: 'Scientists give me everything: even immortality of the soul.' Dali merged art, science and religion in his Hypercube – the unfolding of the fourth dimension into the third, bringing the transcendental into our world.

Science and poetry are more than just a two-way street: they are disciplines that overlap and feed off each other. Practitioners of both of these forms of enquiry are creative, add authenticity to their culture, and their work is the best measure of a civilised society. The conjoining of art and science dates back to Pythagoras. Now, modern science – in particular, the implications of quantum mechanics – opens up new realities.

Given this rich and productive relation, I would like to examine how poetry employs science to artistic ends in the context of selected Australian practitioners. I will survey some recent Australian poetry collections that concern themselves, to a greater or lesser extent, with science. Though not always successful, several of these writers brilliantly merge disciplines, to the advantage of their creative art and the understanding of scientific concepts.

Luke Davies, in his 2005 poetry collection *Totem* (Allen & Unwin, NSW, 2004), is interested in how science can be poetry:

> Time was merely the measure of motion
> with respect to before and after. Meanwhile
> the universe expands. The pine trees creaked.
> The pine cones cracked. On a windless day there was time
> to dream of you. The pine cones snapped open the silence.
> ('Totem Poem,' p. 16)

Our lives are both surrounded by and juxtaposed with numinous events and concepts:

> We dreamed the world worked not in pairs
> but clusters, including the galaxies. Sunlight
> bloomed into gardens from the thin air it rode in on.
> (p. 24)

Davies isn't parading his research or his learning: he conveys the pleasure, the linguistic joy, of using complex words, scientific themes, revelling in the language and its control and release.

The poetry conveys connectedness, yet there are surprises and abrupt changes of course. The jerking pace, the sudden pauses ('And everything stopped working,' p. 12) and rushes ('Things came and went- – the years and all the airports,' p. 13), give the poem its energy and encourage both poet and reader to take stock of the words. The repetitions epitomise the nonlinearity of time that 'Totem Poem' exemplifies.

> *Totem*'s idiom is vital, erotic. It is born of infinity and being. Language itself
>
> emerged: in the Flesh of the Fruit.
> I spoke tongues against your breathlessness …
>
> To be alive I had to praise, to praise I had to
> learn to speak.
> (p. 15)

Davies is not flaunting his reading: he bubbles over with the joy of intelligent scrutiny melded with the hot breath of poetry.

Let's compare this with some other poets in recent years.

Kate Fagan's 2002 collection, *The Long Moment* (Salt Publishing, WA) achieves a successful bond between her research and her idiom. Her language and use of scientific concepts are partners:

> this breath pulls apart a dandelion
> with related intensity
> seed-heads
> springing into maps

leaving speed
to other equations and valencies,
we are splitting prisms
hoping
for slow fantastic
disturbance

... intimacy's accompaniments

respecting machinery
and the way component cogs
tender their own music,
the task
apparently
is no more than cellular
('return to a new physics,' pp. 15–16)

Her poetry is a means of observing and recording – thinking, imagining, 'presencing,' connecting – then observing the recording. Her working manner is to decode eventualities by throwing 'handfuls of syntax and desire a kind of persuasive clarity.' These blended vocabularies allow rich linkages and associations to be uncovered:

There is no end to geometry, the crisp terrain
of triangles your arm marks out across
my lap. Arable and floating, the gentle lake
that pools across your sternum. Syntax, sharp
as something that cannot be held, and therefore
loud as the slip away from tactile certainty.
In the earth, still with flight, sleeping bodies hum
intemporal distrust. Beside them, we are counting
memes, how love makes up for death.
('The waste of tongues')

Wendy Jenkins is another appealing poet who draws from science. She has a clean and modern tone in her *Rogue Equations* (Fremantle Arts Centre Press, 2000).

Melissa Ashley also dips into the atomic world, in *the hospital for dolls* (Post Pressed,

2003). From 'Katherine Mansfield's Eyes': 'the quantum world of the child revealed as amniotic rocking cradle.' Like many users of this word, 'quantum' is meant to give a general sense of something mind-bogglingly tiny – but it is so much more.

Many more poets acknowledge the positive and illuminating use to which science can be put in their art.

Tim Metcalf's first published collection, *Corvus* (Ginninderra Press, ACT, 2001), exhibits a strong intelligence and a broad range of poetic perspective. He explores his experiences through poetry, effectively combining his scientific and artistic training. The first two sections of 'Love in the Information Age' – teasing neurochemical foreplay then cognitive-mechanical coupling – are enjoyable; however, the mathematical third part fails to complete or unify the poem. Metcalf bravely attempts to describe 'the inside arc / of your skull' by giving us an elementary lesson in psychopharmacology, but piling on probabilities and set theory dilutes the equation – and he finally admits, 'I can't intrude.'

Adrienne Eberhard, too, dealing with nineteenth-century Tasmania in *Jane, Lady Franklin* (Black Pepper Press, Vic, 2004), cleverly portrays the period's intellectual conflicts through scientific theories of the day. 'Catastrophism' is a fine poem in the 'Magic of Stones' section of her book, in which Eberhard interestingly explores the uneasy struggle between science and biblical literality.

Science and art are our highest available realities. If they can join and blend in creative and constructive ways, humanity has the best chance of moving forward productively and avoiding catastrophe.

References and Further Reading

Ackerman, Diane *The Planets: A Cosmic Pastoral,* William Morrow & Coy, Inc, New York, 1976

Aitken, Richard *Seeds of Change: An Illustrated History of the Adelaide Botanic Garden,* the Board of the Botanic Garden and State Herbarium, Adelaide, 2006

Angier, Natalie *The Canon: A Whirligig Tour of the Beautiful Basics of Science*, Houghton Mifflin Company, Boston, New York, 2007

Armitage, Simon 'Modelling the Universe: Poetry, Science and the Art of Metaphor' in *Contemporary Poetry and Contemporary Science,* edited by Robert Crawford, Oxford University Press, 2006

Armitage, Simon, *Selected Poems,* Faber & Faber, London, 2001

Ashley, Melissa. *the hospital for dolls,* Post Pressed, 2003

Baker, Janine *Ode to Aquatic Resources*, Fisheries Newsletter, October 1990

Barber, Theodore Xenophon, *The Human Nature of Birds: a Scientific Discovery with Startling Implications,* Bookman Press, Melbourne, 1993

Bate, Walter Jackson, *Coleridge*, Weidenfeld & Nicolson, London, 1969

Battersby, Christine, *Gender and Genius,* The Women's Press, London, 1989

Bell, I.F.A., *Critic as Scientist: The Modernist Poetics of Ezra Pound,* Methuen, London, 1981

Bird, Kai and Martin J. Sherwin, *American Prometheus: The Triumph and Tragedy of J. Robert Oppenheimer*, Atlantic Books, Great Britain, 2009/Alfred A. Knopf Ltd, New York, 2005

Bloom, Harold (ed.), *Percy Bysshe Shelley: Selected Poetry*, New American Library, New York, 1966

Bray, John *Satura, Selected Poetry and Prose,* Wakefield Press, Adelaide, 1988

Bray, John *The Bay of Salamis and other poems*, Friendly Street Poets, Unley 1986

Brock, Brian, *Catharsis,* Pioneer Books, South Australia, 1981

Bryson, John, (ed.) *Matthew Arnold: Poetry and Prose,* Rupert Hart-Davis, London, 1967

Burnell, Jocelyn Bell, 'Astronomy and Poetry' in *Contemporary Poetry and Contemporary Science,* edited by Robert Crawford, Oxford University Press, 2006

Byatt, A.S., *Passions of the Mind: Selected Writings*, Chatto & Windus, London, 1991

Calaprice, A., *The Expandable Quotable Einstein,* Princeton University Press, Princeton, 2000

Campbell, Lewis & Garnett, William, *Life of J. C. Maxwell with selections from his correspondence and occasional writing,* Macmillan, London, 1882

Carroll, Lewis, *The Complete Illustrated Works,* Gramercy Books, New York, 1982

Carson, Rachel, *Silent Spring*, Penguin Books, London, reprinted 1971

Cohen, J.B., *The Triumph of Numbers: How counting shaped modern life,* W.W. Norton & Co, Norton Paperbacks, New York, 2006

Cornwell, John, *Hitler's Scientists: Science, War and the Devil's Pact,* Viking, London, 2003

Crawford, Robert (ed.), *Contemporary Poetry and Contemporary Science,* Oxford University Press, Oxford, 2006

Damasio, Antonio, *Descartes' Error: Emotion, Reason and the Human Brain,* (rev. edn), Vintage Books, London, 2006

Darwin, Erasmus, *The Botanic Garden: a poem in two parts containing the Economy of Vegetation and The Loves of Plants*, Jones & Co, 1825

Darwin, F. (ed.), *The Life and Letters of Charles Darwin,* John Murray, London, 1887

Davies, Luke, *Totem,* Allen & Unwin Ltd, New South Wales, 2004

Davis, Jack et al. (eds.), *Paperbark: A Collection of Black Australian Writing,* University of Queensland Press, St Lucia, 1990

Dawkins, Richard, selected and introduced, *The Oxford Book of Modern Science Writing,* Oxford University Press, Oxford, 2008

de Selincourt, Ernest (ed.), *Wordsworth: The Prelude or Growth of a Poet's Mind*, Oxford University Press, London, 1966

Dixon, Bernard (ed.), *Creation to Chaos: Classic Writings in Science,* published by Cardinal Books, 1991

Doherty, Peter C., *A Light History of Hot Air,* Melbourne University Press, Melbourne, 2007

Dow, Hume (ed.), *Science Speaks: A Selection of English Prose,* F.W. Cheshire, Melbourne, 1962

Dyson, Freeman *Weapons and Hope,* Harper & Row, New York, 1984

Dyson, Freeman, *Disturbing the Universe,* Harper & Row, New York, 1979

Eberhard, Adrienne, *Jane, Lady Franklin,* Black Pepper Press, Victoria, 2004

Eliot, T.S. 'Tradition and the Individual Talent' (1919) in *Selected Essays,* Faber & Faber, London, 1969

Eliot, T.S., *Collected Poems, 1909–1962,* Faber & Faber Ltd, London, 1974

Elson, Rebecca, *A Responsibility to Awe*, edited by Anne Berkeley, Angelo di Cintio and Bernard O'Donoghue, Carcenet Press Ltd, Manchester, 2001

Emsley, John, *Nature's Building Blocks: An A–Z Guide to the Elements,* Oxford University Press, 2001

Fagan, Kate, *The Long Moment*, Salt Publishing, Western Australia, 2002

Fara, Patricia, *An Entertainment for Angels: Electricity in the Enlightenment,* Icon Books, Cambridge, 2002

Fara, Patricia, *Fatal Attraction: Magnetic Mysteries of the Enlightenment,* Icon Books, UK, 2005

Fara, Patricia, *Newton: The Making of a Genius,* Picador, London, 2003

Fara, Patricia, *Sex, Botany and Empire: the Story of Carl Linnaeus and Joseph Banks*, Icon Books, Cambridge, UK, 2003

Fisher, Len, *Weighing the Soul: the evolution of scientific beliefs,* Phoenix Paperbacks, London, 2005

Flannery, Tim, *The Weather Makers: the history and future impact of climate change,* Text Publishing, Melbourne, 2005

Forbes, Peter (ed.), *Scanning the Century: The Penguin Book of Twentieth Century Poetry,* Penguin Books, London, 2000

Ford, George and Monod, Sylvere (eds), *Charles Dickens: Hard Times: An authoritative text, background sources and contemporary reactions, criticism,* A Norton Critical Edition, New York, 1966

Forster, E.M. 'The Machine Stops', *The Eternal Moment and Other Stories,* 1928

Fredman, Stephen (ed.) *The Concise Companion to Twentieth Century American Poetry,* Blackwell Publishing, USA, 2005

Glikson, Andrew, *Dreaming a UniVerse: Gondwanaland Flower: A poetic and photographic journey*, Canberra, ACT revised 1997.

Goldsworthy, Peter *New Selected Poems,* Duffy and Snellgrove, Sydney, 2001

Gribbin, John, *Science: A History 1543–2001,* Allen Lane, London, 2002

Gribbin, John, *Space: Our Final Frontier,* BBC Worldwide, London, 2001

Gribbin, John, *The Fellowship: The Story of a Revolution*, Allen Lane, London, 2001

Gribbin, Mary and John, *From Atoms to Infinity: 88 Great Ideas in Science,* Icon Books, Cambridge, UK, 2006

Hakim, Joy, *The Story of Science, Volume 1: Aristotle leads the way,* Smithsonian Books, Washington, 2004

Hakim, Joy, *The Story of Science, Volume 2: Newton at the Center,* Smithsonian Books, Washington, 2005

Hakim, Joy, *The Story of Science, Volume 3: Einstein Adds a New Dimension,* Smithsonian Books, Washington, 2007

Hall, Donald (ed.) *American Poetry, An Introductory Anthology,* Faber & Faber, London, 1969

Hannaford, Brian D. *Risky Business: Changing a Secondary School,* Wakefield Press, Adelaide, 1986

Harwood, Gwen, *Collected Poems 1943–1995*, University of Queensland Press, St Lucia, 2003

Heath-Stubbs, John and Salman, Phillip (eds), *Poems of Science,* Penguin Books, Middlesex, 1984

Hoffmann, Roald and Torrence, Vivian, *Chemistry Imagined: Reflections on Science,* Smithsonian Institution Press, Washington and London, 1993

Hoffmann, Roald, *Memory Effects*, Calhoun Press, Columbia College, Chicago, 1999

Hoffmann, Roald, *The Same and not the Same*. Columbia University Press, New York, 1993

Holden, Jonathan, 'Poetry and Mathematics' in *The Measured Word: On Poetry and Science,* Kurt Brown (ed.), University of Georgia Press, Athens and London, 2001

Holmes, Richard, *The Age of Wonder,* Harper Press, London, 2008

Holub, Miroslav, *Shedding Life: Diseases, Politics and other Human Conditions,* trans. David Young, Milkweed Editions, Minneapolis, 1997

Holub, Miroslav, *The Dimension of the Present Moment and other essays,* David Young (ed.), Faber & Faber, London, 1990

Holub, Miroslav, *The Vanishing Lung Syndrome,* Oberlin College Press, Ohio, 1990

Hulme, Joy N. *Wild Fibonacci: Nature's Secret Code Revealed,* illustrated by Carol Schwartz, Tricycle Press, Berkeley, 2005.

Jenkins, Wendy, *Rogue Equations*, Fremantle Arts Centre Press, Western Australia, 2000

Jolly, Erica (ed.), *A Broader Vision; Voices of Vocational Education in Twentieth Century South Australia 1897 – 2001,* Lythrum Press, Adelaide, 2001

Jolly, Erica (ed.), *We Came to Marion 1955 – 1995,* Flinders Press, Bedford Park, 1995

Jolly, Erica, *Pomegranates*, Lythrum Press, Adelaide, 2004

Keats, John, *Selected Poems and Letters*, Douglas Bush (ed.), Houghton Mifflin Company, The Riverside Press Cambridge, Boston, 1959

Kemp, Martin, *Visualizations: The Nature Book of Art and Science,* Oxford University Press, Oxford, 2000

Lamb, Karen , Review of *With Love and Fury, Selected letters of Judith Wright, Weekend Australian,* 10–11 March 2007

Lehrer, Tom, 'The Elements' in *Too Many Songs by Tom Lehrer with not enough drawings by Ronald Searle*, Mandarin Paperbacks, London, 1991

Leone Peguero, *Poetry Speaks,* Heinemann Educational Australia, Richmond, Victoria, 1982

Levi, Primo, *The Periodic Table*, trans. Raymond Rosenthal, Penguin, 2000

Lewis, Naomi (ed.), *E. Nesbit's Fairy Stories,* Ernest Benn Ltd, London, 1977

Lightman, Alan, *A Sense of the Mysterious: Science and the Human Spirit,* Pantheon Books, New York, 2005

Lightman, Alan, *Dance for Two: Selected Essays*, Pantheon Books, New York, 1996

Lightman, Alan, *Time Travel and Uncle Joe's Pipe*, Penguin Books, New York, 1986, London, 1980

Lowke, J J. *On the Physics of Lightning,* Proc. IEEE – Plasma science, 2004

MacBeth, George (ed.), *The Penguin Book of Victorian Verse,* Penguin Books, Middlesex, 1969

Macinnis, Peter, *Rockets, Sulfur, Sputniks and Scramjets*, Allen & Unwin, NSW, 2003

Maddox, Brenda, *Rosalind Franklin: The Dark Lady of DNA*, Harper Collins, London, 2003

March, R.H., *Physics for Poets,* McGraw Hill, New York, 1970

Mathews, G.M. (ed.) *Keats: The Critical Heritage,* Routledge & Kegan Paul, London, 1971

Mc Ewan, Ian, *The Child in Time,* Vintage Books, London, 1992

McGough, Roger, *In the glassroom,* Jonathan Cape, London, 1990

McGovern, Iggy, *The King of Suburbia*, The Dedalus Press, Dublin, 2005

Metcalf, Tim (ed.), *Verbal Medicine: Twenty-one Contemporary Clinician-Poets of Australia & New Zealand,* Ginninderra Press, ACT, 2006

Metcalf, Tim, *Corvus*, Ginninderra Press, ACT, 2001

Morley, David, *Creative Recognitions: Science, Writing and the Creative Academy*, LUPAS, on-line journal, Liverpool University Centre for Poetry and Science, at http://www.liv.ac.uk/poetryandscience/essays/creative-recognitions.htm

Muir, Edwin, *One Foot in Eden,* Faber & Faber, London, 1965

Neidjie, Bill, *Gagudju Man*, JB Books, Marleston, South Australia, 2002

Noonuccal, Oodgeroo, *Stradbroke Dreaming*, Angus & Robertson, Australia, 1993

Page, Tony, *Gateway to the Sphinx,* Five Island Press, Wollongong University, NSW, 2004

Pais, Abraham, *A Tale of Two Continents*, Princeton University Press, New Jersey, 1997

Pascal, Blaise, *Pensées*, trans. A.J. Krailsheimer, Penguin Books, London, 1995

Patten, Brian (ed.), *The Puffin Treasury of Verse*, Puffin Books, London, 2006

Peake, Charles (ed.), *Poetry of the Landscape and the Night: Two Eighteenth Century Traditions,* Edward Arnold, London, 1967

Perutz, Max, *Is Science Necessary? Essays on Science and Scientists,* Oxford University Press, Oxford, 1991

Porter, Roy, *Enlightenment: Britain and the Creation of the Modern World,* Allen Lane, London, 2000

Raine, Kathleen, *Collected Poems,* Hamish Hamilton, London. 1956

Reaney, Darryl, 'Dangerous Harmony', *Age* Monthly Review, April 1982

Riordan, Maurice and Turney, Jon, (eds), *A Quark for Mister Mark: 101 poems about science,* Faber & Faber, London, 2000

Rothschild, Miriam 'A liberating bolt from the blue', in *From Creation to Chaos: Classic Writings in Science,* Bernard Dixon (ed.), Cardinal Books, 1989

Rothschild, Miriam, *Butterfly Cooing Like a Dove,* Doubleday, New York, London, 1991

Sacks, Oliver, *Uncle Tungsten: Memories of a Chemical Boyhood,* Picador, 2002

Sandburg, Carl, 'Who do you think you are?', *Poetry Speaks,* Leone Peguero (ed.), Heinemann, Richmond, Victoria, 1982.

Schmidt, Michael, *Lives of the Poets,* Phoenix Paperback, London 1998

Shelley, Mary, *Frankenstein or The Modern Prometheus,* Wordsworth Classics, Hertfordshire, 1993

Smith, Bernard, *Imagining the Pacific: In the Wake of Cook's Voyages,* Melbourne University Press, Melbourne, 1992

Snow, C.P., *The Two Cultures and the Scientific Revolution,* Mentor, Cambridge, Mass. 1959

Stewart, Douglas, *Rutherford and other poems,* Angus & Robertson Ltd, Australia,1962

Tennyson, Alfred Lord, *Poems and Plays,* Oxford University Press, London 1967

Thomas, Lewis, *Et Cetera, Et Cetera: Notes of a Word-Watcher,* Little, Brown and Company, Boston, 1990

Thomas, Lewis, *Late Night Thoughts on Listening to Mahler's Ninth Symphony,* Bantam Books, Toronto, 1984

Thomas, Lewis, *The Fragile Species,* Charles Scribner's Sons, New York, 1992

Thomas, Lewis, *The Lives of a Cell,* Penguin Books, London, 1978

Thomas, Lewis, *The Medusa and the Snail: Notes of a Biology Watcher,* Allen Lane, London, 1980

Thomas, Lewis, *Verse: Can I Ask You Something?,* Library Fellows of the Whitney Museum of American Art, New York, 1984

Watson, James D. *The Double Helix,* Weidenfeld and Nicolson, London, 1968

Wertheim, Margaret, *Pythagoras' Trousers: God, Physics and the Gender Wars,* Fourth Estate, London, 1997

Westfall, R.S., *Memoirs of the life, writings and discoveries of Sir Isaac Newton, Volume 1,* Johnson Reprint Corp., New York, 1965

Wicks, Les, *Stories of the Feet,* Five Island Press, Wollongong, New South Wales, 2004

Williams, Robyn, *Future Perfect: What next and other impossible questions,* Allen & Unwin, Crows Nest, New South Wales, 2007

Wilson, E.O. *Consilience: The Unity of Knowledge*, A.A. Knopf, New York , 1998

Wordsworth, William and Samuel Taylor Coleridge, *Lyrical Ballads,* Derek Roper (ed.), Collins Publishers, London, 1968

Wright, Judith, *Collected Poems 1942–1985,* Angus & Robertson, Australia, 1994

Acknowledgements

First I must acknowledge Emeritus Professor Frank Fenner who supported this project. Without his endorsement the scientists who accepted the invitation to be involved might never have given it a moment's consideration. I thank Professor Tim Flannery for being willing to add his name to that invitation and for giving me permission, when we spoke, to make reference to *The Weather Makers.*

I thank the following Australian scientists for their generosity. They provided responses to our invitation, knowing that I was not offering them a financial reward. I am indebted to Janine Baker, Marcello Costa, Peter C. Doherty, Susannah Eliott, Tim Flannery, Ian Gibbins, John Lowke, Oliver Mayo, David Paganin with the sculptor Marc Rogerson, Ian Plimer, Scoresby Shepherd, Elizabeth Truswell and Juliette Woods.

I appreciate the agreement of scientists, poets, artists and copyright holders who have allowed their poetry and prose to be included. I am indebted to Dr Jocelyn Bell Burnell, Laureate Professor Roald Hoffmann, Professor Alan Lightman and Dr Iggy McGovern.

Among South Australian contributors I thank Howard Groome, Jean Groome, Stephen Lawrence, Graham Rowlands and Paul Wilkins.

The late Dr Denis Grundy, of the School of Education at Flinders University, encouraged me to collect the voices of students (among them Frank Fenner's), teachers and administrators in vocational education in South Australia from 1897–2001. That collection was published as *A Broader Vision.* I have found, in Professor Doherty's call for a 'broader vision', an echo of the voice of a mature-age student who did not allow being labelled a 'tech' student to prevent her from studying at a higher education level.

The readiness of the groups of women and men who form the University of the Third Age at Port Adelaide to continue to come with me as I researched, explored and discovered connections has been essential.

Dr Stephen Brock encouraged me from the beginning. My manuscript was checked at each stage by Professor Ian Gibbins of Flinders University. Elizabeth Mansutti, the third in this trinity of editors, helped me to complete the project. I have been grateful for commentary by Dr Susannah Eliott and David Jolly. Lyn Wilkinson, Senior Lecturer in Curriculum in the School of Education at Flinders University, working with student teachers on integrated approaches to learning, has provided moral support.

I must acknowledge the role of the ABC's Radio National. In particular 'Ockham's Razor', 'The Science Show' and 'All in the Mind'; at times also 'The Book Show', 'Background Briefing', 'Late Night Live' and 'Poetica'. The specialised programs of the ABC's Radio National are most valuable.

I appreciate the willingness to be of assistance shown by Emeritus Professor Anne Edwards, former Vice Chancellor of Flinders University and Professor Martin Westwell, the Director of the Centre for Science Education in the Twenty-first Century.

These acknowledgements must include recognition of the Australian Science and Mathematics School. The 2007 Year 10 and 11 students of the Australian Science and Mathematics School, the Principal, Associate Professor Jim Davies, Terry O'Reilly, Coordinator of Interdisciplinary Curriculum: English and Humanities, and all the teachers who gave their support to the students.

Friends, from all walks of life, have found me books, searched the Internet, bought books on my behalf from the USA and the UK. One translated Voltaire's poem to Emilie du Châtelet about Newton. I have received news cuttings, and sessions downloaded from Radio National. Others have listened to me read parts of a chapter out loud. I thank Geoff Boyce, now working with me on a website to complement the book, Caroline Curnow, Debbie Dixon, Micheline Laigre, Dawn Langman, Stephen Leahy, Michael Luscombe, Reva Luscombe, Yvonne Miels, Viktor Muizulis, Alan Pepper, Ian Purcell, Gillian Rogers, Michael Rogers, Mary Swenson and Tess Young for their assistance.

Publishing a book like this involves an act of faith. *Challenging the Divide* could not have come into existence without the constant support of Michael Deves, the publisher at Lythrum Press.

Erica Jolly

Publishing acknowledgements

In publishing a book of this nature, it has been difficult at times to track the original owner of copyright and obtain permission. All diligent attempts have been made to do so. The publisher would be pleased to learn of any omissions, and will make due acknowledgement in any future editions.

Both the author and the publisher acknowledge the following permissions given by contributors and various authors and publishers, many of whom have been very generous in their co-operation.

Simon Armitage, 'Modelling the Universe', *Contemporary Poetry and Contemporary Science*, Oxford University Press, 2006; Janine Baker, *Circus Earth*, Friendly Street Poets/Wakefield Press, 2008; Jocelyn Bell Burnell; John Bray, *Satura*, Wakefield Press; Brian Brock, *Autumn Peonies*; Michael Brown; Marcello Costa; Sarah Day; Peter C. Doherty; Susannah Eliott; Rebecca Elson, *Responsibility to Awe*, edited by Anne Berkeley, Angelo di Cintio and Bernard O'Donoghue, Carcanet Press Ltd, Manchester, 2001; Kate Fagan; Tim Flannery, *The Weathermakers*; Lisa-Ann Gershwin; Ian Gibbins; Andrew Glikson; Peter Goldsworthy, 'Roy G. Biv', *New Selected Poems*, Peter Goldsworthy, c/o Curtis Brown (Aust) Pty Ltd; Howard Groome; Jean Groome; Gwen Harwood, 'Schrödinger's Cat Preaches to the Mice', *Selected Poems*, Penguin, Australia; Roald Hoffman, *Chemistry Imagined: Reflections on Science, The Same and Not the Same*; Miroslav Holub, 'Animal Rights', 'The Clock', *Vanishin Lung Syndrome*, trans. David Young and Dana Hábová, Field Poetry Series 16, Oberlin College Press; Edward Kravitz; Stephen Lawrence; Primo Levi, 'Almanac', *Collected Poems*, Faber and Faber, 1988; Alan Lightman; John Lowke; Oliver Mayo, *All We Like Sheep*; Iggy McGovern, *The King of Suburbia*, Dedalus Press, Dublin; David Paganin; Ian Plimer; Marc Rogerson; Graham Rowlands; Scoresby Shepherd; Douglas Stewart, 'Rutherford', by arrangement with the Estate of Douglas Stewart, c/o Curtis Brown (Aust) Pty Ltd; Lewis Thomas, 'Computers', © 1973 The Massachusetts Medical Society, from *The Lives of a Cell*, by permission of Viking Penguin, a division of Penguin Group (USA) Inc., 'On Cloning a Human Being', © 1974-1979 Lewis Thomas, from *The Medusa and the Snail*, by permission of Viking Penguin, a division of Penguin Group (USA) Inc., 'Humanities and Science', 'On Matters of Doubt', © 1981 Lewis Thomas, from *Late Night Thoughts on Listening to Mahler's Ninth*, by permission of Viking Penguin, a division of Penguin Group (USA) Inc.; Elizabeth Truswell; Paul Wilkins; Robyn Williams, *Future Perfect: What Next? And Other Impossible Questions*; Juliette Woods; Judith Wright, 'Swamp Plant', 'Words, Roses, Stars', *Collected Poems 1942–1985*, Angus and Robertson; Valerie Yule.

Index

N

O

P

Q

R

S

Lythrum Press
Adelaide

www.lythrumpress.com.au